The Indepe[...]
Guid[...]

United Kingdom

Edited by
Sam Dalley &
Bob Oldfield

The Backpackers Press

ISBN 978-0-9536185-9-0

Independent Hostel Guide 2010: United Kingdom

19th Edition
Editors : Sam Dalley and Bob Oldfield (AKA Sam & Peter Oldfield)

British Library Cataloguing in Publication Data
A Catalogue record for this book is available from the British Library
ISBN   978-0-9536185-9-0

ISBN 978-0-9536185-9-0

9 780953 618590 >

Published by: The Backpackers Press, Speedwell House,
Upperwood, Matlock Bath, Derbyshire, DE4 3PE
www.independenthostelguide.co.uk
Tel: +44 (0) 1629 580427

Printed by: N1 Print
Cover Artwork : Just 30 Ltd www.just30.com
Back Cover Photography : Studio9 Photography www.st9.co.uk
Front Cover Photography : Robert Morris www.robertmorrisimages.co.uk

Internal photographs: Provided by the Independent Hostels

Distributed in the UK by:-
          Cordee Books and Maps, 3a De Montfort Street.
          Leicester, LE1 7HD, Tel: (0116) 2543579
Distributed overseas by:-
          Global Exchange, Australia, Tel: (02) 4929 4688

Printed on paper manufactured from
100% recycled materials.

SYMBOLS

	Mixed dormitories
	Single sex dormitories
	Private rooms
	Blankets or duvets provided
	Sheets required
	Sleeping bags required
	Hostel fully heated (including common room)
	Common room only heated
	Drying room available
	Showers available
	Cooking facilities available
	Shop at hostel
	Meals provided at hostel (with notice)
	Breakfast only at hostel (with notice)
	Meals available locally
	Clothes washing facilities available
	Facilities for less-able people.
	Internet facilities
	Within 1 mile of a Sustrans cycle route
	Within 3 miles of a Sustrans cycle route
	Within 5 miles of a Sustrans cycle route
	Affiliated to Hostelling International
	Member of Lakeland Camping Barns
GROUPS ONLY	Accommodation only for groups

- ▲ No membership requirements
- ▲ Self catering facilities
- ▲ Dorms, private bedrooms and en-suite rooms
- ▲ Groups, individuals and families welcome
- ▲ Great locations for outdoor activities
- ▲ Central city locations for independent travellers
- ▲ Can be booked completely (sole-use) for get-togethers
- ▲ Available for individual nights, weekends or weeks
- ▲ Privately owned
- ▲ Can be YHA affiliated, but are always privately run
- ▲ Eco-conscious
- ▲ Great value
- ▲ Updated daily on **www.Independenthostelguide.co.uk**

pp	per person
GR	Ordnance Survey grid reference
C$	Canadian Dollars

 VisitScotland Quality Assured

 VisitWales Quality Assured

 NI Tourist Board Q.Assured

 VisitEngland Quality Assured

Manchester
122,124

Liverpool
125-129

121
120

94
Oswestry
Shrewsbury

93

90 91,92
05

Ludlow

W A L E S

88 86
Cheltenham

Bristol
50
46
Bath

Minehead
40   *42*   43   *44*   *45*

Barnstaple

M5

Yeovil

A37

37

38

Bude   *36*   Oakhampton   35
Exeter

A30(T)   *33,34*
30   *51*

28,29

Newquay
23,24   A38(T)   *25*   Torbay
26   Plymouth   *32*

15   *21*   *22*
10 *14*   Truro
16 *18,20*

11,12
Penzance

| 0 | | | miles | | 50 |
| 0 | | | kilometres | | 80 |

South England/Midlands

KEY

45 - **Hostel page number**

45 - **Page number of group only accomodation**

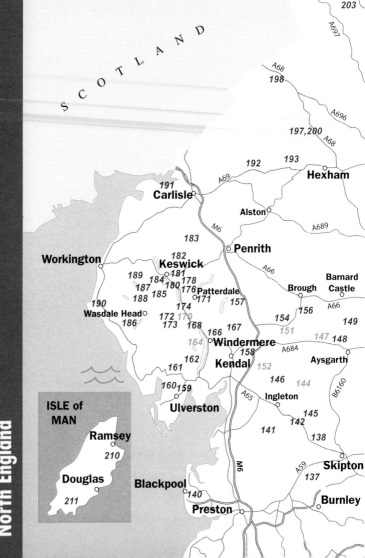

Berwick Upon Tweed *206,208*

204

203

A697

S C O T L A N D

A68
198

A696

197,200 A68

192 *193*

A69

Hexham

191
Carlisle

Alston

M6

A689

183

Penrith

Workington

A66

Barnard Castle

182
Keswick

Brough

189 *181*
184 *178*
187 *180* *176*
188 *185*

Patterdale
171

154 *156* A66

149

190
Wasdale Head

174
172 *170*
173 *168*

157

151

147 *148*

186

166 *167*

Windermere

164

158

A684

162

Kendal

152

Aysgarth

161

146 *144*

B6160

160 *159*

Ingleton

145

Ulverston

A65

142

141

138

ISLE of MAN

M6

A59

Skipton

Ramsey

210

137

Douglas

Blackpool

Burnley

211

140

Preston

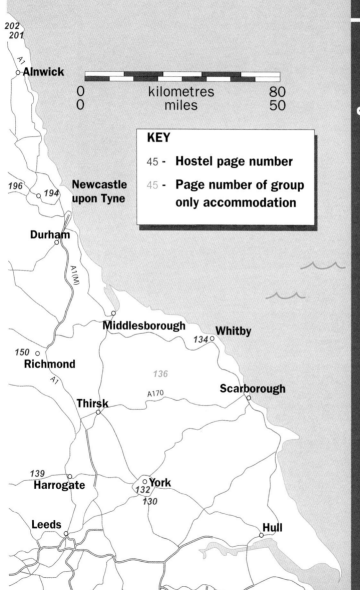

202
201

A1

Alnwick

0   kilometres   80
0   miles   50

KEY

45 - **Hostel page number**

45 - **Page number of group only accommodation**

196   194   **Newcastle upon Tyne**

Durham

A1(M)

Middlesborough   **Whitby**
134

136

150
Richmond

A1

A170

Scarborough

Thirsk

139
Harrogate

132 **York**
130

Leeds

Hull

KELYNACK
BUNKBARN

Kelynack Bunkbarn nestles in the secluded Cot Valley, one mile from the Atlantic Coast in the heart of the Land's End Peninsula Area of Outstanding Natural Beauty. The Barn has one twin room, two two-bedded and one four-bedded bunkroom. Blankets and pillows are provided. There is a toilet/shower room and communal kitchen with full cooking facilities. Adjacent is the bike store and a laundry/drying room shared with the campers on site. We also have a small shop for essentials.

St Just, a mile away, has plenty of food shops and a selection of pubs and take-aways. Kelynack is ideal for coast and moorland walking, spending time on the beaches, birdwatching, rock climbing and exploring the ancient villages, standing stones and tin mining heritage of unspoilt West Penwith.

DETAILS

- **Open** - All year, arrive after 2pm, vacate by 10am. 24 hr access.
- **Number of beds** - 10: 1 x 4 : 3 x 2.
- **Booking** - Booking is advised (25% deposit)
- **Price per night** - Low season £12 per adult, £6 under 12 yrs. High season £12.50 per bed. Exclusive use £110 per night. No meters.
- **Public Transport** - There is a frequent bus from Penzance Rail Station to St Just. The hostel is one mile south of St Just. Free transport from St Just by prior arrangement.
- **Directions** - GR 373 301. The hostel is 200 yards east of the B3306, 1 mile south of St Just, 5 miles north of Land's End and 20 mins walk from coastal path.

CONTACT: Francis or Wendy Grose
Kelynack Camping Park, Kelynack, St Just, Penzance, Cornwall, TR19 7RE
Tel: 01736 787633
kelynackholidays@tiscali.co.uk www.kelynackholidays.co.uk

Y M C A CORNWALL
(PENZANCE)

ENGLAND

West Cornwall is famous for its rugged coastlines, secret coves and long sandy beaches. It offers the chance to relax and unwind, to surf, walk, deep sea dive, horse ride and to visit galleries, small harbours and villages. There are many attractions such as the famous Minack open air theatre.

The YMCA is more than just a hostel, we offer sporting and conference facilities as well as an internet café. Our facilities provide the ideal location for school/ youth groups of any size, for short weekends or for longer holidays. The YMCA has been serving the community of Penwith since 1893, providing an ideal base for you to discover all the area has to offer.
Now available: Isle of Scilly parking from just £2.50 a day!!

DETAILS
- **Open** - All year, 8am to 10pm (except by prior arrangement)
- **Number of beds** - 52: 6x5, 5x4, 1x2
- **Booking** - booking not essential but advisable in Summer
- **Price per night** - Dorm from £16pp, single from £20, twin from £18pp, family rooms from £42. Discount for parties of 15+. 10% discount for students in dormitories.
- **Public Transport** - Penzance train station 15 min walk. Penzance bus station bus service numbers 6A and 6B. Taxi from Penzance centre approx £3.
- **Directions** - From the train / bus stations, turn left towards the centre of town onto Market Jew Street. Turn left and follow Market Jew Street until it becomes Alverton Road. Go straight over the roundabout until you see our sign on the left (approx 200m).

CONTACT: Reception Team
International House, The Orchard, Alverton, Penzance, TR18 4TE
Tel: 01736 334820
admin@cornwall.ymca.org.uk www.cornwall.ymca.org.uk

PENZANCE
BACKPACKERS

Penzance, with its mild climate, its wonderful location looking across to spectacular St Michael's Mount, with all the coach and rail services terminating here, is the ideal base for exploring the far SW of England and the Scilly Isles. Whether you are looking for sandy beaches and sheltered coves; the storm lashed cliffs of Land's End; sub-tropical gardens; internationally acclaimed artists; the remains of ancient cultures; or simply somewhere to relax and take time out, Penzance Backpackers is for you. We are situated in a lovely tree-lined road close to the sea front, with the town centre, bus station and railway station only a short walk away. Accommodation is mostly in small bunk-bedded rooms with bed-linen. Fully equipped self-catering kitchen, hot showers, comfortable lounge, lots of local information and a warm welcome all included.

DETAILS

- **Open** - All year, 24 hours
- **Number of beds** - 30: 2 double, 1x 4 (double + 2 bunks), 3x6, 1x7.
- **Booking** - It's best to phone.
- **Price per night** - From £15 per person. Discount for long stays.
- **Public Transport** - Penzance has a train station and National Express service. 15 mins walk from train/bus station or catch buses 1, 1a, 5a or 6a from Tourist Information/bus/train station. Ask for top of Alexandra Road.
- **Directions** - From Tourist Information/bus/train station either follow Quay and Promenade to mini-roundabout, turn right up Alexandra Rd, we are a short way up on the left; or follow main road through town centre until second mini-roundabout, turn left down Alexandra Rd; we are on right.

CONTACT:
The Blue Dolphin, Alexandra Road, Penzance, TR18 4LZ
Tel: 01736 363836
info@pzbackpack.com www.pzbackpack.com

THE OLD CHAPEL
BACKPACKERS

Zennor is a small picturesque village situated between St Ives and Land's End and is a haven for walkers, bird watchers and anyone who wants a taste of the rural way of life or just simply to relax! The hostel is located very close to the pub and St Ives is nearby for shopping, clubbing, cinemas, restaurants and some of the finest beaches in Cornwall.

The Old Chapel Backpackers has been converted to a very high standard and is perfectly situated for clear views over the sea and moorland. We have four rooms that sleep six people, one room that sleeps four and a family room with double bed. There are washbasins in every room and the hostel is centrally heated throughout. We can offer self-catering and we can provide breakfast, packed lunches and evening meals if required. There is also a café on the premises serving delicious soup, rolls and cakes

DETAILS

- **Open** - All year, winter by prior arrangement, all day
- **Number of beds** - 32: 4 x 6 : 1 x 4 : 1 x family room
- **Booking** - Booking is advisable, 20% deposit
- **Price per night** - From £15 per person all year
- **Public Transport** - There are train stations at St Ives (4 miles) and Penzance (10 miles). Local buses run to/from St Ives every few hours. The taxi fare from St Ives is approximately £5.
- **Directions** - Approximately 4 miles from St Ives on Coastal Road heading towards Land's End.

CONTACT:
Zennor, St Ives, Cornwall, TR26 3BY
Tel: 01736 798307
zennorbackpackers@btinternet.com www.backpackers.co.uk/zennor

St Ives is the jewel in the crown of the beautiful Cornish Riviera, famous for its artistic community, Tate Gallery, picturesque town, harbour, surf beaches and bay. An ideal location for relaxing, surfing (5 minutes walk to Porthmeor Beach), climbing, scuba diving, walking the coast path, fishing, great restaurants, shopping or just relaxing in a quaint Cornish seaside town

St Ives Backpackers was originally a Wesleyan Chapel School built in 1845. The building is based around a central courtyard - ideal for barbecues and socialising. Clean and comfortable surroundings, friendly and informal atmosphere, internet hotspot!. NO CURFEW!!!

Fully equipped kitchen. Bedding provided. Surfboard / wetsuit storage. Regular barbecues. Pool table and ping-pong table.

DETAILS

- **Open** - All year, 24 hours
- **Number of beds** - 62: 8 x 3,6 x 3,5 x 1,3 x 4, 2 x twin, 2 x double.
- **Booking** - Advisable, groups require deposit.
- **Price per night** - Oct-Apr from £11.95, May from £13.95, Sept from £15.95, June from £15.95, Jul-Aug from £17.95. Extra for bank holidays and special events.
- **Public Transport** - Bus: National Express; Train: Mon - Sun 12 per day (change at St Erth); Five minutes walk from bus and train stations.
- **Directions** - Car: Signposted off the A30

CONTACT: Reception
Town Centre, St Ives, Cornwall, TR26 1SG
Tel: (01736) 799444
st.ives@backpackers.co.uk www.backpackers.co.uk/st-ives/index.html

GRANARY
BARN / BACKPACKERS

This is a recent addition to the backpacker's network in Cornwall, approached by a short, tree lined lane off the B3302 road. Our objective is quality accommodation at low cost. The accommodation consists of a dormitory equipped with 8 new beds with mattresses (blankets & sleeping bags required). There is heating, toilet with H&C basin, shower room (hot showers-metered) and communal kitchen with dining area / lounge. There is also a surf-board/ bike store/drying room, huge parking & BBQ area. B&B accommodation is also available in the Farmhouse. The location is minutes from the beach at Portleven (surfing/shops/restaurants/pubs), Helston (Lidl store+ others/pubs/ restaurants). Within easy reach of St.Micheals Mount, Lizard, Lands End and St. Ives. Activities: we can accommodate those who wish to fish (Praa Sands), dive (Porthkerris), walk (loads), Racing Teams (Secure parking area and local CC restorer), cycle, beach. Whatever your pursuit, you will have a friendly welcome, access to a wealth of local knowledge and a commitment to make your stay one to remember for all the right reasons.

DETAILS

- **Open** - All year, all day
- **Number of beds** - 8
- **Booking** - Essential - call to check availability (24 hrs)
- **Price per night** - £7.50 per person. B&B in farmhouse (continental breakfast) £15 per person.
- **Public Transport** - Train & bus stations; Camborne, Redruth and Penzance.
- **Directions** - GR OS Map 103 SW 638 298 on the B3302

CONTACT: Tom
Sithney, Helston, TR13 0AE
Tel: Mobile 07740 514188 (24hrs)
thomas-martin1@sky.com

FALMOUTH
BACKPACKERS

Falmouth's beautiful natural harbour provides a picturesque background to the main street of charming shops, restaurants, cafés and pubs. Voted the 2nd best coastal town, Falmouth is renowned for its sandy beaches, Pendennis Castle, exotic gardens, Arts Centre and the Princess Pavilion. Go sightseeing on ferries to St Mawes, Truro, Flushing and the Helford Passage. On a rainy day visit National Maritime Museum and the Ships and Castle leisure pool. Take advantage of watersports, fishing trips, sailing, diving, with tuition and equipment hire. New owner Judi has moved back from Grenada in the West Indies, to take over Falmouth Lodge. Judi is welcoming guests to enjoy all Cornwall has to offer and looking forward to adding her own character and flavour to the hostel. Relaxed, friendly and clean, Falmouth Lodge Backpackers is just two minutes' walk from the Blue Flag beach of Gyllyngvase and the South West Coast Path and eight minutes' walk into town and the harbour. Free Wi-Fi and internet facilities. Free parking. No curfew. Complimentary tea, coffee and breakfast. Well-equipped kitchen and cosy lounge with TV/DVD and games

DETAILS

- **Open** - All year, 9am to 12pm and 5pm to 10pm
- **Number of beds** - 21: 1 x 2/3; 2 x 4/5; 1 x 6/7; 1 double ensuite (some seaviews)
- **Booking** - Telephone or email in advance
- **Price per night** - From £19 per person
- **Public Transport** - Train - change at Truro for Falmouth Town Station 250 mtrs. National Express to Falmouth. By air - London Stansted/Gatwick to Newquay
- **Directions** - On A39 look for Gyllyngvase Rd on right, then left to Gyllyngvase Ter.

CONTACT: Judi
9 Gyllyngvase Terrace, Falmouth, Cornwall, TR11 4DL
Tel: 01326 319996, mobile 07525 722808
judi@falmouthlodge.co.uk www.falmouthbackpackers.co.uk

TREGEDNA
LODGE

Tregedna Lodge is a recently converted barn, offering comfortable, spacious and flexible accommodation.
Located in the picturesque Maen valley, close to Maenporth beach - a safe, clean, sandy beach with watersports.

Near to Falmouth with a wide range of restaurants, pubs, places of interest. Tregedna is ideally situated for guests to enjoy the many sights and activities that Cornwall has to offer.

4-star graded by English Tourist Board.

DETAILS

- **Open** - All year, all day (please phone between 9am-8pm)
- **Number of beds** - 24: 1x8,1x6,1x2, 2x4 / family (double bed and bunk bed)
- **Booking** - Booking essential. 25% deposit.
- **Price per night** - £18pp (low season) £20pp (July/August). Family rooms £50 per room.
- **Public Transport** - Nearest train stations are within Falmouth, approx 1.5 miles. Nearest bus depot Falmouth. Buses run past Tregedna hourly during summer months, less frequently during winter months.
- **Directions** - By car from Truro take the A39 to Falmouth. Go straight over the double roundabout at Treluswell and straight on (bearing right) at the first of the two roundabouts ahead. At the 2nd, turn left, at the ASDA roundabout go straight across. At the Hillhead roundabout turn right, go straight over the next two roundabouts and continue on this road for approx 2 miles.Tregedna is on your right.

CONTACT: Liz
Tregedna Farm, Maenporth, Falmouth, Cornwall, TR11 5HL
Tel: 01326 250529
tregednafarm@btinternet.com www.tregednafarmholidays.co.uk/lodge.html

For low budget accommodation near Porthtowan, look no further! Porthtowan Backpackers is a small, friendly, family-run place, ideal for surfers, body boarders, walkers, backpackers and students. On Cornwall's North Coast it is only 300 yds from a blue flag beach, one of the best for surfing in Cornwall. At high tide there's lots of sand and at low tide you can walk to Chapel Porth, St. Agnes with a really nice cliff walk back to Porthtowan. Shops and bars are a short walk away. Accommodation comprises a 6 bed room, 4 bed room, double room, and a family room with single bed and triple sleeper (single bunk above a double bed). All rooms ensuite. Also: a communal lounge with 42" TV and kitchenette; storage for surf boards and wetsuits; car parking; roof deck for sunbathing and a barbeque area. Pre-arranged pick-ups from train station £5.

DETAILS

- **Open** - All year, all day
- **Number of beds** - 16-19 : 1x6, 1x4, 1x2, ensuite family room for 4 + futon settee bunk bed in lounge for larger groups (all rooms ensuite).
- **Booking** - Booking is advised by phone or email, with booking fee.
- **Price per night** - Shared room: £20.50pp (4th April to 30 Sept), off peak £18.50pp. 4 nights Mon to Fri £75pp (£66 off peak). Double room: £25pp (£20.50 off peak); 4 nights Mon to Fri £90 (£75 off peak). Family room £82. Continental breakfast included. Sole use available for minimum of 2 days.
- **Public Transport** - Trains at Redruth (4 miles). Buses to village from Truro (Hopleys). Airport at Newquay (Ryan Air, Fly-be, Air South West). Taxis available.
- **Directions** - In the centre of Porthtowan village, between Newquay and St Ives.

CONTACT:
Porthtowan Backpackers, Seamyst, Beach Road, Porthtowan, TR4 8AA
Tel: 01209 891697, Fax: 01209 891697
porthtowanhostel@tiscali.co.uk www.sicklamelazy.co.uk

TRURO
BACKPACKERS LODGE

Truro Backpackers Lodge provides welcoming, family-run accommodation in the heart of Cornwall. Here you will find a comfortable environment and ideal base for your visit to this wonderful county. The house is a rambling 1840's building with many original features and great period charm.
There is a large fully equipped kitchen with an Aga for residents' use. Tea and coffee making facilities are available all day and there is a large comfy lounge with Sky TV to relax in.

The city of Truro provides many attractions and facilities, plus rail and bus links to many other parts of Cornwall. Truro is the capital city of Cornwall and has excellent transport links with the rest of the county, making it a good base for touring. The bus station is just a 5 minute walk away. In addition to the historic Cathedral and popular Theatre, the City boasts many bars and restaurants.

Because the hostel is small advanced booking is essential.

DETAILS

- **Open** - All year, all day
- **Number of beds** - 15: 1x5, 1x4, 1x3, 1x2, 1x1)
- **Booking** - Book in advance by phone.
- **Price per night** - Dorm from £15pp, double room £35, single room from £20pp
- **Public Transport** -   Truro has a train station. Bus station is 5 mins walk. Bus links to many parts of Cornwall.
- **Directions** - See map on website.

CONTACT: Robert Nolan
10 The Parade, Truro, Cornwall, TR1 1QE
Tel: 01872 260857 or 07813 755210
trurobackpackers@aol.com www.trurobackpackers.co.uk

Overlooking one of Newquay's finest beaches, we offer low cost accommodation in the heart of town for international travellers and surfers.

We offer mainly dorm style accommodation, however two twin rooms are available. We have hot showers and board / bike storage can be arranged. There is no curfew, just come and go as you please.

Being centrally based, The Original Backpackers is ideally located for the beaches, the town's many pubs and clubs.

A relaxed atmosphere is guaranteed.

DETAILS

- **Open** - All year (low season group bookings only), all day
- **Number of beds** - 32: 3 x 6 : 2 x 5 : 2 x 2
- **Booking** - Booking is usually essential due to high demand.
- **Price per night** - Off peak from £15pp, peak times from £20pp. Group discounts available off peak.
- **Public Transport** - Newquay has a train station and is served by National Express and an airport
- **Directions** - If driving head towards Fistral Beach, turn right at Tower Garages. Follow this road following outbound traffic, take the second left, signposted Beachfield Ave & The Crescent. Pass in front of The Central, turn right, Beachfield Ave is at the bottom of this road, the hostel is on the right.

CONTACT: Manager
Towan Beach, Beachfield Ave, Newquay, Cornwall, TR7 1DR
Tel: 01637 874668
originalbp@hotmail.com www.originalbackpackers.co.uk

MATTS
SURF LODGE

Newquay is about having fun - and the fun starts here! The Lodge has been open for twelve years and still offers the same easy-going relaxed atmosphere. Newquay is an all year round mecca for surfers, students and travellers, with dramatic cliffs, idyllic beaches and attractions galore. The backpackers is situated at the highest point of the town, only five minutes walk from Central Square with its nightlife and shops. Fistral Beach and the Town beaches are all within ten minutes walk.

All the rooms are clean and comfortable, many with seaview or en-suite facilities. Rates include breakfast, tea /coffee all day and unlimited hot showers. There is a fully equipped kitchen, no curfews, a licensed bar which has good music and 100s of DVDs, plus a games room with pool table and other games. Free car park and secure surfboard and bike storage.

DETAILS

- **Open** - All year, 24 hours
- **Number of beds** - 49:   4 x 6 : 3 x 4 : 1 x 3 : 5 x twin/double
- **Booking** - Recommended for weekends and peak season, but not essential. First night's fee required as deposit.
- **Price per night** - From £8pp (or £10 for en-suite seaview). From £15pp July, August and bank holidays. £45 per week available from September to June.
- **Public Transport** - Local train and bus station. Free pickup when available.
- **Directions** - From coach station walk up St George's Rd, turn right at top. From train station turn left and left again opposite Victoria Hotel onto Berry Rd which leads onto Mount Wise

CONTACT: Matt
110 Mount Wise, Newquay, Cornwall, TR7 1QP
Tel: 01637 874651
matt@surflodge.co.uk www.surflodge.co.uk

Globe Backpackers Plymouth is located just five minutes walk from the ferry port, where boats leave for Roscoff and Santander. The hostel is close to all amenities and a short stroll to the famous Barbican waterfront, Mayflower Steps and city centre. Also near to the bus and railway stations. Excursions to Dartmoor, canoeing on the Tamar River, local boat trips, sailing and walking the coastal paths can be arranged from Plymouth. The theatre, sports/leisure centre, ice-skating rink and National Aquarium are a short walk from the hostel.

Globe Backpackers Plymouth has 4, 6 and 8 bedded dorms, plus 2 double rooms. Bedding and linen is included in the price. Fully equipped self-catering kitchen, TV lounge, separate social room and courtyard garden. Free WiFi. Free tea and coffee.
NO ID. NO STAY (Brits and Overseas all need to produce valid ID).

DETAILS

- **Open** - All year, reception 3.30-11pm, less in winter. No curfew.
- **Number of beds** - 38
- **Booking** - Phone ahead to secure booking
- **Price per night** - From £15pp. Weekly rates available. 50p surcharge for cards.
- **Public Transport** - National Express, local buses and various rail networks.
- **Directions** - From train station walk up Saltash Road to North Croft roundabout. Turn right along Western Approach to Pavilions on your left. From bus station walk up Exeter Street, across roundabout to Royal Parade. Cross road to Union Street, Pavilions on your left. From Plymouth Pavilions walk towards the Hoe, turn left up Citadel Road, the hostel is in 100 metres on the right hand side.

CONTACT:
172 Citadel Road, The Hoe, Plymouth, PL1 3BD
Tel: 01752 225158
info@plymouthbackpackers.co.uk www.plymouthbackpackers.co.uk

TREGOAD PARK
CAMPING BARN

Tregoad Park Camping Barn, situated in rolling countryside on the SE coast of Cornwall, is only 1.5 miles from the pretty harbour village of Looe and close to beaches and great coastal walks. The barn can accommodate up to 32 people in 8 rooms of four beds, making it ideal for families, couples and small and large groups.

Recently refurbished the barn provides all-year accommodation and visitors have access to all the amenities on the park. This includes 55 acres of grounds and, in late spring and summer, a restaurant, bar, shop and outdoor heated swimming pool. In winter the barn is fully heated for added comfort and the coastal paths are wild and wonderful. Check out our website for more details about the barn and camping park.

DETAILS

- **Open** - All year, reception open 9am till 9pm
- **Number of beds** - 32: 8x4
- **Booking** - Please phone or email.
- **Price per night** - Low Season £7, Mid £8, High £11 pp. Per room: (max 4 people) Low Season £25, Mid £30, High £40. Larger groups please call for prices.
- **Public Transport** - Looe train station 1.5 miles, Local buses from Looe stop 500m from site. Taxi from Looe approx £6. Town bus runs to site in July/Aug.
- **Directions** - From Plymouth (A38) to Trerulefoot, turn left at r/bout, 1 mile turn right (A387), after 3 miles road becomes (B3254) Go through "No Mans Land". Tregoad at bottom of hill on left. From East Looe go past garage, turn right to Hessenford (B3254) Follow for 1.5 miles. Tregoad on the right.

CONTACT:
Tregoad Park, St Martins, Looe, Cornwall, PL13 1PB
Tel: 01503 262718
info@tregoadpark.co.uk www.tregoadpark.co.uk/campbarn.htm

BUNKHOUSE
ENGLAND PLUME OF FEATHERS INN

The Plume of Feathers Inn is situated in the moorland village of Princetown which is the main village in Dartmoor National Park. The park covers 368 sq miles and is famous for its rugged beauty, quaint villages, prehistoric remains, and its many peaks, such as High Willhays (2039ft) and YesTor (2030ft).

The Plume is a traditional, family-run inn dating from 1785 with log fires, real ale and plenty of atmosphere. The Alpine Bunkhouse and New Bunkhouse provide comfortable low cost accommodation with bedding included. The Inn also has B&B en-suite accommodation and a 75 tent camping area with toilets and showers. There is a wide range of activities available in the Dartmoor area including sailing, fishing, riding, abseiling, white-water canoeing, climbing, pony trekking and walking.

DETAILS

- **Open** - All year, all day
- **Number of beds** - 42: 2 x 10 5 x 4 1 x 2 1x4
- **Booking** - To secure beds, book in advance with 50% deposit. For weekends 3 to 4 months in advance is advised.
- **Price per night** - From £12pp (bunkhouse), £6.50pp (camping), B&B from £45pp.
- **Public Transport** - Nearest train and National Express services are in Plymouth (17 miles) and Exeter (26 miles). The Transmoor Link bus service between Plymouth and Exeter stops at Princetown, bus fare is £5 - £6. Taxi fare from Plymouth approx £18, from Exeter approx £25.
- **Directions** - The Plume of Feathers Inn is in Princetown village square, next to the Dartmoor National Park High Moorland Centre.

CONTACT:
Princetown, Yelverton, Devon, PL20 6QQ
Tel: 01822 890240, Fax: 01882 890780
pataweir@aol.com

Princetown on Dartmoor is an ideal base for anyone wishing to spend time on Dartmoor whether it is to walk, climb, cycle, kayak or just relax and enjoy the spectacular scenery. Fox Tor Café and Bunkhouse is situated near the centre of the village of Princetown - famous for the prison !

The bunkhouse offers self-catering accommodation for up to 12 in 3 rooms of 4. It is newly decorated, has central heating and a kitchen equipped with microwave, fridge, kettle, toaster and sink. There are separate male and female showers and toilets with underfloor heating. Bunkhouse guests also have the option to use the drying room / store room (big enough for bicycles).

Bunkhouse users can book packed lunches and breakfasts for an early start. No smoking inside.

DETAILS

- **Open** - All year, all day. Arrive from 4pm, leave by 10.30am.
- **Number of beds** - 12: 3 x 4
- **Booking** - Advisable with 50% deposit.
- **Price per night** - From £9.50 per person. Sole use £100.
- **Public Transport** - Trains at Exeter and Plymouth. DevonBus 98 Tavistock-Princetown. Devon Bus 82 Exeter-Plymouth. First 272 Gunnislake-Newton Abbot.
- **Directions** - GR 591 735. Just off the mini roundabout in the centre of Princetown on the Two Bridges road (B3212). 20 mins drive from Tavistock, 15 mins Yelverton, 35 mins Ashburton.

CONTACT: Sam Wyton
Two Bridges Road, Princetown, Yelverton, Devon, PL20 6QS
Tel: 01822 890238
foxtorcafe@aol.com www.foxtorcafe.co.uk

DARTMOOR
EXPEDITION CENTRE

Great for walking, climbing, canoeing, caving, archaeology, painting or visiting places of interest nearby. Dartmoor Expedition Centre has two 300-year-old barn bunkhouses with cobbled floors and thick granite walls. Simple but comfortable accommodation for groups of 4+ only, with bunk beds and a wood burning stove. Radiant heaters (two in each area) and night storage heating (one in each barn). Kitchen area equipped with fridge, water heater, electric stoves and kettles. All crockery and pans provided, and there is freezer space available. Electric appliances are coin operated (£1 coins). Solar hot water system for free showers in wash rooms. House Barn has the living area downstairs and upstairs sleeps 9 plus 5 in an inner cubicle. Gate Barn sleeps 11 downstairs and 10 upstairs. There are two upgraded rooms (1 double, 1 twin). Beds provided with sheet/pillow/pillowcase, sleeping bags needed.

DETAILS

- **Open** - All year, 7.30 am to 10.30 pm
- **Number of beds** - 37: 1 x 1 : 1 x 2 : 1 x 8 : 1 x 5 : 1 x 11 : 1 x 10
- **Booking** - Book in advance with 25% deposit.
- **Price per night** - £13pp (£15 per person in upgraded room). Minimum of 4 people.
- **Public Transport** - Newton Abbot is the nearest train station. In summer there are buses to Widecombe (1.5 miles from hostel). Taxi fare from station £30.
- **Directions** - GR 700 764. Come down Widecombe Hill into the village. Turn right 200yds after school and travel up a steep hill past Southcombe onto the open moor. Continue for one mile until you reach crossroads. Turn right and take first left after 400yds. Hostel is 200yds on left.

CONTACT: John Earle
Widecombe-in-the-Moor, Newton Abbot, Devon, TQ13 7TX
Tel: 01364 621249
earle@clara.co.uk www.dartmoorbase.co.uk

TORQUAY
BACKPACKERS

Torquay is on the English Riviera, famous for warm weather and Mediterranean atmosphere. Turquoise sea, red cliffs, long sandy beaches and secret shingle coves combine to create one of the UK's most beautiful coastlines. It is renowned as a watersport mecca with sailing, water-skiing, windsurfing, diving etc and nightlife with pubs, clubs and restaurants a mere stagger from the hostel which is in the heart of Torquay.

Hostel activities include beach barbecues, jam nights, international food nights and video evenings. There are also trips to Dartmoor exploring emerald river valleys where pixies dwell and the open tor-dotted moors. The hostel offers travellers a friendly, almost family atmosphere. Those who find it hard to leave can easily find work.

DETAILS

- **Open** - Closed Nov 09 till March 2010, 24 hrs. Check in 9-11am and 5-9pm.
- **Number of beds** - 45: 1 x double, 3 x 4, 1 x 5, 3 x 6 , 1 x 8.
- **Booking** - Advised at all times.
- **Price per night** - £8 to £14 per night. £60 to £85 per week.
- **Public Transport** - Torquay can be reached by coach or train from all major towns. From London take a train from Paddington/Waterloo or a coach from Victoria/Heathrow.
- **Directions** - Drivers: follow signs to sea front. Turn left. At junction with lights and Belgrave Hotel, bear left up Sheddon Hill. Next T junction is Abbey Road. Turn left. Hostel is 200m on right.

CONTACT: The Manager
119 Abbey Road, Torquay, Devon, TQ2 5NP
Tel: 01803 299924
jane@torquaybackpackers.co.uk www.torquaybackpackers.co.uk

Sparrowhawk is a small, friendly eco-hostel located within the breathtaking Dartmoor National Park. The hostel is situated in the village centre of Moretonhampstead, 14 miles west of Exeter and can be reached easily by frequent direct bus. Accommodation is in a beautifully converted, fully equipped stable. High open moorland is close by for great hiking, cycling and off-road mountain biking, while the rocky tors rising up on the hilltops offer climbers a challenge. Wild swims in the rivers amongst woodlands or out on the moor is a must for the adventurous traveller. Magnificent stone circles, dwellings and burial sites of ancient civilizations together with wild ponies, buzzards, flora and fauna are all here to be explored. Moretonhampstead has shops, cafés, pubs, good food, live music, and an outdoor heated swimming pool. Dartmoor Way and CTC End2End cycle routes are on the doorstep. Sparrowhawk has solar-heated showers, waste recycling, a secure bike shed and a bus stop nearby.

DETAILS

- **Open** - All year, all day
- **Number of beds** - 18: 1 x 14 plus double / family room
- **Booking** - Book ahead if possible by phone or email.
- **Price per night** - Adults £15. Under 14 £8. Double/family room £36/£45 for 4.
- **Public Transport** - Direct from Exeter Bus 359 or 82. Direct from Plymouth Bus 82. From Okehampton or Newton Abbot Bus 173 or 179. Enquires Tel 0870 6082608.
- **Directions** - From Exeter, take the B3212 signposted on the one-way system at Exe Bridges. From Plymouth head towards Yelverton and then B3212. The hostel is on Ford Street (A382) 100 metres from tourist office.

CONTACT: Alison
45 Ford Street, Moretonhampstead, Dartmoor, Devon, TQ13 8LN
Tel: 01647 440318 - 07870 513570
ali@sparrwohawkbackpackers.co.uk www.sparrowhawkbackpackers.co.uk

BLYTHESWOOD
HOSTEL

Blytheswood Hostel is a detached wooden chalet in secluded woodland overlooking the Teign Valley on the eastern edge of Dartmoor. It is an ideal base for exploring rugged high Dartmoor and the delightful lower slopes rich in wild flowers, butterflies and birds. The surrounding native woodland and nature reserve are home to badgers, deer and otters. There are walks straight from the door (come and see the daffodils in spring) and fishing, golf and cycling nearby. Local attractions include Castle Drogo, The Miniature Pony Centre, Canonteign Falls and picturesque thatched villages. The cathedral city of Exeter is 8 miles away and the beaches of South Devon are 40 minutes drive. Blytheswood Hostel provides flexible accommodation in cosy rooms sleeping between 2 and 8 people in bunks. It is ideal for use by families and groups who can book sole use of the whole hostel. There is a fully equipped self catering kitchen, lounge/dining room, drying room and picnic areas. Duvets and linen provided.

DETAILS

■ **Open** - All year. Reception open 8 to 10.30am and 5 to 8pm (The hostel is closed between 10.30am and 5pm, unless prior arrangement
■ **Number of beds** - 24: 1x2, 2x4,1x6,1x8
■ **Booking** - Booking is essential. Deposit required.
■ **Price per night** - £14pp. Children under 18 £8.
■ **Public Transport** - Trains Exeter. Bus 359 from Exeter + 82 on summer wknds
■ **Directions** - On the B3212 between Exeter and Moretonhampstead, 1mile outside of Dunsford. Approx 100m from Steps Bridge, opposite car park. Please use car park when staying at the hostel.

CONTACT: Patrick and Tracey
Steps Bridge, Dunsford, Exeter, Devon, EX6 7EQ
Tel: 01647 252435
blytheswood@blueyonder.co.uk www.blytheswood.co.uk

EXETER
GLOBE BACKPACKERS ENGLAND

A city centre hostel within easy walk of the beautiful old port, Cathedral, shopping district and a wonderful mix of pubs, clubs, live music, restaurants and café scene. Great for the young and "young at heart" who enjoy a vibrant city centre. Twenty minutes drive to Exmouth with its 2 miles sandy beach for all sail sports, and the same to Dartmoor National Park for walking, climbing, cycling and horse riding. Exeter is also an excellent place to find work and just 2½ hours by train to London. The Globe has some new private rooms: in addition to male, female and mixed dorms there are three large double rooms with additional bunks, sitting area, tea/coffee making facilities, hairdryer and towels. One of these can be used as a twin room and another has a four poster bed. Free WiFi to all guests with laptops. Not suitable for hen and stag groups, DSS, unaccompanied under 18s and families. ID required from everyone.

DETAILS

■ **Open** - All year, check in 3.30 -11pm only, closed 12 - 3.30pm, check out 8.30 -11am, earlier by arrangement
■ **Number of beds** - 42:dorms: 1x10, 1x8, 2x6, private rms 3x4- can use as dbl/twin.
■ **Booking** - To secure booking phone ahead.
■ **Price per night** - £16.50 - £18.75pp, Weekly rates from £75pp. Private rooms from £42 (2 sharing), £75 (4 sharing) 50p charge for cards.
■ **Public Transport** - National Express, local bus companies and rail networks.
■ **Directions** - Bus Station: Cross road, take side turning Southernhay East. Stay on LH side until Southgate Hotel.We are diagonally opposite on other side of junction. From Central Station go down Queen St to High St, turn right and at 1st lights, turn left South St, continue to junction at bottom of hill. Cross at lights, we are on right.

CONTACT:
71 Holloway Street, Exeter, EX2 4JD
Tel: 01392 215521
info@exeterbackpackers.co.uk www.exeterbackpackers.co.uk

You can make your stay whatever you want it to be.

A relaxed place with a variety of bedrooms and large garden.
Close to town, beaches and South West Coastal Path.

An ideal base to see the South West's attractions: The Eden Project, Tintagel Castle, The Tamar Lakes, Dartmoor and Bodmin Moor. There are competition standard surfing beaches nearby. Families with children aged over 5 welcome. Meet old friends or make new ones, on the deck, in the lounge or around the dining room table after cooking up a storm in the fully fitted kitchen.

DETAILS

- **Open** - All year except Christmas week, 8.30am to 1pm and 4.30pm to 10.30pm
- **Number of beds** - 43: 2x6 : 5x4 : 1x3 : 1x2 : 3xdbl
- **Booking** - Advisable, credit card secures booking. Photo ID at check in. (Groups 6 or more by prior booking)
- **Price per night** - From £14pp dorm rooms (single night supplement)
- **Public Transport** - To Bude: From Exeter Via Okehampton X9. From Plymouth X8. From Newquay X10 (changing at Okehampton). From Bideford 85. All buses- First Bus Company. There are train and bus links from London to Exeter.
- **Directions** - From A39, head into Bude down Stratton Rd past Morrisons on your right, follow the road down past Esso garage. Take the second road on the right, Killerton Road (before the Bencollen Pub). Continue up to the top of the road and Northshorebude is on the corner on your left. Turn into Redwood Grove and parking is the first on the left.

CONTACT: Sean or Janine
57 Killerton Road, Bude, Cornwall, EX23 8EW
Tel: 01288 354256 or 07970 149486
info@northshorebude.com www.northshorebude.com

A former Victorian school, Elmscott is surrounded by unspoilt coastline with sea views of Lundy Island. This property offers a next-to-nature retreat. Great for walking, cycling, surfing and bird watching. There are amazing rock formations and many quiet lanes to explore. The famous fishing village of Clovelly is a few miles away with its cobbled streets and pretty harbour. Also nearby is Hartland Abbey where Sense and Sensibility was filmed. Elmscott is located a few minutes walk from the South West Coast Path which passes many spectacular coves and river mouths. The accommodation is in one unit of 20 beds and another of 12. It has mixed dorms, single sex dorms and private rooms.

In winter it is only available for groups (of up to 35 people). There is a kitchen, a well stocked shop in summer and a games room close by. Self catering only.

DETAILS

- **Open** - All year (groups only in winter), 24 hours
- **Number of beds** - 32 (35 in winter): 1 unit of 20: 2x6, 2x4; 1 unit of 12: 1x6, 1x4, 1x2. Extra 3 bed room available for sole use bookings in winter.
- **Booking** - In summer book direct with the hostel by phone or email. In winter book via the YHA website, or for last minute sole use bookings call the owners.
- **Price per night** - Adult £15 to £20, under 16's £12.50 to £15.50 (discounts for YHA members). Enquire for special prices for groups or longer stays.
- **Public Transport** - Nearest trains Barnstaple (25 miles). Buses from Barnstaple to Hartland (4 miles from hostel). Phone hostel for taxi service.
- **Directions** - The hostel is in the small hamlet of Elmscott 4 miles from the village of Hartland. Grid Ref 231 217.

CONTACT: John & Thirza Goaman
Elmscott, Hartland, Bideford, Devon, EX39 6ES
Tel: 01237 441276, Hostel 01237 441367
john.goa@virgin.net www.elmscott.org.uk

YARDE ORCHARD
CAFÉ AND BUNKHOUSE

Yarde Orchard lies at the highest point on North Devon's Tarka Trail. Two of the National Cycle Network routes - Devon Coast to Coast (route 27) and the West Country Way (route 3) also pass our gate. The bunkhouse offers accommodation for upto 14. Camping is available for small tents between the orchard trees with the option of using our 2-person vango ridge tents. A fire pit and barbecue are available for guests to use with a nominal charge for locally sourced charcoal/fuelwood.

Yarde Café offers a hearty homecooked menu with an emphasis on local produce and a licensed bar offering Devon ales and ciders and an affordable wine list. The bunkhouse is open all year round with the café available for breakfast, lunch and supper (everyday through the summer and easter holidays, weekends and half-terms out of season).

DETAILS

- **Open** - All year, all day
- **Number of beds** - 14: 1x6, 1x4, 1x4 (family) + cot
- **Booking** - Book by phone or email
- **Price per night** - bunk/sleeping bag £12 per night (£8 under 18), family room £40 per night, exclusive use £140 1st night, £120 subsequent nights.
- **Public Transport** - 118 bus (Barnstaple-Tavistock), alight at Gribble Inn. Trains: Barnstaple station (with cycle hire) then 18 miles along Tarka Trail to Yarde.
- **Directions** - By car: From Great Torrington take A386 towards Hatherleigh. After 2 miles at Gribble (118 bus stops here), take minor right turn signed Petersmarland, Petrockstowe. By bike: Yarde Orchard is located on NCN routes 3 & 27 at East Yarde

CONTACT: David Job
Yarde Orchard, East Yarde, Petersmarland, Torrington, Devon, EX38 8QA
Tel: 01805 601778 Mob: 07972 786306
info@yarde-orchard.co.uk www.yarde-orchard.co.uk

OCEAN
BACKPACKERS

Ocean Backpackers is a clean, homely hostel with a relaxed atmosphere and no curfews. It's situated in a quaint North Devon town built around an ancient fishing harbour. Central to the harbour itself, the bus station, high street, pubs, restaurants and many surfer's favourites- Woolacombe, Croyde and Saunton. Surf's down? Don't despair! Try other local activities such as quad biking, paint balling, kayaking, coasteering, horse riding and mountain biking. Adrenalin not your thing? Then take a trip to Lundy Island (a national marine reserve) and spot rare birds, seals, dolphins and basking sharks. It's wonderful walking country! The coastal path between Woolacombe and Lynton is breathtaking and Exmoor has an abundance of walks through Britain's most spectacular scenery. Hostel facilities include lounge, free internet access, self-catering kitchen, surf board storage and a car park. Ilfracombe has plenty of summer work so why not come and hang out here for a while.

DETAILS

- **Open** - All year, reception 9am-10pm. No curfew.
- **Number of beds** - 44:- 1x8, 5x6, 1 x double, 1 x double & bunk.
- **Booking** - Booking advised but not essential.
- **Price per night** - From £10-14 in dorm. Double/Twin £30 - £35 per room.
- **Public Transport** -   Direct coaches from London Victoria/Heathrow/Plymouth/ Exeter. By train take the Tarka line to Barnstaple then bus to Ilfracombe.
- **Directions** - From M5 take A361. From Cornwall take A39 to Barnstaple then follow the signs to Ilfracombe. Ocean Backpackers is by the harbour opposite the bus station. For more detailed directions go to our website and click on directions.

CONTACT: Chris and Abby
29 St James Place, Ilfracombe, Devon, EX34 9BJ
Tel: 01271 867835
info@oceanbackpackers.co.uk www.oceanbackpackers.co.uk

EXMOOR
BASECAMP

Exmoor Basecamp is a converted barn giving comfortable, high standard bunkhouse accommodation. There are 2 large dormitories each sleeping 8 in bunkbeds and a 2 bedded leaders' room. There are excellent hot showers, drying room, lounge/eating area, fully equipped kitchen and a barbecue. The Basecamp is situated at Countisbury on the North Devon coast. The surrounding countryside includes the dramatic Watersmeet Valleys, moors of Exmoor and coastal paths. Lynton and Lynmouth are the nearest villages and the Atlantic surf beaches are within easy reach. The Basecamp is owned and managed by The National Trust and a free night's accommodation can be earned for each day's conservation work arranged with local wardens. Other local activities are walking, horse riding, boat trips, fishing and cycling. However you spend your time the basecamp is ideal for getting away from it all.

DETAILS

- **Open** - All year, 24 hours
- **Number of beds** - 18: 2x8, 1x2
- **Booking** - Booking essential with £50 deposit
- **Price per night** - £120 midweek nights, £160 Fri/Sat/Sun nights. £50 for later departures. 10% discount for 4+ nights (except Easter, Christmas & New Year).
- **Public Transport** - The nearest train and coach stations are in Barnstaple (approx. 20 miles), From there take a local bus to Lynton. Buses to Countisbury are very limited and summer only. Taxis from Lynton approx £5.
- **Directions** - From Minehead follow A39 to Countisbury. We are on the left after the Blue Ball Inn. From Lynmouth we are first building on right. Car park is opposite.

CONTACT: Karen
Countisbury, Lynton, Devon, EX35 6NE
Tel: 01598 741101 / 07974 829171
exmoor.basecamp@nationaltrust.org.uk www.nationaltrust.org.uk/basecamps

Base Lodge is ideally situated for exploring Exmoor, The Quantocks and The North Devon Coast by mountain bike or foot. Excellent off and on road mountain biking for all levels. Guided mountain biking and secure lock up facilities. Exmoor affords excellent scenic moor and coastal views and the 600+ mile-long South West Coastal Path starts here in Minehead. Other activities can be arranged including mountain biking, navigational training, climbing, surfing, pony-trekking and natural history walks and talks.

Base Lodge is clean, comfortable and friendly, providing a shared fully equipped kitchen and dining room. Local pubs and restaurants are all within walking distance.

DETAILS

- **Open** - All day access once booked, bookings taken by e-mail or phone or take a chance and call in. All day access, reception open from 3pm
- **Number of beds** - 23: 2x7,1x5, 1x3, 1x1
- **Booking** - Advisable. Deposit required for groups or exclusive use.
- **Price per night** - Dorms £15, private twin or single £17pp. Exclusive use of Base Lodge from £250. Family room discount.
- **Public Transport** - Coach station 5 min walk. Buses from Taunton, Exeter and Tiverton. Train station: Taunton (26 miles). Steam railway from Taunton to Minehead.
- **Directions** - With the sea behind you, drive/walk up The Parade until you reach Park Street, continue straight on until you reach a fork. Take the right hand into The Parks (Baptist Church on your right). Only limited parking is available.

CONTACT: Wendy or Graham
16 The Parks, Minehead, Somerset, TA24 8BS
Tel: 01643 703520 or 0773 1651536
togooutdoors@hotmail.com www.togooutdoors.com

CAMPBELL ROOM
ENGLAND GROUP ACCOMMODATION

The Campbell Room offers self-catering group accommodation for scouts and other youth organisations, schools and universities, training courses, and groups of walkers, cyclists and others. Sheltered at the mouth of a rural valley on the edge of the Quantock Hills Area of Outstanding Natural Beauty, the building offers a main activity hall which can also sleep 18 on comfortable mattresses, 2 bedrooms each sleeping 3, a fully equipped kitchen, washrooms, showers, drying room, a campfire area and space for 1 or 2 tents.

Many routes for walking, hiking and mountain biking pass close to the centre and a swimming pool is nearby. Groups with transport can access many attractions and activities including beaches with rock pools and fossils, the coastal resort of Minehead, the West Somerset Railway, Wells Cathedral, Glastonbury Tor, Wookey Hole, Cheddar Gorge, Dunster Castle, Cricket St Thomas Wildlife Park, Exmoor, and the county town of Taunton.

DETAILS

- **Open** - All year, by arrangement
- **Number of beds** - 24: 1 x 18 : 2 x 3
- **Booking** - Booking essential, one month in advance with deposit.
- **Price per night** - £3.95pp (2 leaders free for groups over 12), min £48 per night
- **Public Transport** - Train and bus stations at Bridgwater. Take the bus to Nether Stowey, just over 1 mile from the Campbell Room.
- **Directions** - GR ST 187381. M5 junction 23 or 24 Bridgwater. A39 west to Nether Stowey, follow signs to Over Stowey. From church follow road 300m east, then 400m south (toward Forest Trail Ramscombe). Centre at T junction (W of Aley, TA5 1HB)

CONTACT: Pat Briggs
36 Old Rd, North Petherton, Bridgwater, Somerset, TA6 6TG
Tel: 01278 662537
info@campbellroom.org.uk www.campbellroom.org.uk

Larkshall is the Cerberus Spelaeological Society's headquarters and offers excellent modern facilities. As well as for members it is available for use by guest individuals or groups wanting accommodation on Mendip. It makes an ideal base for caving as well as many other outdoor activities including walking, cycling, climbing etc. It is also a good base for anyone wanting to explore the Somerset countryside and within very easy reach are the famous tourist attractions of Wells, Wookey Hole, Cheddar Gorge and Caves, and the city of Bath. The accommodation provides all the home comforts with a kitchen/dining room, large lounge, and showers and changing facilities. For anyone so inclined the central corridor can be traversed using the climbing holds fitted along the wall. There are two guest communal bunkrooms with ample space to sleep large groups in comfort.

For those that prefer, it is possible to camp, and there is a large car park.

DETAILS

■ **Open** - All year, 24 hours. Key available by prior arrangement.

■ **Number of beds** - 31 (1 x 12 + 1 x 19). Unlimited camping available.

■ **Booking** - Advisable. Email preferred via website, or phone or write.   Non refundable deposit of £20 a night required.

■ **Price per night** - £5. Sole use of bunkrooms £60 and £95. Min 2 nights at wknds.

■ **Public Transport** - There is a bus stop near the crossroads in Oakhill on the A367. Taxis are available in Shepton Mallet, Wells and Frome

■ **Directions** - Larkshall is 4 miles north of Shepton Mallet and 15 miles south of Bath off the A367. At crossroads in Oakhill take road to Stoke St Michael. Larkshall is about one mile from Oakhill on the right (ST 6505 4720).

CONTACT:
Larkshall, Midway, Stoke St Michael, Somerset, BA3 5JE
Tel: 0845 475 0954
hostelbookings@cerberusspeleo.org.uk www.cerberusspeleo.org.uk

BATH
YMCA

Bath YMCA offers a warm welcome and the best value accommodation. From its central location all the sights of this World Heritage City are easily reached on foot. Bath is also an ideal base for the explorer. Staying longer brings Stonehenge, Wookey Hole Caves, Cheddar Gorge, the southern reaches of the Cotswolds, and more exciting destinations all within reach. With a total of 210 beds, we have a great deal of experience in making all our guests feel comfortable. We have a fully air conditioned lounge area, colour TV and restaurant which offers a varied lunch menu at special YMCA subsidised prices. Laundry, lockers, pool and football table, telephone fax and internet facilities are available. The Health and Fitness suite provides a steam and sauna room and new equipment with a qualified staff team who have worked hard to create a club atmosphere. 'Fitness with Fun' is our motto. Couples, families, groups and backpackers' are all welcome, you don't have to be young or male. All these facilities and the YMCA's traditional sense of community will make your stay a truly memorable one.

DETAILS

- **Open** - All year, 24-hour reception
- **Number of beds** - 210: 2x14, 1x12, 3x10, 7x4, 6x3, 40x2, 11x1
- **Booking** - Credit card guarantees.
- **Price per night** - From £17pp dorm bed, inc. light breakfast.
- **Public Transport** - Bath has a train station and is served by National Express.
- **Directions** - Located approximately ½ mile from rail and bus station. Broad Street is located near the Podium Shopping Centre off Walcott Street.

CONTACT: Reception
International House, Broad Street Place, Bath, BA1 5LH
Tel: 01225 325900, Fax: 01225 462065
stay@bathymca.co.uk www.bathymca.co.uk

48 SWANAGE AUBERGE
BUNKHOUSE

ENGLAND

Swanage Auberge, the bunkhouse that cares, is a refuge for climbers, walkers and divers. Situated at the eastern end of the Jurassic Coast with excellent walking, diving and rock climbing on the doorstep. The bunkhouse is in the centre of Swanage town, a stones throw from the South West Coast Path and all local amenities - pubs, shops, restaurants etc. Swanage Auberge is totally self contained with central heating, fully equipped self catering kitchen, drying and laundry facilities and a meals service if required. There are two bunk rooms, one with 4 standard bunks and the other with 6 alpine style places (3 and 3). There is also accommodation for 4 and a family room in the adjoining house. Pillow and towel provided and bedding is available for hire. There are two showers, loos and washrooms and an area to hang and wash wetsuits. There is a rucksack and boot rack in the entrance corridor. Sandals are provided. Parking for 2 vehicles is usually available when booking (first come first served basis). Price includes cereal breakfast and beverages. Packed lunches available (see website for further details).

DETAILS

- **Open** - All year, opens 5.30pm (all day once booked in)
- **Number of beds** - 17: 1x6, 2x4, family room (dbl + single)
- **Booking** - Book by phone or email. Booking form online. 20% deposit required.
- **Price per night** - £16 pp including cereal breakfast and free tea or coffee. Group rates available. Hire of duvet with sheets £2.50 per week. Credit cards not accepted.
- **Public Transport** - Bus from Poole or Wareham. Train service to Wareham.
- **Directions** - At the end of the first left hand alley off Mount Pleasant Lane.

CONTACT: Pete or Pam
45 High Street, Swanage, Dorset, BH19 2LX
Tel: 01929 424368, mobile 07711117668 , Fax: 01929 424368
bookings@swanageauberge.co.uk www.swanageauberge.co.uk

BRISTOL
BACKPACKERS HOSTEL

  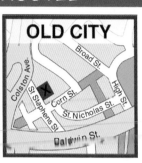

City Centre hostel - clean & comfy beds - free linen & hot showers - big kitchen - free tea, coffee & hot choc - indoor bicycle storage.

Late night basement bar - piano & guitar room - dvd lounge - cheap internet machines - free laptop wireless access - luggage storage room - laundrette.

Run by backpackers for backpackers - mixed/single sex dorms - private rooms - no curfew after check in

DETAILS

■ **Open** - All year, reception hours 9am -11.30pm (No curfew)
■ **Number of beds** - 90: Bunk bed accommodation in private twin, private triple or 6, 8 and 10 bed dorms.
■ **Booking** - Most cards, phone or walk in.
■ **Price per night** - £16pp. Private rooms from £36. See website for discounts.
■ **Public Transport** - See below.
■ **Directions** - Located in 'Old City', the historic centre of Bristol. From Bristol Central Bus Station (Marlborough St) 7 mins walk. Follow pedestrian signs to 'Old City' then see map above. From Bristol Temple Meads train station 12 mins walk. Follow pedestrian signs to 'Old City' then see map above. Or take bus number 8 or 9 to the 'Centre Promenade'. Disembark at The Bristol Hippodrome. From Airport take the 'Shuttle' to the Central Bus Station. By road follow signs for Baldwin Street in the city centre.

CONTACT:
17 St Stephen's Street, Bristol, BS1 1EQ
Tel: 0117 9257900
info@bristolbackpackers.co.uk www.bristolbackpackers.co.uk

The David Donald Field Studies Base offers accommodation for educational, family and other groups in a converted 1940 RAF radar station, renovated with central heating and double glazing. It sleeps 24 but up to 30 if some wish to camp and share the indoor facilities. There is a well equipped kitchen, a spacious community room, a drying room, picnic area, BBQ / campsite area, a games area and lots of parking. There are ramps to the main building and adapted toilets for wheelchair users, but for these the drive to the centre is very difficult without a car. This is an outstanding area for environmental studies and is also popular with groups or families enjoying a relaxing break, reunions, walking, outdoor actvities and other social events. It is within an SSSI, and has Lulworth Cove, Durdle Door, The Arne Nature Reserve, Purbeck Marine Reserve, Corfe Castle, Poole Harbour and lots of other interesting sites nearby.

DETAILS

- **Open** - All year ,
- **Number of beds** - 24: 1x2, 1x2 ensuite, 1x9, 1x11 plus limited camping.
- **Booking** - Booking required with £200 deposit. Phone for availability. Forms can be downloaded from website and returned to P&D Adv Centre, Recreation Road, Parkstone, Poole, BH12 2EA,
- **Price per night** - Prices for 2010: whole centre from £300 per night. £5 per person for numbers exceeding 24, up to a maximum of 30. Bed linen £5 per person.
- **Public Transport** - Train to Wareham. Wilts & Dorset Buses to Worth Matravers.
- **Directions** - Arriving in Worth Matravers from Kingston bear right by duck pond into Pikes Lane. After Renscombe Farm road turns sharp right then left onto Renscombe Rd. 200m further the driveway to the base is on the right. OS SY967777

CONTACT: David Donald Field Studies Base
Off Renscombe Rd, Worth Matravers, Isle of Purbeck, Dorset BH19 3LL
Tel: 01202 710701
enquiries@dorsetadventure.co.uk www.dorsetadventure.co.uk

AVON TYRRELL
ACTIVITY CENTRE

Avon Tyrrell Activity Centre is set in 65 acres of private grounds in the heart of the New Forest National Park. The centre is committed to providing fun, educational and activity holidays and breaks to all groups of people regardless of age and ability in a secure and safe environment.

Our Grade 1 listed house can provide full board for groups of between 15 and 110, mostly in dormitory style bedrooms. There are also twin rooms, some with ensuite facilities. Our self catering wooden lodges range from 6, to 12, to the largest 14 berth lodge. Groups can also stay on our camp site nestled amongst the pine trees, which is open between April and October. Families and day visit groups are also welcomed. All our accommodation has disabled access and disability equipment is available to guests in both the house and lodges at no extra cost.

DETAILS

- **Open** - All year, all day
- **Number of beds** - 110 in Main House 6,12 and 14 berth lodges, large campsite
- **Booking** - Booking essential.
- **Price per night** - Please visit our website for 2010 prices, special offers and late deals.
- **Public Transport** - Trains at Christchurch, New Milton and Brockenhurst (6,7 & 10 miles).
- **Directions** - GR SU 185 003. The Centre is half way between the villages of Burley and Bransgore.

CONTACT:
Bransgore, Hampshire, BH23 8EE
Tel: 01425 672347, Fax: 01425 675108
info@ukyouth.org www.avontyrrell.org.uk

Britain's only island city, Portsmouth is a unique blend of seaside resort and naval heritage. Portsmouth and Southsea Backpackers is the city's only independent hostel for travellers. It offers a friendly cosmopolitan atmosphere within easy reach of the major tourist attractions including the ships (Victory, Mary Rose and Warrior), the D Day museum, and the new Gunwharf Quays. It is only 150m from the beach and in an area containing an excellent variety of pubs, restaurants and clubs. The accommodation is mostly in small dorms for 4 people, but there are also twins, doubles and family rooms, some with en-suite facilities. All hot showers are free. We have a large social area which has Freeview TV, an internet facility, pool, darts and a dining area. There is a fully equipped kitchen, BBQ, seating in the garden area and secure cycle storage.

DETAILS

- **Open** - All year, service: 8am to 11pm
- **Number of beds** - 68: 1x8, 1x6, 10x4, 7x2
- **Booking** - Advisable, groups require deposit
- **Price per night** - From £15pp, £34 per room (double/twin), £38 (double ensuite)
- **Public Transport** - From any bus or train station catch a bus to Southsea and get off at the Strand. Walk back the way the bus has come and Florence Road is 2nd left. If there are 2+ people get a taxi. Ferries from Portsmouth go to France, Spain, the Channel Islands, and the Isle of Wight.
- **Directions** - From the M27 take the M275 to Portsmouth and follow signs to the seafront. Drive along the seafront until blue glass building (The Pyramids) and turn left. Turn right at mini roundabout and Florence Road is then 1st on the left.

CONTACT: Sammi
4 Florence Road, Southsea, Portsmouth, Hants, P05 2NE
Tel: 023 92832495, Fax: 023 92832495
info@portsmouthbackpackers.co.uk www.portsmouthbackpackers.co.uk

WETHERDOWN
HOSTEL

The Wetherdown Lodge is part of The Sustainability Centre which promotes environmental awareness and low impact living. It is on top of the South Downs, and is an award-winning example of an eco-renovation and a comfortable place to stay, just a few steps from the South Downs National Trail. A clean, bright, friendly hostel, open to all. Ideal for family get-togethers, walkers, cyclists, business away-days and wedding parties. The hostel has spacious communal areas, comfortable bedrooms with hand basins & all linen provided & separate bathrooms / toilets throughout. A 'help yourself' breakfast is included in the price, available from 8am. There is a small fully equipped self-catering kitchen. Packed lunches available by order. The centre has large grounds with woodland trails, a guided walk and cafe open thurs-sun. Camping is also available all year round with tipis and yurts for hire. Within 2 miles of the hostel are 4 country pubs, local shops, Chinese, Indian & Pizza takeaways.

DETAILS

- **Open** - All year, all day
- **Number of beds** - 34: 10 x 3, 2 x 2
- **Booking** - Book by telephone or online.
- **Price per night** - Shared rooms (twin/triple) £22.50pp Group booking (8+) £19.50pp. All prices include linen & breakfast.
- **Public Transport** - Trains at Petersfield, 6 miles (£10 by taxi). From station 38 bus to Clanfield or the 52 or 67 to East Meon.
- **Directions** - GR 676 189. From A3 take Clanfield turn (brown sign). Turn right after Rising Sun in Clanfield. At top of hill, turn left signed Droxford.

CONTACT: Hazel, Rob or Mark
The Sustainability Centre, Droxford Road, East Meon, Hampshire, GU32 1HR
Tel: 01730 823549, Mob: 07884 258713, Fax: 01730 823168
accommodation@sustainability-centre.org www.sustainability-centre.org

Gumber Bothy is a converted traditional Sussex barn on the National Trust's Slindon Estate in the heart of the South Downs. It provides simple overnight accommodation or camping for walkers, riders and cyclists, just off the South Downs Way. The bothy forms part of Gumber Farm and is 5 minutes walk from Stane Street, the Roman Road that crosses the South Downs Way at Bignor Hill. Facilities include platforms in 3 dorms sleeping up to 27, good hot showers and basins, kitchen/diner with gas hob and washing up facilities, a few pots and pans provided.

Paddock for friendly horses and racks for bikes.
Wheelchair accessible (please phone for details).
Sorry, but as we're a sheep farm, no dogs and most definitely NO CARS.
Not suitable for under fives.

DETAILS

- **Open** - March to October (inclusive), flexible
- **Number of beds** - 27: 1 x 18, 1 x 5, 1 x 4 plus overflow area
- **Booking** - Booking by telephone. Booking required for groups with 50% deposit.
- **Price per night** - £10.00 (adult), £5.00 (under 16s).
- **Public Transport** - Train stations, Arundel (urban) 5 miles, Amberley (rural) 4 miles, Chichester (8 miles). National Express stop at Chichester. Buses 84 and 85 from Chichester, stop at Fontwell and then it is a 3 mile walk to the Bothy. Taxi fare from Arundel to Northwood Farm is approx £10, followed by a 2 mile country walk.
- **Directions** - OS Map LR197 or E121 GR 961 119, Nearest car park GR 973 129. No vehicular access. One mile off South Downs Way on Stane Street bridleway

CONTACT: Bothy Warden
Slindon Estate Yard, Slindon, Arundel, West Sussex, BN18 0RG
Tel: 01243 814730
katie.archer@nationaltrust.org.uk

PUTTENHAM
ECO CAMPING BARN

The Camping Barn is a traditional Surrey timber barn in Puttenham village on the North Downs Way and Sustrans NCN22 cycle route. It is located in the Surrey Hills Area of Outstanding Natural Beauty with delightful cycling and walking routes all around. There is a fully equipped self-catering kitchen, a shower, toilets and foam covered sleeping platforms, all to a high standard. Electricity and hot water included but bring your own towel and sleeping bag (or hire one - £2.50 a stay). Evening meals are available in the village. The Barn has many sustainable features including solar panels and rainwater collection for flushing toilets. The Barn is wardened. NO CARS ON SITE. Excellent cycle shed. Young people under 18 are welcome but must be accompanied by a responsible adult.

DETAILS

- **Open** - Easter to October, 1700 to 1000
- **Number of beds** - sleeping platforms for 11
- **Booking** - booking is essential
- **Price per night** - £12 adults, £10 under 18. Sole use by arrangement. £2 'green' discount if arriving by foot, bicycle or public transport.
- **Public Transport** - Trains (08457 484950) at Wanborough (3.5 km), Guildford (7 km) and Farnham (9 km). The X65 Stagecoach bus (0845 1210180) from Guildford and Farnham drops you within 1 km of the barn. Alight at Puttenham turn (Hogs Back) and walk south to village.
- **Directions** - GR SU 933 479. Turn off A31 south onto B3000 then take first right into village. The Camping Barn is signposted immediately opposite the church.

CONTACT: Louisa Hall
The Street, Puttenham, Nr Guildford, Surrey, GU3 1AR
Tel: 01306 877 964, Fax: 01306 877964
bookings@puttenhamcampingbarn.co.uk   www.puttenhamcampingbarn.co.uk

SurreyHills

Area of Outstanding Natural Beauty

Sustainable
Development
Fund

www.surreyhills.org

KIPPS
BRIGHTON

Kipps Hostel - Canterbury, one of the highest rated hostels in Britain now has a hostel in Brighton. There are 8 quality, well equipped private bedrooms all featuring TV, clock radio, CD player and wash basin and 2 ensuite dormitory rooms for groups or individuals.

The hostel is situated in Central Brighton with views of the Royal pavilion, close to all attractions, the pier and beach.

Guests can relax on the roof terrace or in the lounge area and enjoy a continental breakfast in the dining area or a drink at the bar. We also offer a self catering kitchen, nightly events and friendly knowledgable staff.

DETAILS

- **Open** - All year, reception 8am-11pm – No Curfew
- **Number of beds** - 36: 1x1, 6x dbl, 1x twin, 1x3, 1x8, 1x10
- **Booking** - Please book by phone or email or online.
- **Price per night** - From £15.00 per person per night
- **Public Transport** - We are close to Brighton Train Station and Bus Station. From Train Station: exit and walk ahead down the main street for a few minutes, turn into Church Street (on your left) and walk along Church Street until the end, the Hotel is opposite. From Bus Station: exit onto Old Steine Road and turn left towards the Grand Pavillion. At the far end of the Pavillion and opposite is the hotel.
- **Directions** - Take the M23, then A23 towards Brighton Town Centre. The Hotel is opposite the Royal Pavillion on Grand Parade.

CONTACT: Reception
76 Grand Parade, Brighton, BN2 9JA
Tel: 01273 604182
brightonroyalhotel@gmail.com www.kipps-brighton.com

THE GLADE
AT BLACKBOYS

The Glade is a quiet retreat in the heart of rural East Sussex, just over an hour's drive from south London and 45 minutes from Brighton and the south coast. This former YHA hostel is set in an acre of its own grounds, close to the intersection of the Weald and Vanguard Ways and a short drive from the climbing crags at Harrisons Rocks and Bewl outdoor centre. The small dorms and private location make it ideal for sole-use, for family re-unions, parties or corporate team-building groups.

When the hostel is open to all, the pleasant lounge/dining room, with its wood burning stove and relaxed atmosphere, makes a great place to socialise. The kitchen is fully equipped for self-catering, with cookers, ovens, fridges, toasters, microwaves and a small freezer. All bedding is provided, but all guests have to bring their own towels. Outside there is a secure bike shed and picnic benches which are great for al-fresco eating. There is also woodland parking space for several cars.

DETAILS

- **Open** - All year, closed between 10am and 5pm (when not in sole use)
- **Number of beds** - 30:1x6,1x5, 2x4,3x3, 2x1
- **Booking** - Please enquire by phone or email.
- **Price per night** - Sole use £395 per night. At all other times, £15 per adult and £10 for under 16s. Family room discounts available.
- **Public Transport** - Stagecoach Bus 318 stops at Blackboys Village 0.5 miles from hostel. Trains at Buxted 2.5 miles away. National Express at Uckfield 4 miles away.
- **Directions** - From Blackboys village take Gun Road and look for signs.

CONTACT: Alan
The Glade, YHABlackboys, Gun Road, Blackboys, Uckfield, Sussex, TN22 5HU
Tel: 01825 890607
blackboys@yha.org.uk www.the-glade.co.uk

Coldblow Farm is situated on the Kent Downs just north east of Maidstone. The farm today provides a range of self-catering accommodation for both people and horses! The long distance trail, the North Downs Way, runs along the southern boundary of the farm and the Pilgrims Way is just a short distance away. The farm is surrounded by a network of public footpaths, bridleways and byways. The accommodation comprises: two Bunkhouse Barns, sleeping 10 (3 rooms, 2, 4 & 4) or 41 (7 rooms, 4 x 8 bunks, 3, 2 & 4 beds); Camping Barn sleeping 15 on sleeping platforms; Flint Cottage (studio style, sleeping two); a Camping Paddock and 18 Stables for horses and ponies. All barns have fully equipped kitchen/dining rooms and central heating. Log burners in the Camping Barn and Flint Cottage. Toilets and showers (on meters) in all barns and for Camping Paddock, but the Camping Barn shares washing facilities of small bunk barn. Eco and Disabled Friendly Lodge also available.

DETAILS

- **Open** - All year, reception 9am till 6pm
- **Number of beds** - New Barn 41: 4x8, 1x4, 1x3, 1x2; Old Barn 10: 2x4, 1x2 ; Camping Barn 15: 1x15; Cottage 2; Eco Lodge 8:
- **Booking** - Advanced booking essential, with full payment.
- **Price per night** - Camping Barn £8.50, Bunkhouses £14.50, Cottage £60 (for 2).
- **Public Transport** - Bearsted is the nearest train station (2 miles by road or path).
- **Directions** - From Thurnham at the Black Horse Pub crossroads take the Pilgrims Way signposted to Hucking. Turn next left at staggered crossroads into Coldblow Lane, Coldblow Farm is half a mile up hill on right. If towing or in large vehicle ring us

CONTACT: Booking Office,
Coldblow Lane, Thurnham, Maidstone, Kent, ME14 3LR
Tel: 01622 730439
coldblowfarm@btconnect.com www.coldblow-camping.co.uk

PALACE FARM
HOSTEL

Palace Farm Hostel is a relaxing and flexible hostel on a family run arable and fruit farm. It is situated in the village of Doddington, which has a pub, in the North Kent Downs Area of Outstanding Natural Beauty. The area is great for walking, cycling (cycle hire available £5 a day) and wildlife. The location is central for exploring Canterbury, Rochester, Chatham, Leeds Castle and the many other historic towns, villages and castles in Kent. The accommodation in converted farm buildings, consists of six fully heated en-suite rooms sleeping up to 30 guests. The rooms surround an attractive courtyard garden with lawns, patio and barbecue area, ideal for families and groups. The en-suite rooms cater for all age groups and those with disabilities. There are quality double beds & 3ft bunk beds. Duvets, linen and continental breakfast included. Small tent only campsite. Green Tourism Business Scheme GOLD Award winner.

DETAILS

- **Open** - All year, 8am to 10pm flexible, please ask
- **Number of beds** - 30: 1x8, 1x6, 2x5, 1x4, and 1x2
- **Booking** - Advised, not essential mid week.
- **Price per night** - From £14 child, £18 adult (private rooms). Reduction for groups staying for 3 or more nights, please ask.
- **Public Transport** - Trains at Sittingbourne (London Victoria to Dover). Buses from Sittingbourne station to Doddington two hourly (Mon-Sat), last buses 16.30 & 17.30.
- **Directions** - From A2 between Sittingbourne and Faversham turn south at Teynham, signed to Lynsted. Go through Lynsted and over M2 bridge, take 2nd turning right into Down Court Rd. Farm is 90 metres on left.

CONTACT: Graham and Liz Cuthbert
Down Court Road, Doddington, Sittingbourne / Faversham, Kent, ME9 0AU
Tel: 01795 886200
info@palacefarm.com   www.palacefarm.com

KIPPS
CANTERBURY

Kipps is an ideal home from home for backpackers, visitors or small groups looking for self-catering budget accommodation in Canterbury. It is a short walk to the town centre and the historic attractions including the renowned Canterbury Cathedral. Canterbury also makes an ideal base for day trips to Dover, Leeds Castle and the many local beaches.

Facilities include dining room, TV lounge with digital TV, a garden, a fully equipped kitchen, a small shop offering breakfast and other food items, bicycle hire. Free WIFI & broadband access. Rooms include single/double/twin/family & dorms of up to 8 beds (most en-suite). Camping available in summer. Free on-street parking. Kipps have now opened a hostel/hotel in Brighton, opposite the Royal Pavilion and close to town (see page 60).
For further information visit www.kipps-brighton.com

DETAILS

- **Open** - All year, no curfew, reception 7.30am to 11pm
- **Number of beds** - 51:- 2 x 1, 2 x 2, 1 x 3, 1 x 5, 1 x 6,1 x 7, 2 x 8, 1 x 9
- **Booking** - Advance booking recommended. Book online.
- **Price per night** - Dorms £16pp, Singles £22pp, Doubles £37, Quads £50. Weekly and winter rates available. Credit cards accepted.
- **Public Transport** - Canterbury East train station on London Victoria to Dover line, is ½ mile by footpath (phone hostel for directions). The local C4 bus stops by the door of the hostel. Taxi from coach/rail stations is £3.
- **Directions** - By car :- Take B2068 to Hythe from City Ring Road (A28). Turn right at first traffic lights by church. Kipps is 300 yds on left.

CONTACT: Reception
40 Nunnery Fields, Canterbury, Kent, CT1 3JT
Tel: 01227 786121
kippshostel@gmail.com www.kipps-hostel.com

ALL STAR
HOSTEL

ALL STAR HOSTEL is a new hostel very close to Kilburn Tube Station (only 15 mins from Central London) and the 24 hour bus routes. Completely refurbished with brand new facilities including pressure showers, fully fitted kitchens, wooden floors, lounge room with Sky TV, free internet, laundry facilities (free soap powder), and security lockers in all the rooms. Choose from 6 bed dorms, female only rooms, double rooms with TV/DVD, or private studio apartments. FREE tea and coffee, FREE toast and jam breakfast, FREE WIFI.The All Star Hostel will offer you a comfortable homely stay with a friendly atmosphere at great prices for your trip to London.

Accommodation London also operates over 300 STUDIO apartments and shared antipodean houses in North West London, with secure private rooms. They provide a great atmosphere with other working holidaymakers to give you that feel for London living.

DETAILS

- **Open** - All year, office hours 8am 6pm Mon-Sat. Sundays 9am-5pm .
- **Number of beds** - 100+ beds plus apartments and houses.
- **Booking** - Book online.
- **Price per night** - Minimum of 4 nights stay. Dorms from £15, private rooms from £20pp. Long term from £10 a night. £15 check-in fee on Sundays.
- **Public Transport** - Close to Kilburn Tube Station on the Jubliee Line (zone 2). Free pick up from tube station (office hours only). Frequent bus services including a night bus from the city .
- **Directions** - Located a short distance from the main arterial roads through the city.

CONTACT: Reception
39 Chatsworth Road, London, NW2 4BL
Tel: 0208 459 6203 , Fax: 0208 451 3258
info@accommodationlondon.net www.accommodationlondon.net

Piccadilly Backpackers Hostel is literally a hop, skip and a jump from Piccadilly Circus. London's most central hostel for travellers on a budget! Soak up the atmosphere from this vibrant area, as famous as the capital itself. Our award winning hostel, spread over 5 floors, is surrounded with London's attractions, including the famous nightspot Leicester Square, the trendy area of Soho, shops of Oxford Street, and London's renowned Theatre Land.

Heaps of free facilities include wide screen TV, lockers, luggage storage and the all important breakfast, with access to high speed internet and a dedicated Travel shop and more! Come join us for a cheap drink in our funky bar - and nightly party events organised daily. You're sure to have an awesome time! Overall, Piccadilly Backpackers offers an unbeatable blend of value, comfort and security, and is undeniably the greatest portal for visitors to London!

DETAILS

- **Open** - All year, 24 hours
- **Number of beds** - 700
- **Booking** - Advisable, groups require deposit
- **Price per night** - From £12
- **Public Transport** - One minutes walk from Piccadilly Circus tube station.
- **Directions** - Take exit 1 from Piccadilly Circus tube station, head down Sherwood Street, Piccadilly Backpackers is on your right just after Piccadilly Theatre. By car follow signs for central London, then to Piccadilly Circus, then follow signs to nearby NCP car park.

CONTACT: Reception
12 Sherwood Street, Piccadilly, London, W1F 7BR
Tel: 0207 434 9009, Fax: 0207 434 9010
bookings@piccadillybackpackers.com www.piccadillybackpackers.com

PALMERS
LODGE

Palmers Lodge is a unique Grade II listed building. A three million pound refurbishment has turned this house, the former home of Samuel Palmer (Huntley & Palmers) into a stunning hostel. Guests can enjoy modern facilities, such as FREE internet, whilst admiring the beautiful oak flooring, fireplaces and ceilings! The Lodge has a 24hr reception, bar, restaurant, large lounge, full security card access, generous car park and plenty of showers! With Swiss Cottage tube just across the road the heart of the city is just minutes away whilst, if you fancy a really late night, we are also on the Night Bus route from Trafalgar Square. Winner Silver Award, Visit London best hostel 2006. Nominated for Visit London best hostel 2007. Constantly in Hostels.com top 10 hostels worldwide since July 2006.

DETAILS

- **Open** - All year, 365 days, 24 hours
- **Number of beds** - 273 : 3x2 6x4,4x6,4x8,2x10,3x12,3x14,1x19,1x18,1x24,1x28
- **Booking** - Booking is advised but not essential. Deposit for first night is preferred. Photo ID is required at check in.
- **Price per night** - £14.00 to £24.00 per person, including breakfast.
- **Public Transport** - Next to Swiss Cottage and Finchley Road stations. Leave Swiss Cottage tube exit 2, At the top of the stairs turn to face the main road. College Crescent goes up on your right. Also on bus routes for Stansted and Luton airports.
- **Directions** - Palmers Lodge is located just off the A41 which can be accessed from the M1, M25 or A1. Simply stay on the A41 towards central London and turn left just before Swiss Cottage tube; drive round to the left along College Crescent.

CONTACT: Reception
40 College Crescent, Swiss Cottage, London, NW3 5LB
Tel: 0207 483 8470, Fax: 0207 483 8471
reception@palmerslodge.co.uk www.palmerslodge.co.uk

DOVER CASTLE
HOSTEL AND FLATSHARES

Dover Castle Hostel and Flatshares offers backpackers great value short and long stay accommodation in central London. Located close to London Bridge in the centre of the city we are walking distance to sights such as Tower Bridge, St Paul's Cathedral, London Dungeon, Shakespeare's Globe, Tate Modern and the London Eye. Prices include free breakfast and free wifi. The hostel has a guest kitchen and common room, free luggage room, a laundry service as well as a late guest bar with pool table and super drink offers. Guests wanting to stay in London for longer can rent rooms in Dover Castle house / flatshares. These furnished houses and flats are a short bus ride to London Bridge in zone 2 South East London. Single occupancy double rooms cost £115 per week and twin rooms cost £75 per week per person inclusive of bills and wifi for a 6 week minimum stay. More info at www.london99.com for more info on the flatshares. Short or long term guests can find their home in London with Dover Castle!

DETAILS

■ **Open** - All year, 24 hours. No Curfew
■ **Number of beds** - 68: 1x4, 2x5, 1x8, 2x10, 2x12
■ **Booking** - Booking advisable in summer. Credit card secures bed.
■ **Price per night** - £12-£17 pp incl. breakfast. Discounted weekly rates available
■ **Public Transport** - Nearest main line station is London Bridge. Take underground Northern Line to Borough. The hostel is opposite Borough underground station between London Bridge and Elephant and Castle. 10 mins from Waterloo Station.
■ **Directions** - From Borough underground station cross the road to Great Dover Street, we are 1 minute walk and located on the right hand side.

CONTACT: Sallie Stone
6 Great Dover Street, Borough, London, SE1 4XW
Tel: 020 74037773, Fax: 020 77878654
dovercastle@hotmail.com www.dovercastlehostel.com

ACE HOTEL
LONDON

Located in trendy Kensington, Central London, Ace Hotel sets a new standard for budget accommodation in the UK. The hotel spans four beautiful Victorian town houses, has it's own bar, garden and hot-tub and provides the latest amenities, security and comfort for the independent traveller. Ace Hotel London's latest contemporary budget accommodation offers a clean, friendly and vibrant place to stay at a very reasonable price.

We offer a wide range of bunk-bedded rooms varying from 2 beds to 8 beds, of which some are ensuite and some standard. Our double ensuite bed rooms have television, bathrobes, fridge, and private patio. All rooms have security lockers, high quality beds and electronic swipe card access making them comfortable, modern and secure. Come and stay with us and see for yourself why Ace Hotel is an ACE place to be.

DETAILS

- **Open** - All year, 24 hours
- **Number of beds** - 163: 1x8, 9x6, 17x4, 1x3, 11x2, 1xdouble
- **Booking** - Credit card guarantees bed, full payment upon arrival. Groups (10+) 50% deposit and the remaining balance paid 1 month prior to arrival.
- **Price per night** - Rates starting from £19.00 per person per night. Weekly rates available.
- **Public Transport** - 5 mins walk from West Kensington and Barons Court tube sts.
- **Directions** - From West Kensington turn right out of tube station onto North End Rd. Cross and continue down North End Rd, take next left Gunterstone Rd. From Barons Court turn left out of the station and cross over the main road. Walk straight down the road past the college and take the first right down Gunterstone Road.

CONTACT:
16-22 Gunterstone Road, West Kensington, London, W14 9BX
Tel: 0207 602 6600, Fax: 0207 602 1021
reception@ace-hotel.co.uk www.ace-hotel.co.uk

GENERATOR
LONDON

Generator
HOTEL LONDON

The Generator is London's largest, liveliest and funkiest hostel with over 800 beds and is famous for its party atmosphere. We are open 24 hours a day, 365 days a year with friendly staff who are always on hand to help. Just minutes from Covent Garden and Leicester Square, The Generator is located in the heart of Bloomsbury. There is a late bar (open 6pm to 2am) which provides the perfect environment to meet young travellers from all over the world. Other facilities include a laundry, chill out room, games room with pool tables and satellite TV, internet café, safety deposit boxes and free luggage storage on departure. Continental Breakfast is free for everyone, as are bed sheets & 24hour hot showers and a walking tour of London. Accommodation is available in singles, twins, triples, quads plus both small and large dorms.The hostel is generally suitable for 18-35s. It is a must-stay hostel for all backpackers if you want to meet loads of people from all over the world and party the night away.

DETAILS

- **Open** - All year, 24 hours
- **Number of beds** - 840
- **Booking** - With credit card- 48 hr cancellation.
- **Price per night** - From £15 per person in a dorm room.
- **Public Transport** - Kings Cross/Euston Station are both approx 5 minutes walk from the hostel. The nearest National Express station is Victoria and the closest tube station is Russell Square.
- **Directions** - From Russell Square Tube cross onto Marchmont Street, walk to traffic lights and turn right onto Tavistock Place - the hostel is at number 37.

CONTACT:
Compton Place, (off 37 Tavistock Place), Russell Square London, WC1H 9SE
Tel: 0207 388 7666
london@generatorhostels.com www.generatorhostels.com

CLINK
HOSTEL

Clink is all about reinvention. Not only have we restored a 200 year old courthouse to create a stylish backpackers, we have also changed the traditional perception of youth hostels. With its utterly cool interior, modern facilities and high-tech pod beds, Clink is a far cry from the generic hostel.

What makes us exceptional: The Courtroom Lounge… chill out where The Clash were on trial. The Prison Cells…sleep it all off in an authentic prison cell, whether in solitary confinement or with your partner in crime. The Internet Lounge/TV Lounge… write your own story from the place that inspired Charles Dickens to create Oliver Twist.

Each pod bed has a personal light, a safety locker and a storage box combining comfort, security and privacy. Stylish in-house bar: happy hours and entertainment every night! Stay and judge for yourself…

DETAILS

- **Open** - All year, 24 hours - no curfew or lockouts
- **Number of beds** - 600: 4-16 bedded, triple, twin, single, ensuite, cell rooms(for 2).
- **Booking** - Book online, by email or by phone.
- **Price per night** - From £10pp including FREE breakfast. Group discounts.
- **Public Transport** - Just around the corner from King's Cross Station with direct links to Heathrow, Luton, Gatwick, Victoria, the Eurostar and one change to Stansted.
- **Directions** - King's Cross station is 5 mins away by foot. Exit the station, walk down King's Cross Road for 500m and you'll find us on your left.

CONTACT: Reception
78 Kings Cross Road, King's Cross, London, WC1X 9QG
Tel: 020 7183 9400, Fax: 020 7713 0735
info@clinkhostel.com www.clinkhostel.com

ASHLEE
HOUSE

Stay in stylish, modern cheap accommodation with great facilities and relaxing lounge areas. Feel right at home with a diverse mixture of international travellers. You'll also find yourself a stone's throw from the British Museum, Covent Garden, Bloomsbury and Camden Market or just minutes away from the bright lights of Piccadilly Circus and Leicester Square.

Security is excellent with coded entrances to the building and the rooms. There is also a fully equipped self-catering kitchen. And we can even get you on the guest list of some of London's hottest nightclubs! So if it's the real London experience you're looking for come to Ashlee House and start living it!

DETAILS

- **Open** - All year, 24 hours - no curfew or lockouts
- **Number of beds** - 3 large dorms, 6 dorms, 12 small dorms and 4 private rooms
- **Booking** - Advanced booking recommended.
- **Price per night** - From £9pp including FREE breakfast. Group discounts.
- **Public Transport** - Kings Cross has excellent public transport: underground, local buses and direct links with all major airports - Heathrow, Gatwick, Luton and Stansted. Only 20 mins from Waterloo International and Victoria.
- **Directions** - King's Cross Station is 2 mins away by foot. From the station take the exit for Grays Inn Road, departing the exit McDonald's will be on right. Keep McDonald's right, walk straight ahead, passing an exchange bureau, the police station and KFC. The road curves to the right - this is Grays Inn Road - the hostel is 200 metres up the road on the right, opposite The Royal Throat Nose and Ear Hospital.

CONTACT:
261-265 Gray's Inn Road, King's Cross, London, WC1X 8QT
Tel: 020 7833 9400, Fax: 020 7833 9677
info@ashleehouse.co.uk www.ashleehouse.co.uk

HARLOW
INTERNATIONAL HOSTEL ENGLAND

Harlow International Hostel is situated in the centre of a landscaped park and is one of the oldest buildings in Harlow. The town of Harlow is the ideal base from which to explore London, Cambridge and the best of the South East of England. The journey time to central London is only 35 minutes from the hostel. National Cycle Route One passes our front door. We are the closest hostel to Stansted Airport. There is a range of room sizes from single to eight bedded, many with their own washing facilities. Self-catering facilities, refreshments and a small shop are all available. During your visit you can relax with a book from our large collection or enjoy a board game with other guests. A children's zoo, assault course and outdoor pursuit centre are available in the park.

Meals provided for groups. Airport parking available.

DETAILS

■ **Open** - All year, 8am-12pm (check in 4-10.30pm)

■ **Number of beds** - 32: 2x1 : 5x2 : 1x4 : 1x6 :1 x 8

■ **Booking** - Advance booking (can be taken 18 months in advance) is recommended. Deposit of £2pppn of stay.

■ **Price per night** - £14.00 per adults, Family rooms £55 (sleeps 4), £65 (sleep 5), £76 (sleep 6). Please check our website for latest prices and discounts.

■ **Public Transport** - The rail station is only 800m from hostel with links to London, Cambridge & Stansted Airport. Buses connect to London and airports.

■ **Directions** - J7 of M11 take A414 into Harlow. At the 4th roundabout take 1st exit (First Ave). Drive to 4th set of traffic lights. Immediately after lights turn right (School Lane). Hostel is on left opposite Greyhound Pub.

CONTACT: Richard or Iku
13 School Lane Harlow, Essex, CM20 2QD
Tel: 01279 421702
mail@h-i-h.co.uk www.h-i-h.co.uk

COURT HILL
CENTRE

Just 2 miles south of Wantage and only a few steps from the historic Ridgeway National Trail, The Court Hill Centre enjoys breathtaking views over the Vale of the White Horse.

Reclaimed barns surround a pretty courtyard garden, on the site of a disused rubbish dump! Offering accommodation to families, groups and individuals, a popular year-round destination. We offer evening meals, breakfasts, and picnic lunches, all prepared using as much local produce as possible. Meals are served in the beautiful high-roofed dining room which retains the impressive proportions and atmosphere of the old barn. Before and after your meal relax in the cosy sunken lounge with a log fire when it's chilly. We offer pitches for small tents, and can accommodate small groups by arrangement. A meeting/classroom is also available.

DETAILS

- **Open** - Open all year round, to check availability please call 01235 760253.
- **Number of beds** - 59: 1x15, 1x9, 1x6, 1x5, 6x4, 1x2
- **Booking** - Essential 24 hours in advance.
- **Price per night** - Adult £17, Under 18 £13
- **Public Transport** - Train, Didcot Parkway 10 Miles. Stagecoach, 32/A, X35,36 from Didcot Parkway to Wantage 2 Miles. There is no direct connection to the centre.
- **Directions** - From the M4 Jct 14, follow signs to Wantage. From Oxford A420 and A338 through Wantage. The Courthill Ridgeway Centre is accessed from the A338 close to Letcombe Regis

CONTACT: Reception
Courthill, Letcombe Regis, Wantage, OX12 9NE
Tel: 01235 760253
info@Courthill.org.uk www.Courthill.org.uk

OXFORD
BACKPACKERS

UNDER NEW MANAGEMENT. Oxford Backpackers is a purpose built hostel, in the heart of Oxford, the leading university town of England. The hostel is two minutes walk from the train and bus stations and close to the Tourist Information Centre and all the City's attractions. It is safe, clean and friendly. Small dorms with individual pin code locks, fully equipped kitchen, well supplied bar, laundry, games room, internet access and organised activities add to the experience.

Oxford City is steeped in history and culture. You can explore Christ Church, Magdalen and New College of the University, the Bodleian Library, the Oxford Story and Britain's oldest museum the Ashmolean Museum. Or explore the canals and quiet villages of the Cotswolds.

DETAILS

■ **Open** - All year, 24 hour access, service 8am until 11.30pm.
■ **Number of beds** - 120
■ **Booking** - Booking is advised in summer (April to Sept), 7 days in advance with deposit by credit card.
■ **Price per night** - From £13 per person. Discounts for longer stays and groups. Discounts when you book ahead to Bath Backpackers hostel (01225) 446787.
■ **Public Transport** - Oxford has train and National Express services. Hostel is 100m from train station and easy walking distance from the coach station.
■ **Directions** - From train station turn left and walk 100 metres, hostel is on your right. From Oxford coach station turn right, hostel is over the bridge 100 metres on your left. By road follow signs to the train station.

CONTACT:
9a Hythe Bridge Street, Oxford, OX1 2EW
Tel: 01865 721761, Fax: 01865 203293
oxford@hostels.co.uk www.hostels.co.uk

CENTRAL
BACKPACKERS OXFORD ENGLAND

Central Backpackers, Oxford's premier Backpackers Hostel accommodation. Awarded one of Europes Top Hostels 2007 and 2008 by Hostelworld.com also recommended by Let's Go and Lonely Planet Guide books. Central Backpackers brings a new level of comfort and security to the hostel experience. With a huge range of free services and facilities everything you need to make your trip safe, comfortable and enjoyable. Free continental breakfast, internet and wi-fi. Located in the centre of Oxford's historical university city. Central Backpackers is less than a 5 minute walk from the bus station, train station, Oxford's Castle/Prison complex, museums and vibrant student nightlife. Central Backpackers is Australian and Canadian owned and operated. All staff members are backpackers with extensive travel experience. Look for our new Backpackers Hostel opening March 2010 in Cambridge!

DETAILS

- **Open** - All year, 24 hours. No curfew
- **Number of beds** - 50: 1x12, 3x8, 1x6, 2x4
- **Booking** - Advisable, essential in high season.
- **Price per night** - From £14 per person.
- **Public Transport** - Oxford Tube bus company leaves London every 12 mins and costs £12-15 return, Oxford Express buses offer direct services to and from Heathrow, Gatwick and London Airports. Trains from Paddington every 10-20 mins.
- **Directions** - Bus: (3 mins) turn right onto George St, follow the road around to the left. Take first right onto Park End St. Train: (3 mins) Look to your left and see Royal Oxford Hotel. Park End St runs down the right side of the hotel. Give us a call if lost.

CONTACT: Reception
13 Park End Street, Oxford, OX1 1HH
Tel: 01865 242288
oxford@centralbackpackers.co.uk www.centralbackpackers.co.uk

RAMBLERS' RETREAT
WENDOVER HOUSE

ENGLAND

Wendover House is a residential school set in the heart of the Chiltern Hills, right on the Ridgeway Path. At weekends and school holidays the Ramblers' Retreat welcomes walkers and holiday makers into the school. The retreat has one dormitory with five curtained bedspaces, a private room for one, a well-equipped kitchen and plenty of washing facilities. The school is situated around an 18th century manor house with 22 acres of land. It is easily accessible by road and there is a direct rail link to London Marylebone only a few minutes walk away. Wendover Village is an old market town set in an Area of Outstanding Natural Beauty. It has lots of historic buildings with excellent pubs and restaurants only 5 minutes walk from the school. As well as the Ridgeway Path there are 33 miles of public rights of way crisscrossing the parish

DETAILS

- **Open** - Weekends and school holidays, all day
- **Number of beds** - 6: 1 x 5, 1 x 1
- **Booking** - Book minimum of 24 hours in advance. No deposit required (payment by cash or cheque only).
- **Price per night** - £12 per person. Optional bedding pack (inc towel) £3
- **Public Transport** - Wendover station on the Marylebone to Aylesbury line is 6 mins walk. Trains run approximately twice an hour. Local bus service from Aylesbury runs twice an hour and hourly at weekends.
- **Directions** - Wendover House is just off the A413 in the centre of Wendover. If arriving from Aylesbury, travel through Wendover in the direction of Amersham. Look for turning signed "St Mary's Church". Drive past the church and look for school.

CONTACT:
Wendover House School, Church Lane, Wendover, Bucks, HP22 6NL
Tel: 01296 622157 (school hours), 01296 626065 or 01296 625319
office@wendoverhouse.bucks.sch.uk www.wendoverhouse.bucks.sch.uk

Foxholes Castle Bunkhouse at Bishops Castle is situated within a relaxed, family-run campsite, surrounded by glorious views of South West Shropshire's beautiful hill country.   Within a few minutes walk of the Shropshire Way, Offa's Dyke Path, the Sustrans cycle network and the lively town of Bishop's Castle it is ideal for families, couples, walkers, cyclists and photographers. The bunkhouse is a 8m x 3m heated area, divided in half by a petition with an open doorway. There is a single bed and one set of bunks in each section (no bedding is provided). In heated buildings next to the bunkhouse (shared with the campsite) are wet room, showers, fridge, freezer and washing-up sink. A second set of showers and toilets are 30 seconds walk away. There is good accessibly for wheelchair users. There is an outside table, seating and space for a BBQ. There are no cooking facilities but there are lots of pubs, restaurants, cafes and take-aways 5 minutes walk away in Bishops Castle.

DETAILS

■ **Open** - All year, 24 hours
■ **Number of beds** - 6: 2 x 3
■ **Booking** - Bookings by phone or send an email.
■ **Price per night** - £10 per person or £40 for whole bunkhouse (sleeps 6).
■ **Public Transport** - Trains at Craven Arms (12 miles). Buses from Shrewsbury to Bishops Castle (5 mins walk from bunkhouse) every 2 hours.
■ **Directions** -   Bishop's Castle is on the A488 about 20 miles south of Shrewsbury, and 35 miles from the M54. Foxholes is on the B4385 Montgomery Road just north of the town. Look for our sign, and follow our driveway for half a mile. GR SO 324 897

CONTACT: Chris or Wendy Jones
Foxholes Camping, Montgomery Rd, Bishops Castle, Shropshire, SY9 5HA
Tel: 01588 638924, mobile 07890 231351
foxholes.castle@googlemail.com www.foxholes-castle.co.uk

BERROW HOUSE
ENGLAND BUNKHOUSE & CAMP SITE

Berrow House is situated in Hollybush between Rugged Stone Hill and Midsummer Hill in the Malvern Range. It is ideally suited for families, groups and individuals (including those with special needs) who want easy access to the countryside. The Forest of Dean, the Welsh border and the start of the Worcestershire Way Walk are near, with the towns of Malvern, Ledbury, Tewkesbury, Worcester, and Gloucester all within a half hour drive. The bunkhouse has sleeping accommodation for 5 in the main room and 3 more beds on the upper floor. The main room has heating and easy chairs. The adjacent kitchen/dining room has hot water, cooker, cutlery, crockery and cooking utensils. Toilets, dryer and shower are adjacent. The Fold is a separate building which has sleeping accommodation for 4 in two rooms, a fully equipped kitchen, heating, toilet, shower and a cloakroom. The Nook (caravan) has a double and single bed and uses the bunkhouse facilities. Camping, picnic area, water garden and car park are also available.

DETAILS

- **Open** - All year, 24 hours
- **Number of beds** - 8 (Bunkhouse), 4 (The Fold), 3 (The Nook) and 8 tents.
- **Booking** - Not required for individuals
- **Price per night** - £10 per person.
- **Public Transport** - Nearest train station and National Express service are in Ledbury, which is 3 miles from the hostel and would cost approx. £5 in a taxi.
- **Directions** - Take A449 from Ledbury towards Malvern. Turn right on to A438 through Eastnor. Berrow House is behind phone box in Hollybush (yellow sign).

CONTACT: Bill or Mary Cole
Hollybush, Ledbury, Herefordshire, HR8 1ET
Tel: 01531 635845, Fax: 01531 635845
berrowhouse@tiscali.co.uk www.berrowhouse.co.uk

BERROW HOUSE

CAMPING

CARAVANS

BUNKHOUSE

WOODSIDE LODGES
BUNKHOUSE

Woodside Lodges is a landscaped park with lakes, grass and woodland managed to encourage wildlife. In addition to the Scandinavian pine wood lodges and campsite there is a modern barn converted into self catering units for walkers and cyclists. This bunkhouse has 5 units, 4 sleeping 2 and 1 sleeping 4 (additional camp beds are available). Each unit has a cooking area with kettle, toaster, microwave, 2 electric rings, fridge and basic utensils. Electric is by coin meter and bedding can be provided for an extra charge (or bring your own sleeping bag). The toilets and showers are shared with the campsite. Close to the Herefordshire Trail, the Malvern Hills and the Forest of Dean the area is ideal for walkers. Nature lovers will enjoy the site with its backcloth of mixed woodland, wild flowers, pools and waterfalls where fishing, wild swimming and picnics can be enjoyed. The nearby town of Ledbury is famous for its black and white buildings, cobbled streets and Poetry Festival.

DETAILS

- **Open** - All year, All day
- **Number of beds** - 12 : 4x2, 1x4
- **Booking** - Booking in advance advised.
- **Price per night** - Telephone for prices
- **Public Transport** - Public transport is available within 1/2 mile
- **Directions** - From Junction 2, M50 take the A417 to Ledbury. At the first roundabout turn left following Leadon Way (the by-pass). At the third roundabout turn left into Little Marcle Road. Go past the factory and take the right turn signposted Falcon Lane & Baregains Lane. Woodside Lodges is the sixth entrance on the right.

CONTACT: Woodside Lodges Country Park
Woodside Lodges, Falcon Lane, Ledbury, Herefordshire, HR8 2JN
Tel: 01531 670269
info@woodsidelodges.co.uk www.woodsidelodges.co.uk

BRIDGES LONG MYND
YOUTH HOSTEL
ENGLAND

This small hostel, once the old village school, is tucked away in the Shropshire Hills with the Long Mynd to the east and Stiperstones to the west. It is an ideal spot for ramblers with the Shropshire Way passing close by and a great network of uncrowded paths to explore. Walkers on the Shropshire Way may see wild poinies, woodpeckers, skylarks, ravens and various birds of prey. Small towns nearby worthy of a visit include Ludlow, Much Wenlock, Bishops Castle and sleepy Montgomery. There's also the Acton Scott working farm museum and The Bog former mining centre close by, and a pub next door serving food.

The hostel has a good kitchen, a lounge with wood fire, books and games, a drying room, a food shop and a large garden. One ensuite room has some facilities for the disabled, phone to discuss your requirements. Meals are available and camping is allowed.
PLEASE CONTACT THIS HOSTEL BY PHONE OR POST

DETAILS

- **Open** - All year, Reception 8-10 am, 5-10 pm. Hostel closes at 11pm.
- **Number of beds** - 37: 1x4 ensuite, 1x2 ensuite,1x8, 1x10, 1x12
- **Booking** - Telephone to book. No credit or debit cards accepted. Cheques must be made payable to Bridges Youth Hostel not YHA.
- **Price per night** - Adults £15. Under 18's £11
- **Public Transport** - Trains at Church Stretton (5 miles).
- **Directions** - From Church Stretton, take 'The Burway' road uphill. Take right fork at top of Long Mynd. From Shrewsbury take road via Longden and Pulverbatch, then left by Horseshoe Inn. Access from Church Stretton over the Long Mynd Hill is not advisable in bad weather during winter

CONTACT: Bridges Youth Hostel
Ratlinghope, Shrewsbury, Shropshire, SY5 0SP
Tel: 01588 650656 Fax: 01588 650531

All Stretton Bunkhouse offers comfortable self-catering accommodation with underfloor heating for small groups of up to 10 people. It has easy access to the Long Mynd which offers walks and bike rides for all levels of fitness. There are local stables where you can book horse riding by the hour or day. It is within easy reach of the busy town of Church Stretton and all its facilities, and just 10 minutes walk from the local pub (but please always book meals as they are not very big). Takeaway food can be ordered from Church Stretton.

There are three bedrooms in the bunkhouse: Synalds and Cardoc have two bunks (sleeping 4) and Novers has two singles. A cot is also available. The well equipped kitchen has cooker, microwave, toaster, kettle and fridge. There is a shower, two toilets and a tumble dryer. The track up to the property is steep and rough so wheelchair access is difficult.

DETAILS

- **Open** - All year, 5pm to 10.30pm. Reception 5pm to 9pm.
- **Number of beds** - 10 plus 1 cot.
- **Booking** - Book by phone, post or online.
- **Price per night** - £17.50, £15 under 18's. £3 discount for all YHA members.
- **Public Transport** - Trains to Church Stretton from Shrewsbury, Hereford and Cardiff. Station 1.2 miles walk (or taxi) from Bunkhouse. National Express buses to Shrewsbury, hourly local buses from Shrewsbury to Church Stretton via All Stretton.
- **Directions** - 300m on right going up Batch Valley road (off the B4370, a mile north of Church Stretton).

CONTACT:
Meadow Green, Batch Valley, All Stretton, Shrops, SY6 6JW
Tel: 01694 722593   Mob: 0781 5517482
info@allstrettonbunkhouse.co.uk   www.allstrettonbunkhouse.co.uk

WOMERTON FARM
BUNKHOUSE

Womerton Farm Bunkhouse is situated right next to the Longmynd, an AONB in the heart of the Shropshire Hills. Our bunkhouse offers a small select accommodation to sleep 8, 6 in bunks downstairs and a double fold-down sofa bed upstairs. There is a fully equipped kitchen and living area upstairs.

We are 3 miles from Church Stretton, 12 miles from historic Shrewsbury and 15 miles from Ludlow, food capital of Shropshire. There are many local attractions such as Acton Scott Working Farm Museum, Stokesay Castle, Museum of Lost Content and Discovery Centre. The LongMynd is fantastic for walking, mountain biking and horse riding. Horses can be field-accommodated if arranged in advance. Well behaved dogs that are not moulting allowed. For photo gallery, directions and details please visit our website at www.womerton-farm.co.uk

DETAILS

- **Open** - All year, all day. Closed from 11 am to 4pm on change over days.
- **Number of beds** - 9: 1x6, 1x1 + double sofa bed in living area
- **Booking** - Booking recommended to guarantee a place.
- **Price per night** -   £80 Christmas / New Year, £80 Easter to Sept, £60 off peak. Stay 3 nights get next 1 to 3 nights half price. Phone or email for midweek offers.
- **Public Transport** - Nearest train and bus station is Church Stretton (3 miles). Taxi fare is about £10.
- **Directions** - From Church Stretton follow A49 north. Past coffee shop and craft centre take a left turn signed Lower Wood. From Shrewsbury on A49 south, pass though Leebotwood then take the right turn signed Lower Wood. Follow this road for 1 mile, cross a cattle grid onto the Long Mynd and we are the first farm on the right.

CONTACT: Ruth or Tony
Womerton Farm, All Stretton, Church Stretton, Shropshire, SY6 6LJ
Tel: 01694 751260
ruth@womerton-farm.co.uk www.womerton-farm.co.uk

Stokes Barn is located on top of Wenlock Edge, an Area of Outstanding Natural Beauty in the heart of Shropshire countryside. Two bunkhouses are available, the Threshing Barn (sleeping 28) and the Granary (sleeping 16). These offer comfortable, centrally heated, dormitory accommodation for a wide range of groups and provide an ideal base for corporate groups, field study groups, universities, schools, stag and hen parties, walkers or just a relaxing reunion with friends or family.

The Ironbridge World Heritage Site is only 6 miles away and is a great attraction. Walk to the historic town of Much Wenlock to visit shops, pubs and sports facilities. Situated only a few miles from Church Stretton and the Long Mynd the barn is in a walking / cycling haven. Many activities available. Have a relaxing and enjoyable stay.

DETAILS

- **Open** - Feb-Dec (closed in Jan), all day
- **Number of beds** - Threshing Barn 28: 1x12,1x10,1x6 Granary 16:1x10,1x4,1x2
- **Booking** - Deposit required.
- **Price per night** - Barn: £270 per night mid week. £720 for the weekend (2 nights) . Granary: £192 per night mid week. £480 for the weekend (2 nights).
- **Public Transport** - Trains at Telford (10 miles) and in Shrewsbury (10 miles). National Express coaches call at Shrewsbury from London, call 0839 142348 for information. Midland Red buses stop in Much Wenlock, enquires 01952 223766.
- **Directions** - GR 609 999. From the M6 take M54 Telford following Ironbridge Gorge signs. A4169 to Much Wenlock, joining A458 for Shrewsbury. The Barn is signed at Newton House Farm (TF13 6DB) on the Much Wenlock to Shrewsbury Rd.

CONTACT:
Stokes Barn, Newtown Farm, Much Wenlock, Shropshire, TF13 6DB
Tel: 01952 727491 ext 2, Mob: 07973 329889
info@stokesbarn.co.uk www.stokesbarn.co.uk

SPRINGHILL FARM
BUNKHOUSE

Springhill Farm Bunkhouse is on a hill farm at 1475ft above sea level, near the Shropshire / Wales border with beautiful views over the Ceiriog Valley and Berwyn Mountains. Great for walking and activity breaks or just to relax. Available onsite are cycle hire, archery and horse riding. The main bunkhouse can sleep around 20, and the 2 smaller self catering cottages can sleep up to 10 more. There is also a separate large room with its own kitchen which can be used for meetings or as a camping barn. The bunkhouse has underfloor heating, entrance hall with w/c and drying room, large kitchen, dining room and sitting room. There are 5 bedrooms sleeping 1-8 people.Outside is a large patio and lawn, BBQ and hot tub.
Your own horse and pets are welcome on request.

DETAILS

- **Open** - All year, all day (please don't phone after 9pm)
- **Number of beds** - 30+: 20 (bunkhouse) + two cottages + camping barn
- **Booking** - Advisable, deposit required
- **Price per night** - £17pp (including bedding but not towels)
- **Public Transport** - Nearest train station Chirk (8 miles). Nearest bus service is in the village Glyn Ceiriog (2.5 miles). Transfer can be arranged.
- **Directions** - GR SJ 210 346. On the A483 from Wrexham, take the third exit on the first roundabout (Macdonalds). At the next roundabout take the first exit, continue into Chirk, and then turn right for Glyn Ceiriog. After 6 miles you will arrive at Glyn Ceiriog. At the mini roundabout turn left, go over the bridge, and then straight away turn right into a small lane. Continue up the hill for about two miles, do not turn off.

CONTACT: Sue Sopwith
Springhill Farm, Selattyn, Oswestry, Shropshire, SY10 7NZ
Tel: 01691 718406
sue@springhillfarm.co.uk   www.atspringhill.co.uk

HATTERS HOSTEL
BIRMINGHAM
ENGLAND

In the heart of Birmingham, in the city's thriving Jewellery Quarter, Hatters is clean, modern and comfortable, combining the facilities of a hotel with the fun and character of a hostel. We offer a range of great-value accommodation to suit the needs and budget of any traveller, including secure, private en suite rooms, as well as beds in shared en suite dormitories. All of the rooms are clean, light and stylish. Each of the private rooms is individually decorated with its own unique charm and character.

The hostel has a great location, within easy reach of all that Birmingham has to offer, including the shops, nightlife and live music venues. The National Indoor Arena (NIA) is just 0.6 miles (1 km) away and Broad Street is just a 10-minute walk from the front door. Free tea, coffee, toast and jams are available 24-hours a day on an all-you-can-eat basis.

DETAILS

- **Open** - all year , 24 hours
- **Number of beds** - 100 (all ensuite): 8 private rooms, 2 x 12 bed, 1 x 10 bed, 7 x 6 bed, 2 x 4 bed
- **Booking** - Booking not essential but recommended, especially on weekends. Photo ID (ie passport, ID card or driving license) required at check in.
- **Price per night** - From £14.50 Please contact the hostel directly for groups
- **Public Transport** - 15 minutes walk northwards from New St train station, 20 mins from Digbeth coach station. Nearest trains at Snow Hill station (5 mins).
- **Directions** - From New St. Station go left onto New St., take 5th right onto Bennett's Hill, then 2nd right onto Colmore Row and finally 2nd left, Livery St.

CONTACT:
92-97 Livery Street, Birmingham, B3 1RJ
Tel: 0121 236 4031
birmingham@hattersgroup.com www.hattersgroup.com/birmingham

BIRMINGHAM
ENGLAND CENTRAL BACKPACKERS

Birmingham Central Backpackers is Birmingham's first and best independent backpackers hostel and THE place to stay while exploring the Brilliance of Birmingham. Located a minute's walk from the National Express coach station, 1 minute from the buses to the NEC and Airport and a mere 7 minute walk to New Street train station, our location can't be beaten for convenience. Rooms include 4-8 person dorms, a pod dorm and singles and privates. Friendly international staff, two cosy common rooms for relaxation, guest kitchen, free breakfast and nightly snack buffet, free Wi-Fi and budget computer stations, gigantic cinema screen with over 600 movies to choose from, Playstation 3, Nintendo Wii, pool, travel information centre, outdoor patio and guest-only bar. So when in Birmingham make us your place to stay, you won't regret it!

DETAILS

- **Open** - All year, check-in from 2pm-11pm. Common area open 8am-12am
- **Number of beds** - 80: 11 rooms of 4-8 beds 1x3, 3x2, 2x1 + pod dorm
- **Booking** - Book by phone, email or online. 2% credit card fee, 40p debit card fee for bookings of £50 or more.
- **Price per night** - £16 weekdays, £17 Fri and Sat, inc. linen, light breakfast and nightly snack buffet.
- **Public Transport** - Digbeth coach station and New Street train station near by.
- **Directions** - From Digbeth coach station take Milk Street (Big Bulls Head on corner). Hostel located above Billy's Bar, one block down. From New Street Station, walk down New Street through the Bull Ring and down the steps to the markets. Take a left at the markets and go to the traffic light. Cross over the light to the Digbeth High Street. Walk 4 blocks, and turn left onto Milk Street.

CONTACT: Ian and Jen Randall
58 Coventry Street, Digbeth, Birmingham, B5 5NH
Tel: 0121 6430033 Mobile: 07756 829970
info@birminghamcentralbackpackers.com www.birminghamcentralbackpackers.com

ACKERS
ADVENTURE

Only 2 miles from the centre of buzzing Birmingham lies Ackers Adventure, a centre for adventurous activities. Set in 70 acres of semi-rural land the centre has a 100m dry ski slope, climbing walls, archery course and canoeing on the Grand Union Canal which runs straight though the site. Ackers Residential Centre (ARC) and Ackers Adventure are run by a charitable organisation that offers subsidised rates to schools and youth groups but also welcomes family groups, corporate groups and clubs. The purpose-built centre, opened in 2008, has 9 sleeping rooms, a fully equipped kitchen, refectory area with chairs and tables and a recreation room with a TV & DVD player, activity games, chairs & tables and comfortable seating. Facilities include ample secluded parking, showers and changing rooms, disability lift, cafeteria, function room, picnic and BBQ area. All groups get sole use of the centre. A stay at Ackers Adventure could be combined with a visit to The Sea Life Centre, Cadbury World, Thinktank, The Bull Ring shopping centre, National Motorcycle Museum, the NEC as well as art galleries, museums and theatres.
Instructor led activities and lessons are available.

DETAILS

- **Open** - All year, 24 hours. Office staffed 10am -5pm (9pm on weekdays).
- **Number of beds** - 26: 4x4, 5x2
- **Booking** - Please book by phone.
- **Price per night** - From £125 for sole use of centre. Prices may increase in March 2010 (see website or phone for latest prices).
- **Public Transport** - A few minutes walk from Small Heath rail station.
- **Directions** - Entrance off the Small Heath Highway (dual carriageway), see signs

CONTACT:
Ackers (ARC), Waverley Canal Basin, Small Heath, Birmingham, B10 0DQ
Tel: 0121 772 5111 Fax: 0121 766 7870
info@ackers-adventure.co.uk www.ackers-adventure.co.uk

OLD RED LION

Visitors to Castle Acre are entranced by the special atmosphere of this medieval walled town which lies within the outer bailey of an 11th-century castle. Castle Acre is on the Peddars Way, an ancient track now a long distance path. The Old Red Lion, a former pub, is centrally situated and carries on the tradition of serving travellers who seek refreshment and repose. Guests can stay in private rooms or dormitories, where bedding and linen are provided free of charge. There are quiet areas (with wood burning stoves) for reading, meeting other guests and playing. There are two large areas: the flint and timber walled converted pub cellar (see photo), suitable for yoga; and The Garden Room with kitchen and toilet adjacent, ideal for group use: celebrations, classes, courses, workshops and retreats. There is a ground floor double room with disabled use toilet. Sole occupancy of premises may be hired; rates negotiable. Drying facilities. Good local shops, pubs etc. Tourism concern supporter. No smoking.

DETAILS

- **Open** - All year, all day access. Arrival times by arrangement.
- **Number of beds** - 24: 1x10, 1x6, 2 x double (1 en-suite), 2 x twin
- **Booking** - Useful but not essential
- **Price per night** - £18pp if staying for 3+ nights, otherwise £20pp. Private rooms from £25pp. All prices include linen and breakfast.
- **Public Transport** - Train stations at King's Lynn & Downham Market (14 miles). Buses from King's Lynn to Swaffham. Daily National Express coach between Victoria Coach Station & Swaffham. Norfolk Bus info 0500 626116. Taxi from Swaffham £7.
- **Directions** - GR 818151. Castle Acre is 3.5 miles north of Swaffham (A47) on the A1065. The hostel is on left, 75yds down from Bailey Gate in village centre.

CONTACT: Alison Loughlin
Bailey Street, Castle Acre, Norfolk, PE32 2AG
Tel: 01760 755557
oldredlion@yahoo.co.uk www.oldredlion.org.uk

DEEPDALE GRANARY
GROUP HOSTEL
ENGLAND

A perfect base for groups to stay, explore and absorb the stunning North Norfolk coast. Deepdale Granary is a self-contained 17th century building sleeping 18 in four bedrooms with a fully fitted kitchen and dining/sitting room. Part of the award winning Deepdale Farm, right on the coast in the heart of an Area of Outstanding Natural Beauty. We have excellent pubs nearby, both traditional and chic. Great restaurants and miles of unspoilt beaches and dunes. The Norfolk coast is perfect for walking and cycling with miles of coast path and picturesque villages. Take time to discover our heritage sites including the Sandringham and Holkham estates or enjoy birdwatching in the tranquil beauty of the unique saltmarsh. The Granary is fully heated, has showers, a drying room and solar water heating. Next-door Dalegate Market has shops, a supermarket, and a brilliant café serving locally sourced food. Camping and Tipis also available.

DETAILS

- **Open** - All year, all day. Collect key from Deepdale Information.
- **Number of beds** - 18: 2 x 6 : 1 x 4 : 1 x 2.
- **Booking** - Essential, 20% deposit, balance in advance. See website for details
- **Price per night** - From £144 per night, for up to 18 people.
- **Public Transport** - Trains / coaches at King's Lynn (25 miles) then excellent Coastal Hopper bus to Burnham Deepdale. Coastal Hopper services the coast from King's Lynn to Cromer, including Sandringham. Travelline 0870 608 2 608.
- **Directions** - GR 803443. On A149 coast road, halfway between Hunstanton and Wells-next-the-Sea. Beside Deepdale Garage & opposite Deepdale Church.

CONTACT:
Deepdale Information Centre, Burnham Deepdale, Norfolk, PE31 8DD
Tel: 01485 210256
info@deepdalebackpackers.co.uk www.deepdalebackpackers.co.uk

Eco friendly award winning backpackers hostel on the beautiful north Norfolk coast. Escape the smog of the cities to this stunning part of the world. We offer private ensuite rooms (double, twin, triple, quad and family), single sex and mixed dorms. There's so much to do here, adrenaline sports, great pubs and restaurants, miles of sandy beaches. Deepdale is a perfect base for walking and cycling with miles of coast path, the famous big skies and quaint fishing harbours. Or just come and chill. Our facilities are second to none, all rooms are en-suite, we have a fully equipped farmhouse kitchen and a really cosy lounge with a TV and a woodburner for cooler nights. There's a lovely courtyard with barbeques for summer evenings. Deepdale is a working farm and eco-friendly with recycling, underfloor heating and solar water. Next-door Dalegate Market has shops, a supermarket, and a brilliant café serving locally sourced food. Camping and Tipis also available

DETAILS

- **Open** - All day every day, collect key from Deepdale Information.
- **Number of beds** - 50: 5 x dbl, 1 x twin, 1 x triple, 1 x quad plus dorms
- **Booking** - Pre-booking recommended. Max group size 12. See website.
- **Price per night** - From £9.50 (£63 per week) dorm room. £28 twin/double room.
- **Public Transport** - Train and coaches at Kings Lynn (25 Miles). Coast Hopper bus to Burnham Deepdale on the coast road from Kings Lynn to Cromer, stops at Sandringham, Holkham and Titchwell Bird Reserve. Travelline 0870 6082608
- **Directions** - GR 803443 On A149 Coast road halfway between Hunstanton and Wells-next-the-Sea. Beside Dalegate Market, opposite Deepdale Church.

CONTACT:
Deepdale Information Centre, Burnham Deepdale, Norfolk, PE31 8DD
Tel: 01485 210256
info@deepdalebackpackers.co.uk www.deepdalebackpackers.co.uk

BROOK HOUSE
BARN

Brook House Barn provides comfortable, self-catering accommodation ideally suited for families, groups or individuals. This high standard barn conversion has a fully equipped kitchen/dining area, drying room, utility, and a large lounge with panoramic views over the Wolds countryside. There are 2 bedrooms on the ground floor and 3 bedrooms and a small lounge on the first floor. The bedrooms have a mix of beds and bunks, bed linen is provided and all have en-suite shower rooms. A two bedroom (4/5 person) cottage converted to a similar standard (graded Visit Britain 4 *) is also available. The village of Scamblesby, at the heart of the Lincolnshire Wolds and on the Viking Way, has footpaths, bridle ways and meandering country lanes. The historic market towns of Louth and Horncastle are 10 mins drive, Lincoln, Boston and the Coastal Beaches are 1/2 hour away. Cadwell Park racing circuit, Market Rasen racecourse and the Battle of Britain and Aviation Heritage centres are nearby.

DETAILS

- **Open** - All year, flexible accesss.
- **Number of beds** - 22
- **Booking** - Booking advisable, 20% deposit, balance 1 month prior to visit.
- **Price per night** - From £20pp, family and group rates available. Whole barn hire Fri Sat Sun, 2 nights £325 per night, 3 nights £270 per night. Mon to Thurs, 2 nights £250 per night, 3 or 4 nights £220 per night. Whole barn £1500-00 per week.
- **Public Transport** - Trains: Lincoln, Grimsby. Coaches: Louth, Horncastle. Interconnect 6 (0845 234 3344) calls at Scamblesby and other villages in the Wolds.
- **Directions** - Scamblesby village is just off the main A153 Horncastle to Louth rd.

CONTACT: The Strawsons
Watery Lane, Scamblesby, Nr Louth, Lincolnshire, LN11 9XL
Tel: 01507 343266
enquiry@brookhousefarm.com www.barnbreaks.co.uk

THE IGLOO
BACKPACKERS HOSTEL

Centrally located within easy walking distance of the city's historical sights and entertaining sounds, the Igloo is Nottingham's most popular choice for the budget-minded traveller. On offer to overseas jobseekers, backpackers and youth groups is a clean, safe and warm overnight stay in a large, listed Victorian house. Just £15 per night buys a whole host of homely comforts; bunk bed dorms, hot power showers, lounge with TV, films, internet stations and WiFi, games room with pool table, fully-equipped kitchen, free tea & coffee, laundry facilities and good company. Open in outlook and open all day all year, it is the ideal home-from-home for hostellers seeking rest and recuperation before pursuing the exploits of Robin Hood or enjoying the energetic nightlife of this popular university city. Check out our web site.

DETAILS

- **Open** - All year, all day
- **Number of beds** - 36: 1x6; 1x8; 1x10; 1x12
- **Booking** - Essential during summer months. Groups must confirm by email or by phone with deposit.
- **Price per night** - £15pp. £60 per week after 7 nights stay. Seasonal discounts.
- **Public Transport** -   Direct, regular trains from London etc. National Express to Broadmarsh bus station. From bus/train stations 20mins walk, £4 taxi ride or catch tram to Trent Uni (4th stop), take next R (Peel St), follow to Golden Fleece pub.
- **Directions** - From the Tourist Information Centre (Market Square) turn right out of TIC, take next left onto Cumber Street, keep walking straight on for ten mins, past the Victoria Shopping centre, untill you reach the Golden Fleece Pub. The igloo is directly opposite. Entry is on the side of the buidling.

CONTACT: Igloo Backpackers Hostel
110 Mansfield Road, Nottingham, NG1 3HL
Tel: 0115 9475250
reception@igloohostel.co.uk www.igloohostel.co.uk

The Reckoning House camping barn has been renovated to a high standard including double glazing and insulation. It is situated on the edge of Lathkill Dale, 3 miles from Bakewell. Lathkill Dale is a nature reserve managed by English Nature to protect a variety of flora and fauna as well as some outstanding geological features. Horse riding, fishing, golf and cycle hire are all available locally. There are also many local walks including the Limestone Way.

It has a cooking area, 4 calor gas rings (gas supplied) a washing up sink with hot water, a toilet, wash basin, storage heaters in all rooms and shower inside the barn. Upstairs there are two separate rooms with bunkbeds.

DETAILS

- **Open** - All year, by arrangement
- **Number of beds** - 12
- **Booking** - Sole use bookings only, in advance (min 2 nights at weekends). 10% deposit, balance 2 weeks before arrival.
- **Price per night** - £8.50 per person. Sole use £85 per night, Reduction for sole use on Sun (excluding bank holidays), Mon, Tue, Wed or Thurs nights.
- **Public Transport** - Train stations at Buxton (10 miles) and Matlock (13 miles). National Express drop at Bakewell. Local buses (enquiries 01332 292200) go to Bakewell from Monyash, Over Haddon, Matlock and Buxton.
- **Directions** - GR 184 666. Take the B5055 out of Bakewell towards Monyash. Continue for 3 miles. After passing Haddon Grove Farm holiday cottages (the second set of cottages on right), take the first turn left at the signpost to Haddon Grove. Bear left at the bottom of the lane. The camping barn is the first on the left in a half mile.

CONTACT:
Mandale Farm, Haddon Grove, Bakewell, Derbyshire, DE45 1JF
Tel: 01629 812416
julia.finney@virgin.net www.mandalehouse.co.uk

BARN FARM
BARNS AND CAMPSITE

Barn Farm is a working farm in the village of Birchover with fine views over the Derwent valley. Nearby are Stanton Moor with Victorian stone carvings and Nine Ladies stone circle; Robin Hood's Stride and other bouldering and climbing areas; the Limestone Way; a village shop and two pubs which serve food. Four camping barns are available: Sabine Hay has 15 bunkbeds arranged around a communal space with fully fitted kitchen; Hill Carr and Warren Carr have a similar arrangement with 15 and 12 single beds respectively. Stables Barn has 6 bunkbeds. All bunkhouses have self-catering facilities, are heated and have private bathroom and shower facilities in adjacent barns. Also available: two ensuite double-bed units, the Garden Room and the Gatehouse Barn. There's also space for camping (no single sex groups), caravans and campervans with good showers, toilets and laundry facilities. Barn farm also offers indoor or outdoor storage for caravans and campervans.

DETAILS
- **Open** - All year, accommodation available all day.
- **Number of beds** - 52: 1x15, 1x15, 1x12, 1x6, 1x2, 1x2 plus camping.
- **Booking** - Booking advisable 50% deposit.
- **Price per night** - Hill Carr £150, Sabine Hay £140, Warren Carr £240, Stables Barn £100. Garden Room £45/ night; Gatehouse Barn £85/night (min.2 nights) Weekly rates available. Camping £7.50pp (£5pp DofE groups).
- **Public Transport** - The 172 bus from Bakewell to Matlock runs approx. hourly.
- **Directions** - From the A6 between Matlock and Bakewell take the B5056. Follow signs for Birchover, continue past the Druid Inn to farm sign at the top of the village.

CONTACT:
Birchover, Matlock, Derbyshire, DE4 2BL
Tel: 01629 650245
gilberthh@msn.com www.peakdistrictonline.co.uk

SHEEN
BUNKHOUSE

Sheen Bunkhouse is a newly converted barn in a quiet corner of the Peak District, close to the beautiful Dove and Manifold valleys. Comprehensively equipped, it offers a large TV lounge, well-equipped self-catering facilities and two bunkrooms with wash basins. Toilets and showers are conveniently located for both rooms.

Passing close by the barn, the Manifold Valley Track, Tissington Trail and High Peak Trail provide easy access to beautiful countryside, ideal for families and cyclists. Dovedale, the Upper Dove Valley and the remote and mysterious moorlands around Flash and Longnor offer stunning scenery for walkers. Visit the markets and parks at Buxton (8 miles), Leek (10 miles) and Bakewell (12 miles) for a great day out. Other attractions include Alton Towers (35mins by car) and the famous Opera House and show caves at Buxton.

DETAILS

- **Open** - All year, 24 hours access, reception 8-10am, 5-9pm
- **Number of beds** - 14: 1x8, 1x6
- **Booking** - Book by phone or email
- **Price per night** - From: Adults £14.00, Under 16's £9.50.
- **Public Transport** - Train station at Buxton. Daily bus operated by Bowers from Buxton to Hartington passes close to bunkhouse.
- **Directions** - On the B5054 between Hartington and Hulme End take the turning to Sheen (also signposted for 'Staffordshire Knott'). The bunkhouse is on the right 200yds after the pub.

CONTACT: Graham Belfield
Peakstones, Sheen, Derbyshire, SK17 0ES
Tel: 01298 84501, Fax: 01298 84501
grahambelfield@fsmail.net

MOORSIDE FARM
BUNKHOUSE

Moorside Farm is a 300-year-old farmhouse set 1200 feet up in the beautiful Peak District National Park on the Derbyshire/Staffordshire border and approximately five miles from the historic town of Buxton. Sleeping accommodation is provided in two areas, one for 14 - this is alpine style with pine clad ceiling and a pine floor with bunk beds. The second area has 6 beds, also in bunks and is an ideal room for a small group or family. Downstairs there are showers, toilets and a large dining / general room. The farmhouse has full central heating and drying facilities are available. We provide a three course breakfast, a packed lunch and a substantial dinner in the evening, vegetarians are catered for. A small kitchen is available for making tea and coffee. Ample parking space is provided.
All bookings have sole use of the accommodation.

DETAILS

- **Open** - All year, 24 hours
- **Number of beds** - 20: 1 x 14 : 1 x 6
- **Booking** - Booking with deposit required with two weeks' notice
- **Price per night** - £29.00 per person, bed, breakfast and evening meal included. £19.00 per person bed and breakfast. (min 4 persons)
- **Public Transport** - Nearest train station Buxton. Take bus to Longnor or Travellers Rest. Bus enquiries 01332 292200.
- **Directions** - GR SK 055 670. Leave A53, Buxton to Leek road, at Travellers Rest, take 4th lane on left, down to T junction, take first left, Moorside Farm is first right entrance.

CONTACT: Charlie
Hollinsclough, Longnor, Buxton, Derbyshire, SK17 0RF
Tel: 01298 83406
moorsidefarm@yahoo.co.uk www.moorsidefarm.com

Bushey Heath Farm is a family run smallholding in the heart of the Peak District, central to all the popular visitor centres, but just off the beaten track. Offering a summer campsite, self-catering static caravan and 'top of the range' bunkbarns for up to 14 people. Incorporating a ground source heat pump, a wind turbine for electricity and rainwater harvesting for wc flushing. We have developed the farm in an environmentally sensitive way so visitors can experience practical sustainable ideas. The static caravan has two bedrooms and shower/wc and can sleep up to 6. The Hen House Bunk Barn has two bedrooms with bunks for 4 in each. The Little Barn has a large single bedroom with bunks for 6 people. Both barns have luxury shower rooms and a combined fully equipped kitchen/diner open area downstairs. Sleeping bags required. Good dogs accepted.

DETAILS

- **Open** - All year. Campsite May till October, opening hours by arrangement
- **Number of beds** - 8: Hen House, 6: Little Barn, 6: Static caravan, 80 Pitches.
- **Booking** - Camping at Bank Hols only. Bunkhouse early with deposit advisable.
- **Price per night** - Camping Adult £5, Child £3, Vehicle £2. Static Caravan £220-£300 per week, short breaks available. Hen House - sole use £120-£140pn. Little Barn – sole use £90-£105pn. Weekends sole use only.
- **Public Transport** - Nearest trains at Hope (4 miles), Nearest buses in Tideswell (2 miles). Bus numbers 65, 66, x67, 173, 177, 197, 202.
- **Directions** - GR SK 146 785. From Tideswell take Manchester Road past Star Pub and cross over A623, road stops at farm. Going west along A623, 1.5 miles past the Anchor Pub turn right at cross roads in 's' bends..

CONTACT: Rod Baraona or Lisa Thomas
Tideswell Moor,Tideswell, Buxton, Derbyshire, SK17 8JE
Tel: 01298 873007, Mobile: 07710 163376
rod@baraona.freeserve.co.uk www.busheyheathfarm.co.uk

PEAK DISTRICT
HOLIDAY BARN

This extremely impressive holiday barn with 6 bedrooms comfortably sleeps up to 24. Situated in the heart of the Peak District, perfectly positioned for large groups to stay together and celebrate: wedding parties, family re-unions, birthdays, stag and hen parties, walking holidays etc. Also perfect for corporate residential or team building courses.

Recently converted to an extremely high standard while retaining many of the barn's original features. Fully insulated with double glazing and central heating throughout. 6 bedrooms including king sized 4 poster bed (all bed linen included), 3 bathrooms, a large multi-fuel log burner, plenty of off-road parking. Outside is a lawned garden with BBQ, fire pit and outdoor pizza oven. One all year round price with no additional increases for seasonal variations, school holidays, bank-holidays etc (excluding Christmas and new years eve). During mid-week periods no matter what the size of your group the barn is the perfect venue with our 'mid-week flexibility package' (see website).

DETAILS

- **Open** - All year round, all day.
- **Number of beds** - 24 : 2x king size, 3x double, 14 large bunks
- **Booking** - Booking required with £200 bond.
- **Price per night** - From £35pp midweek. 2 night weekend £1680 inc VAT.
- **Public Transport** - Stations on Sheffield to Manchester railway within 7 miles. Transpeak bus Nottingham to Manchester stops at Ashford (4 miles).
- **Directions** - Situated on the A623 in Wardlow Mires, next to the pub. OS 182757

CONTACT: Amanda Gregory
Wardlow Mires, near Tideswell, Buxton, Derbyshire, SK17 8RW
Tel: Booking enquiries: 07525 051 226 (Amanda), 07791667027 (Mark)
bookings@peakdistrictholidaybarn.co.uk   www.peakdistrictholidaybarn.co.uk

THORPE FARM
BUNKHOUSES

Thorpe Farm Bunkhouses are situated a mile northwest of Hathersage, on a family run mixed dairy farm which makes its own ice cream. The bunkhouses are 2 miles west of Stanage Edge. Other popular climbing and walking areas are nearby. Castleton is 6 miles up the Hope Valley and Eyam is 6 miles southwest.

Each bunkhouse has dormitories with individual bunks each with mattress and pillow. There is some sleeping space in the sitting rooms and room for camping outside. The bunkhouses have heating, drying facilities, hot showers, toilets, electric / gas cooking, fridges, freezers, electric kettles, toasters etc. The Byre is all on one level with disabled facilities.

DETAILS

■ **Open** - All year, no restrictions
■ **Number of beds** - Old Shippon 32: 2x12, 2x4. Byre 14: 1x6, 2x4. Old Stables 14: 1x8, 1x6. Pondside 14: 1x8, 1x6
■ **Booking** - Essential for weekends.
■ **Price per night** - From £10pp. Sole use from £100 per night.
■ **Public Transport** - Train station at Hathersage, 10 mins walk from bunkhouse. Bus service 272 operates from Sheffield to Hathersage. Weekends only bus service 257 operates from Sheffield via Stanage & Snake Pass to Hathersage. Details phone Busline 01298 230980 or 01246 250450.
■ **Directions** - GR 223 824. If walking from A6187/A625 in Hathersage turn right (just past the George Hotel) up Jaggers Lane, turn second right up Coggers Lane and fifth turning on left (signed Thorpe Farm). If driving follow the road from Hathersage towards Hope for ¾ mile, then turn right into private drive (signposted Thorpe Farm).

CONTACT: Jane Marsden
Thorpe Farm, Hathersage, Peak District, Via Sheffield, S32 1BQ
Tel: 01433 650659
jane@hope-valley.co.uk www.thorpe-bunk.co.uk

PINDALE FARM
OUTDOOR CENTRE
ENGLAND

The Centre is situated one mile from Castleton in the heart of the Peak District. It comprises a farmhouse pre-dating 1340 and lead mine buildings from the 1850s, which have been completely rebuilt from a near derelict condition. The Centre now offers 5 different kinds of accommodation. The farmhouse offers traditional bed and (an AGA cooked) breakfast. The Barn has 6 independent self-catering units, the lower 3 of these can accommodate people with certain physical disabilities. The old Lead Mine Engine House, our logo, is a self-catering unit sleeping 8. The Powder House, originally the mine's explosive store, is a small camping barn with basic facilities for up to 4 people. A campsite, adjacent to the Centre, has showers, hot water, and toilet facilities. The Centre is the ideal base for walking, climbing, caving, horse riding etc. Instruction is available if required. Well behaved pets welcome.

DETAILS

- **Open** - All year (Camping March-October), 24 hours
- **Number of beds** - 64 bunkbeds plus camping and B&B
- **Booking** - Early booking (deposit) is best.
- **Price per night** - Camping £5 pp, Powder House £6 pp, Engine House and Barn £11 pp, B&B £25 pp with four poster bed and an AGA breakfast.
- **Public Transport** - Hope has a train station. The nearest National Express service is in Sheffield. Approximate taxi fare to Sheffield is £15-£20. On local buses ask for Hope. Hope is 15 minutes walk from the hostel.
- **Directions** - GR 163 825 From Hope follow cement works signs, turn off main road between church and Woodroffe Arms.

CONTACT:
Pindale Lane, Hope, Hope Valley, Derbyshire, S33 6RN
Tel: 01433 620111, Fax: 01433 620729
pindalefarm@btconnect.com

HOMESTEAD
AND CHEESEHOUSE

These two bunkhouses are situated on a small mixed farm in the middle of Bamford, just 3 miles from Stanage Edge. The Derwent Dams are between 1.5 and 7 miles further up the valley. Castleton is 5 miles to the north, Chatsworth House and Park 10 miles to the south west.

Both bunkhouses have individual bunks each with mattress, fitted sheets and pillow, gas central heating and drying facilities. Homestead has 22 beds in 3 rooms, and 2 bathrooms with 2 toilets and showers in each, a large dayroom with oak seating and a fully equipped kitchen with gas cooker. Cheesehouse is a self-contained bunkhouse with four bunks, ideal for a small family or group. It has a shower and toilet and is equipped with a kitchen having cooking rings, a microwave oven, toaster and kettle. The Bunkhouses are 2 minutes walk from two pubs. Sorry, no dogs (working dogs on site).

PLEASE CONTACT THIS HOSTEL BY PHONE OR POST.

DETAILS

- **Open** - All year, no restriction
- **Number of beds** - Homestead 22: 1x10, 2x6. Cheesehouse 4: 1x4.
- **Booking** - Recommended for weekends.
- **Price per night** - £10 per person. Sole use: Homestead £170, Cheesehouse £36.
- **Public Transport** - Nearest train station Bamford, 10 mins walk. Bus 274 & 275 operates Sundays Bamford to Sheffield or Castleton. Bus 272 Bamford to Sheffield and Castleton. Bus 175 Bamford to Bakewell.
- **Directions** - The farm is in the centre of Bamford on South View Lane (turn off A6013 at the 'Country Stores').

CONTACT: Helena Platts
The Farm, Bamford, Hope Valley, S33 0BL
Tel: 01433 651298

THE OLD SMITHY
CAMPING BARN

The Old Smithy is a camping barn or 'stone-tent' situated in the village of Burwardsley, which is mid-way along the Sandstone Trail in Cheshire. The central section of the Sandstone Trail takes in Beeston and Peckforton castles. The barn is also on NCR45 Mercian Way cycle route.

The Old Smithy offers basic accommodation to groups of walkers, cyclists and others visiting this part of Cheshire. It is on Burwardsley Road, on the outskirts of the village, close to the Post Office. The Old Smithy provides space for up to eight people, with an area for cooking, washing up, a toilet and sleeping platform. There is no electricity or hot water. You will need to bring your own sleeping bag and roll mat, a cooker, food and matches. Lighting is via lanterns (provided) but you will need a torch. You can buy food and pre-book food parcels at the Burwardsley Village Post Office . The nearest pub is The Pheasant Inn (it has its own website).

DETAILS

- **Open** - All year, 24 hours. Pre-arrange arrival times.
- **Number of beds** - 8: 1 x 8
- **Booking** - Bookings by phone or email.
- **Price per night** - £4.00 per person per night.
- **Public Transport** - The nearest train station is Chester (10 miles) with an hourly bus service to Tattenhall (2 miles).
- **Directions** - The Barn is on Burwardsley Road, on the outskirts of the village, close to the Post Office. Grid reference: 513 569 OS Landranger No.117

CONTACT: Mandy Geall
Burwardsley Village Store, Harthill Road, Burwardsley, Cheshire CH3 9NU
Tel: 01829 770359
mandy_geall@hotmail.com

Chester Backpackers is located just a few minutes walk from the ancient heart of the historic city of Chester in an original Tudor coaching inn (formally the Waterloo Inn). We offer clean, comfortable rooms most of which have en-suite facilities, with freshly laundered linen provided as standard. Free tea and coffee, free left luggage facilities and well-equipped rooms make Chester Backpackers an ideal base for walking the Roman walls of Chester, exploring the nearby Welsh mountains and dramatic coastline or day trips to Liverpool and Manchester. We can also assist with finding work for longer-term travellers and our attractive long-term rates make it an ideal location to spend time in this beautiful city. We are open 24 hours with no curfew, and our friendly well-trained staff (travellers themselves) are on hand to offer help and advice.

DETAILS

- **Open** - All year, 24 hours , no curfew
- **Number of beds** - 32: 1 x 18 : 1 x 8 : 2 x 2 : 2 x 1
- **Booking** - Book by phone or email. Strongly recommended at weekends, 2 to 4 days notice advisable at other times
- **Price per night** - Dorm £15pp (£17 at weekend), Single £25pp (£30 at weekend). Dbl/ twin £40 per room (£45 at weekend). Long term rates available.
- **Public Transport** - Hostel is 10 mins walk from train station and National Express coach station. Liverpool and Manchester airports are 30 mins drive away.
- **Directions** - From train walk up City Rd. At ring road (nr Last Orders) bear left into Boughton (A41). Hostel 100 metres on left. From National Express walk up Union St with park on right, turn right at major junction. Hostel 100m on left. Car park at rear.

CONTACT:
67 Boughton, Chester, CH3 5AF
Tel: 01244 400185
sales@chesterbackpackers.co.uk www.chesterbackpackers.co.uk

HATTERS
MANCHESTER

Recently refurbished to its 100 year old splendour and winner of the Manchester Tourism Customer Care award, The Hatters has firmly established itself as the city's favourite funky hostel. Located in the Northern Quarter in the heart of the city centre, this is an ideal spot to start exploring the north west of England. Hatters caters for independent travellers and groups. It has a fully serviced kitchen with seating for groups of up to 50 and free all-day continental breakfast. There is an internet cafe and free wireless connection.

Let the knowledgeable and friendly staff guide you to the best that this great city has to offer, from live music and football to restaurants, shopping, museums, pubs and clubs. Three star graded with Visit Britain.

DETAILS

■ **Open** - All year, 24 hours
■ **Number of beds** - 150: 1x18, 7x10, 6x8, 1x6, 2x4, 2x2, 3x1
■ **Booking** - Booking recommended, essential for groups with deposit. ID is required at check in. Booking not essential for individuals.
■ **Price per night** - From £14.50 in an 18 bed dorm, £15.50 in a 8 to 10 bed dorm, £17.50 in a 4 to 6 bed dorm and from £25 per person in private rooms.
■ **Public Transport** - We are located only 5 minutes from Piccadilly railway station which is in the city centre. The main bus and tram station is on Piccadilly Gardens which is literally around the corner.
■ **Directions** - Coming into Manchester follow signs for Piccadilly Station. Newton Street is at the top of Portland and London Piccadilly Road.

CONTACT:
50 Newton Street, Manchester, M1 2EA
Tel: 0161 236 9500
Manchester@hattersgroup.com   www.hattersgroup.com

HILTON CHAMBERS

ENGLAND

Welcome to Hilton Chambers - Manchester's introduction to posh hostels. Located in the Manchester's bohemian Northern Quarter in the city centre, this fresh and airy hostel offers hotel-style facilities while maintaining the fun and character of a hostel. We boast ensuite dormitories, internet access, a self-catering kitchen, a free, light, all-day breakfast, free luggage storage and much much more! Let our welcome be your guide as we give you insider hints and tips so you can experience the real Manchester and all it is famous for. We are just a stone's throw from live music, entertainment, nightclubs, bars, museums, and shops too. The famous Manchester United Stadium "Old Trafford" is just 15 minutes away by tram and City of Manchester Stadium is a short bus trip away (or a brisk walk).
Come and pay us a visit soon.

DETAILS

- **Open** - All year, 24 hours
- **Number of beds** - 155 = 3 x triple ensuite, 3 x double ensuite, 4 x twin ensuite, 1 x 10 bed ensuite, 3 x 8 bed ensuite, 7 x 6 bed ensuite, 1 x 4 ensuite, 1 x 8 standard, 4 x 6 standard, 2 x 4 standard
- **Booking** - Booking not essential but recommended, especially at weekends. Photo ID (ie passport, ID card, driving license, etc) is required on check in
- **Price per night** - From £15. Please contact the hostel directly for groups
- **Public Transport** - Only 5 minutes from main train and coach stations.
- **Directions** - From Piccadilly Square follow Oldham St. At third crossroads turn right onto Hilton St. Hostel is on left after a few more steps.

CONTACT: Reception
15 Hilton Street, Manchester, M1 1JJ
Tel: 0161 236 4414
Hilton@hattersgroup.com www.hattersgroup.com/hilton

Welcome to The Hatters Hostel Liverpool UK. At Hatters Hostels we like to look after people, it's that simple. Newly opened and in one of Liverpools most historic buildings in the Culture Capital!.

Lay your head down in comfort and let us show you the Liverpool we love, right on our doorstep! The hostel is situated smack bang in the city centre a close walk to all shopping areas as well as the liveliest nightlife areas.

All rooms have ensuite facilities, with bedding provided. Light breakfast is included and self catering is possible in the guests kitchen with free fair trade tea and coffee. Towels are available for hire. Valuables can be handed in for safekeeping, and there is lockable luggage storage for larger items.

To stay at The Hatters all you require is current photo identification.

DETAILS

- **Open** - All year, 24 hour reception. Check in after 2pm, check out before11am.
- **Number of beds** - 72 rooms
- **Booking** - Group bookings require 1st nights payment as deposit (non refundable). Other bookings securable by deposit or card number.
- **Price per night** - 6 bed rooms from £16.50 / £17.50 weekends. 4 bed rooms £17.50 / £18.50; Triples £25; Doubles £27.50 /£35.
- **Public Transport** - Less than 20 minutes walk from city centre main transport links. 2 airport buses leave from just around the next corner.
- **Directions** - On Mount Pleasant roughly half way between Metropolitan Cathedral and Lime Street Train Station

CONTACT: Reception
56-60 Mount Pleasant, Liverpool, L3 5SH
Tel: 0151 709 5570
liverpool@hattersgroup.com   www.hattersgroup.com/Liverpool/

EMBASSIE
ENGLAND LIVERPOOL BACKPACKERS

The Embassie is a terrace house in an unspoilt Georgian square used in the filming of 'In the Name of the Father'. The house was built in 1820 and until 1986 it was the Consulate of Venezuela. Only 15 minutes walk from city centre. Liverpool is known for its nightlife, a student population of 70,000 ensures a lively scene, bands start playing at 11pm and bars are regularly open till 2am.

Hostellers have a key to come and go, the hostel is clean, safe and staffed 24 hours. Bedding is provided (including sheets) and free coffee, tea, toast and jam are available 24 hours, eat as much as you want.

International, or UK regional travellers only, NO LOCALS.

DETAILS

- **Open** - All year, 24 hr access with key.
- **Number of beds** - 40
- **Booking** - Booking is not essential for individuals. Groups larger than 6 should book (20% deposit).
- **Price per night** - £15 (Sunday to Thursday), £17.50 (Friday), £20 (Saturday).
- **Public Transport** - Liverpool has a train station and is served by National Express Coaches. A £3.50 taxi fare will bring you from the train or bus station to the hostel door, (good idea if you have a heavy rucksack).
- **Directions** - From the Anglican Cathedral (the third largest in the world) continue uphill along Canning Street away from the city centre. This will bring you into Falkner Square (15-20 mins). The hostel has a red door and is by a phone box.

CONTACT: Kevin
1 Falkner Square, Liverpool, L8 7NU
Tel: 0151 7071089
embassie@gmail.com www.embassie.com

INTERNATIONAL INN

ENGLAND

The International Inn is a multi award-winning hostel in a converted Victorian warehouse, located in the heart of Liverpool City Centre's cultural quarter. Liverpool has a wealth of attractions for visitors and you will find theatres, heritage, two Cathedrals as well as the City's renowned nightlife venues just a stone's throw away. The Hostel is also ideally located for visiting students, being opposite the University.

The International Inn provides fully heated accommodation in en-suite dormitories of 2, 4, 6, 8 and 10 beds. Private fully furnished apartments also available and newly opened cocoon pod hotel rooms. Facilities include a café, fully equipped kitchen, TV/DVD/games lounge, laundry, baggage store, internet access and information desk. There are no curfews to curtail your evening's fun.

DETAILS

- **Open** - All year, all day
- **Number of beds** - 103: 4x2, 5x4, 2x5, 1x6, 1x7, 4x8, 2x10 plus apartments
- **Booking** - Advisable at the weekend
- **Price per night** - From £15 (dorm) or £18 per person in twin room. Price includes tea, coffee, toast'n'jam 24hrs.
- **Public Transport** - Liverpool Lime Street Station 10 minutes walk away. National Express Station 10-15 minutes walk.
- **Directions** - From Lime St Station take the Skelhorn St exit. Turn left up hill and continue along Copperas Hill. At Main Road jnct. turn right along Russell St, continuing along Clarence St then Rodney St. At jnct. of Hardman St (HSBC bank on corner) turn left. South Hunter St is 2nd on left. The hostel is 20m up on the right.

CONTACT:
South Hunter Street, (off Hardman Street), Liverpool, L1 9JG
Tel: 0151 709 8135
info@internationalinn.co.uk www.internationalinn.co.uk

NABURN STATION

ENGLAND

Naburn Station is a converted railway station situated on the Trans Pennine Trail and Sustrans cycle route 65. It offers high quality accommodation ideal for cyclists and walkers. It also provides the perfect base for exploring the many delights of York and North Yorkshire with easy access to the city, the moors, the dales and the coast. The local village pub provides basic groceries and good food and there are other pubs and shops within easy walking and cycling distance. Cycle and boat hire are available locally and there are riding stables in the village. Facilities include a well equipped kitchen, a laundry and drying room, off road parking, secure bike storage and internet access. All bedding and towels are provided. No smoking. Pets and children welcome.

DETAILS

- **Open** - All year, 24 hours
- **Number of beds** - Singles/twins/double and up to 4 beds
- **Booking** - Advised in summer and bank holidays
- **Price per night** - £15pp, under 14s £10. Incl. bedding, towels, tea and coffee. Camping £5 per person. 10% discount for cyclists.
- **Public Transport** - Trains at York (5 miles) and Selby (10 miles). Arriva bus 42 between Selby and York stops at bottom of the drive. Collection can be arranged from either station and local bike hire is available.
- **Directions** - On A19 from York turn right at sign to Naburn just before A64 ring road junction. From A64 Selby junction follow A19 towards York. Take first left signed Naburn. Just before the village go under the old railway bridge and turn immediately left. On Sustrans cycle route 65, 5mins walk from Naburn village centre.

CONTACT: Ann
Station House, Naburn, York, YO19 4RW
Tel: 01904 636531 mob: 07779 352201
Saturn65@btinternet.com   www.naburnstation.org.uk

ACE HOTEL
YORK

Ace Hotel York is situated in Micklegate, the oldest part of York and its main entrance. This grand Grade 1 Georgian building was built in 1752 as a 'Town House' for the very wealthy John Bouchier of Bennigborough Hall. The Hotel has many impressive features including a stone flagged entrance hall leading to a grand carved sweeping staircase. With its panel rooms, vaulted cellar & fabulous Rococo ceiling depicting Shakesphere & Newtons Heads, the hotel holds a wealth of history and architecture. The oak beamed basement holds a television lounge, games room & sauna which leads onto a private courtyard. Ace Hotel York is the top end of budget accommodation. The Hotel is situated only 5 minutes form the main train station and rests within York city walls. It offers fantastic views of York including the oldest Gothic Cathedral (the Minster) and is surrounded by the walls themselves. This city centre hotel offers a number of budget rooms & dormitories all with exquisite views.

DETAILS

- **Open** - All year, 24 hours
- **Number of beds** - 129: 1x14, 4x10, 3x8, 6x6, 1x4, 3x2, 1xfamily, 1xdouble
- **Booking** - Credit card guarantees bed, Groups (10+) 50% deposit.
- **Price per night** - Rates starting from £19.50 per person. Weekly rates available.
- **Public Transport** - 5 mins walk from rail and bus stations.
- **Directions** - By car: from A64 take A1036 into York. Continue straight past race course and into Micklegate. We're 100 metres along on the left opposite the church. From rail station: turn right out of the station for 300 metres. Take the first left through the medieval gate into Micklegate. From coach station: head up the hill towards the traffic lights. At the end of Rougier St turn right onto Micklegate.

CONTACT: Reception
Micklegate House, 88-90 Micklegate, York, YO1 6JX
Tel: 01904 627720, Fax: 01904 339350
reception@ace-hotelyork.co.uk www.ace-hotelyork.co.uk

WHITBY BACKPACKERS
AT HARBOUR GRANGE

Harbour Grange is Whitby's long established, friendly backpackers hostel. It is beautifully situated on the River Esk, in Whitby itself, and only 5 minutes walk from train and bus stations. The hostel is all on the ground floor and has good facilities for self-catering with a dining area and a separate lounge area, both big enough to seat 24 people. There are 5 dormitories and family rooms are available on request. The hostel is open all day but so that everyone can have a chance of a good night's sleep there is a curfew at 11.30 (quiet at midnight). The premises are non-smoking.

Whitby is a beautiful little fishing town surrounded by beaches and moorland. Here you can find stunning views from cliff walks and visit lovely villages like Grosmont where steam trains run from Whitby to Pickering and Goathland where Heartbeat is filmed. Take a look at where Captain Cook lived and the Abbey that has stood as a landmark for 800 years.

DETAILS

- **Open** - 1st April - 31st Oct. Open all year for groups booked in advance. Hostel open all day. Check in 5pm-9pm.
- **Number of beds** - 24: 1 x 2 : 2 x 4 : 1 x 6 : 1 x 8.
- **Booking** - Booking advised for weekends and for groups, 10% deposit.
- **Price per night** - From £17 per person. Sole use £290 a night.
- **Public Transport** - Whitby has a train station and a bus station.
- **Directions** - From Whitby train and bus stations: cross the bridge and turn right. Follow the river. First right after 'The Bottom House' pub.

CONTACT: Birgitta Ward-Foxton
Spital Bridge, Whitby, North Yorkshire, YO22 4EF
Tel: 01947 600817, Mobile 0777 9798611
backpackers@harbourgrange.co.uk www.whitbybackpackers.co.uk

BRANSDALE
MILL

Bransdale Mill is a converted water mill at the head of an unspoiled and hidden valley in the North York Moors. Accommodation is basic but comfortable. It is an ideal base from which to get away from it all and to enjoy peace and tranquillity in beautiful countryside. There are many fine walks in the surrounding area, which is rich in wildlife. The nearest towns are Kirkbymoorside and Helmsley, both 10 miles away, and the North Yorkshire coast can be reached within an hour. The local pubs are 8 miles away, both of which serve food. Local attractions include the North Yorkshire Moors Railway; Heartbeat Country; National Trust properties at Nunnington, Rievaulx, Bridestones, and the Yorkshire Coast; Pickering and Helmsley Castles and Duncombe Park. The surrounding farmland is owned by the National Trust and let to tenant farmers; please respect the working life of the Dale.

DETAILS

■ **Open** - All year, All day
■ **Number of beds** - 13: 1 x 7 : 1 x 6.
■ **Booking** - Essential, minimum of two weeks in advance. Contact: Peakside, Ravenscar, Scarbourough, YO12 0NE.
■ **Price per night** - £120 per group (discounts may be available for small groups - please contact for details).
■ **Public Transport** - National Express to Pickering. Local buses Malton (18 miles) and Kirkbymoorside. Taxi Kirkbymoorside approx £10.
■ **Directions** - From Kirkbymoorside Market Place, left at the mini roundabout, take left fork to Fadmoor, continue 9 miles. Just before the head of Bransdale see a gate with sign 'Basecamp', follow track to Mill.

CONTACT: Anne Deebank
Bransdale, Fadmoor, York, YO62 7JL
Tel: 01723 870423
anne.deebank@nationaltrust.org.uk

EARBY HOSTEL
FRIENDS OF NATURE ENGLAND

The Friends of Nature (FoN) invite you to stay in this beautiful historic cottage in the peaceful village of Earby, Lancashire. Earby FoN House is a cosy cottage with a picturesque garden, stream and waterfall close to the Pennine Way. An ideal stop for the Pennine Way walker, as a base for local day hikes and for cyclists and those interested in the countryside and local heritage. Particularly suited to individuals, families and small groups. We have 2 comfortable lounges, a well equipped kitchen and seating for 18 in the dining areas. Real ale pub and meals nearby. Breakfast café in village and late stop Co-op. Secure bike storage. On-line booking. Visit Britain 3* Hostel, 'Walkers Welcome', and 'Cyclists Welcome'. FoN is one of Europe's oldest env. groups with 600k members and 800 houses across Europe. Under 16s must be accompanied by responsible adult aged 18 or over and of same sex if in shared dormitory.

DETAILS

- **Open** - From 2 weeks before Easter until 1st November (during winter open for sole-use bookings by arrangement) , 7am to 10am and from 5pm to 11pm
- **Number of beds** - 22 beds in 1x2, 2x6 and 1x8 bed rooms.
- **Booking** - Real-time live web bookings up until 5pm daily. Verbal bookings can only be held until 6pm daily. Book via web-site, e-mail or phone
- **Price per night** - Adults from £16 and under 18's from £12. Members of Friends of Nature, IFN and YHA pay discounted members rates
- **Public Transport** - Skipton-Burnley bus (hourly) drops ½ mile from Hostel. Skipton rail station for Leeds and Settle–Carlisle line, and Colne for Manchester
- **Directions** - Grid Ref SD915469. Geo-Coords 53.918065, -2.13064. 7 miles west of Skipton. In Earby village off the A56 Skipton-Colne road, 300m past Red Lion pub.

CONTACT: Manager
9-11 Birch Hall Lane, Earby, Lancashire, BB18 6JX
Tel: 01282 842349
earby@thefriendsofnature.org.uk www.thefriendsofnature.org.uk

AIRTON
QUAKER HOSTEL

Airton Quaker Meeting House has been used by Friends since the 1650s. The adjoining hostel was originally a stable and barn. The stable was converted into a wartime evacuee hostel in 1940 and used as a holiday hostel from 1943 with a modernisation in 1983. The meeting house is still used for worship.

The hostel is situated in the centre of Airton, a beautiful Yorkshire Dales village on the banks of the River Aire. The Pennine Way passes the village, and Malham Cove, Janet's Foss and Gordale Scar are in walking distance. The hostel has a self-catering kitchen / common area and 3 rooms, 2 with 4 bunks, 1 with 6. Blankets and pillows are provided but you must bring your own sleeping bag. There is a farm shop and café at Airton (closed Mondays) and more facilities in Gargrave. Parties of children (except families) must be accompanied by two adults. No animals permitted except guide dogs.

DETAILS

- **Open** - All year, no restrictions
- **Number of beds** - 14: 2 x 4 ; 1 x 6
- **Booking** - Advance booking is recommended with a deposit of 10%.
- **Price per night** - £10 (adults) £5 (Children under 12). Exclusive use of the hostel is available for a supplement charge.
- **Public Transport** - Nearest train stations Gargrave (4.5miles), Skipton (8.5miles). Buses from Skipton to Malham pass through Airton. Approx taxi fare from Skipton £12.
- **Directions** - GR 904 592 Block of buildings in Airton Village, on the right hand side of the road, leading down to the river bridge.

CONTACT: Mr or Mrs Parker
The Nook, Airton, Skipton, North Yorkshire, BD23 4AE
Tel: 01729 830263
bobminor@aol.com

Situated in the Yorkshire Dales amidst stunning landscape overlooking Thruscross Reservoir in a designated Area of Outstanding Natural Beauty on the edge of the Dales National Park, this self-catering accommodation centre offers excellent facilities for up to 30 people in 9 bedrooms with bunk beds. Leaders' en-suite accommodation has private catering, dining and lounge facilities. The centre is fully centrally heated. There are 4 showers, 4 hand basins and 4 toilets. There are no extra charges for heating, lighting and hot water. The well-equipped kitchen includes a 4-oven Aga cooker, two fridges and a freezer, together with all the cooking utensils and equipment. 3 star Hostel. Ideal for Team Building Courses, Schools, Scouts, Guides and family parties etc. Located only 12 miles from Harrogate and Skipton, 30 miles from the City of York. Tourist Board inspected and managed by the owners. All groups must be accompanied by an adult (25+).

DETAILS

- **Open** - All year, flexible
- **Number of beds** - 30 :- 4 x 2 : 3 x 4 : 1 x 6 : 1 x 4 en-suite
- **Booking** - Advisable at weekends
- **Price per night** - £12.50 pp. Sole use £270 (Sat/Sun/Bank Hol), £200 any other night, £600 for 4 nights midweek. Sunday night, if staying for 2+ nights £150.
- **Public Transport** - Nearest train stations are at Harrogate and Skipton, both 12 miles from the hostel. Taxi fare from either station would be approximately £22.
- **Directions** - GR 146 575. Leave A59 at Blubberhouses, signed West End 2.5 miles. Do not turn off, centre is on left side.

CONTACT:
West End, Summerbridge, Harrogate, HG3 4BA
Tel: 01943 880207
m.verity@virgin.net www.westendoutdoorcentre.co.uk

THE FYLDE
INTNL. BACKPACKERS

Welcome to The Fylde, Blackpools first 4 star Nationally Accredited Backpackers Hostel. Centrally located, we are ideal for walkers, cyclists, travellers and families looking for budget accommodation within Lancashire, the Wyre and the Fylde. Blackpool is famed for its tower, sandy beaches, piers, trams and fairgrounds, but it has lots more to offer: cinemas, nightclubs, galleries, parks and the world famous Illuminations. Recently refurbished, The Fylde has a variety of modern, spacious and clean ensuite private rooms.

Facilities include a comfortable Sun Lounge, a spacious Dining Room, a Games Room with full sized pool table and free parking for guests. For further information on our accommodation see our website

DETAILS

■ **Open** - Closed for Xmas, reception 8.00am until 10pm, check out by 11am
■ **Number of beds** - 28: 3x4, 1x3, 4x dbl, 2x twin, 1x1
■ **Booking** - Not essential but advisable for weekends, school holidays and Blackpool Illuminations. Credit card no. secures booking.
■ **Price per night** - Sun-Thurs £18pp. Weekends (for 2 night stay) £45pp (£39pp in low season). All prices include breakfast. Reductions for longer stays.
■ **Public Transport** - Trains at Blackpool North (1 mile, £4 by taxi). Talbot Road Coach Station (20 mins walk, £4 by taxi). Airport (3 miles, £8 by taxi or bus).
■ **Directions** - Turn off M55 at junction 4. Turn right at the roundabout and keep straight for about 3 miles. After four sets of traffic lights you will see CSL furniture shop. Continue along Park Road, passing Coin Age Laundry and some small B&B's. At the next set of lights on Park Road you will see Kingsley Court. Turn left at the lights on to Palatine Road and we are on the left side.

CONTACT: Vicky or Kate Easley
93 Palatine Road, Blackpool, Lancashire, FY1 4BX
Tel: 01253 623735
enquiries@blackpoolbackpackers.com   www.blackpoolbackpackers.com

Roeburndale Camping Barn is situated in a secluded meadow on the banks of the River Roeburn, and surrounded by native woodlands. It is a good miles walk (45mins) from the car park through woods and over a swing bridge. It is ideal for walkers, study groups or as a quiet retreat.

There are two floors and a balcony overlooking the river. The upstairs has bunk beds for 16 people (double, triple and some single beds). Downstairs there are table and chairs, gas cooker and wood burning stove (wood available at £3 per bag). Plenty of eating utensils are provided. There are simple washing and compost toilet facilities. Outside there is a field and a small fireplace. There is also a yurt and a 10 bed study centre for hire - ring (015242) 21880. No dogs.

DETAILS

- **Open** - March to November (inclusive), 24 hours
- **Number of beds** - 16: 1x16 + camping
- **Booking** - At weekends sole use bookings for 2+ nights get priority. Individuals and single night bookings are only available at short notice. Pay sole use rates to secure booking in advance.
- **Price per night** - Sole use: £120 for 3 night weekend (Fri,Sat,Sun); £40 for a single night. Individuals £4.50 per person (only available at short notice).
- **Public Transport** - Trains at Lancaster (12 miles) and Wennington (3 miles). Hourly buses from Lancaster bus station to Hornby or Wray, then 1 hour walk to barn.
- **Directions** - GR SD 611 650. 12 miles east of Lancaster, Junction 34 on M6. Take A683 then B6480 to Wray or Hornby.

CONTACT: Jane McArthur
Backs Bottom Farm, Roeburndale West, nr Wray, Lancaster, LA2 9LL
Tel: 08454 585795 or 015242 22214
roeburndalecampingbarn@phonecoop.coop www.middlewood.org.uk

DALESBRIDGE

Dalesbridge is located on the A65 at Austwick, on the edge of the Yorkshire Dales National Park, just five miles from both Ingleton and Settle. It is a comfortable venue for those visiting the Yorkshire Dales, whether you are a family, a group or an individual. The six bed units have a kitchen area with a cooker, fridge, washing up sink, shower and toilet. Crockery, cutlery and cooking pots are provided and there is a seating area in the middle of the room. The four bed units have a shower and toilet, small seating area with kettle, toaster, microwave, crockery and cutlery. These rooms are ideal for the smaller group not requiring full self-catering facilities. Utilising all the units provides group accommodation for up to 40. You will need to bring your own sleeping bag and pillow, alternatively bedding is available to hire. We have a great deal to offer: bar, drying room, functions, B&B, and campsite.

DETAILS

- **Open** - All year, reception open 9am - 5pm
- **Number of beds** - 40
- **Booking** - Advance booking with deposit
- **Price per night** - £15 per person. £84 for 6 bed unit; £56 for 4 bed unit.
- **Public Transport** - Settle railway station is 5 miles away and Clapham station 1.5 miles. There are infrequent buses but if you would like collection from either railway station please give us a call.
- **Directions** - GR 762 676. The hostel is on the main A65. When travelling from Settle towards Ingleton we are situated on the left hand side between the two turnings into Austwick.

CONTACT: Jon
Austwick, Nr Settle, LA2 8AZ
Tel: 015242 51021
info@dalesbridge.co.uk www.dalesbridge.co.uk

THE OLD SCHOOL
BUNKHOUSE

Situated 4.5 miles from Ingleton in Yorkshire Dales limestone country. Located between Ingleborough and Whernside with superb views of both, the bunkhouse makes an ideal base for sporting or nature holidays. The area is well known for it's scenery including the Three Peaks walk, (Ingleborough, Pen-y-ghent and Whernside), the waterfalls walk and for having some of the best caves and potholes in the country including the famous Gaping Ghyll system and the White Scar show cave.

This is a stone property, which has been converted from an old school, with much of the character remaining and provides self-catering accommodation for up to 30 people. The property comprises lounge, drying room, 4 shower rooms with hand basins and toilets, well equipped kitchen / dining room with industrial cooker, toaster, fridge, freezer, dishwasher, microwave, and payphone. No pets allowed in bunkhouse. Nearest pub 100 yds.

DETAILS

- **Open** - All year, 24 hours
- **Number of beds** - 30 (5 x 6)
- **Booking** - Early booking advised for popular times. £100 deposit for 2 nights. 25% for 3 nights or over.
- **Price per night** - £200 per night (sole use) with an extra £10 per person for groups over 20 people. Minimum of 2 nights at weekends.
- **Public Transport** - Ribblehead station 1 mile. No buses.
- **Directions** - 4.5 miles on the B6255 Ingleton to Hawes Road, just after Chapel-Le-Dale village on left hand side. 11 miles from Hawes on B6255.

CONTACT: Clare and Peter Fox
Chapel-le-Dale, Ingleton, Carnforth, Lancs, LA6 3AR
Tel: 01729 823835
pfox119@btinternet.com www.oldschoolbunkhouse.co.uk

This newly-built bunkroom situated close to the Golden Lion Hotel in the idyllic village of Horton in Ribblesdale is available either for groups or individuals. It is in an ideal location for walking the Pennine Way, climbing the 3 Peaks (Pen-y-ghent, Ingleborough & Whernside), caving in the many potholes, exploring the Settle to Carlisle Railway, fishing at the nearby Helwith Bridge, clay pigeon shooting at Coniston Cold or for a relaxing weekend away with friends. The bunkroom consists of 2 large bedrooms each with at least 20 beds, 4 shower rooms (1 having disabled facilities) and a drying room. Self catering facilities will be available from Jan 2010. There is plenty of parking space and a ¾ acre field for recreation (ideal for BBQs or picnics). Any bookings are welcome small or large: schools, colleges, universities, 4x4 groups, cyclists, hen/stag parties, all are welcome. The Golden Lion Hotel and other cafes are close-by if you require cooked breakfasts, packed lunches or bar snacks. The village has a Post Office / Stores, Cafe / Tourist Information Centre, two hotels and a useful rail link to Leeds & Carlisle.

DETAILS

- **Open** - All year, all day. Please arrive before 10pm, let us know if this is a problem. Check out by 10am.
- **Number of beds** - 40 : 2 x 20
- **Booking** - Bookings only confirmed by payment
- **Price per night** - £15pp. Discounts for group bookings and charities.
- **Public Transport** - The Settle to Carlisle train stops in the village.
- **Directions** - In the village of Horton on the B6479 to the north of Settle.

CONTACT: Carl & Susan Johnson
1 Chapel Lane, Horton in Ribblesdale, Settle, North Yorkshire, BD24 0HA
Tel: 01729 860380 Mob: 0787 0849419
johnson@jsusan.orangehome.co.uk www.3peaksbunkroom.co.uk

WHERNSIDE MANOR
BUNKHOUSE

ENGLAND

The beautiful Dentdale Valley is the ideal place for walking, caving, climbing or just enjoying the stunning views. Three good pubs, 3 cafés and a shop just a stroll away give you the best of both worlds.

The bunkhouse is set in the grounds of historic Whernside Manor, a grade 2 listed building. This is an English Tourist Board approved bunkhouse, well equipped with cooker, microwave, crockery and pans. All you need is food and sleeping bags (these can be hired). Everyone loves the hot shower rooms and drying rooms. There is also a camping area for larger groups.

Barbeque and outdoor eating area for hot days, cosy and heated in winter.

The perfect place for a get together.

DETAILS

- **Open** - All year, 24 hours
- **Number of beds** - 12: 1 x 12
- **Booking** - Booking essential with 25% deposit
- **Price per night** - £10pp Group use £100.
- **Public Transport** - Dent Station 3 miles. Coach station Kendal 15 miles. Local bus Wednesdays and Saturdays to and from Kendal and Dent.
- **Directions** - Leave M6, junction 37. Follow Sedburgh Road for approx 5 miles, then Dent road for 3 miles. Turn right in centre of Dent, past George and Dragon, follow road for 1.25 miles.

CONTACT: Angela Johnson
Whernside Manor, Dent, Sedburgh, Cumbria, LA10 5RE
Tel: 015396 25213
whernsidemanor@aol.com www.whernsidemanor.com

Harris House is the outdoor pursuits centre of the William Hulme's Grammar School (Manchester). The centre occupies an old village school, with attached headmaster's house, on the edge of the hamlet of Hardraw.   It is a grade II listed building built in 1875 in attractive Dales stone. Ample parking is available in the old playground and the large schoolroom is used for communal activities. The well appointed and practical accommodation is centrally heated throughout and can accommodate groups of up to 34. Hardraw has a camp site, a café and the Green Dragon Inn (adjacent to Hardraw Force waterfall).   Many groups use these facilities to complement their visit. The café offers good value, substantial home cooking for groups. In the locality are opportunities for caving, rock climbing, fell walking and cycling (secure storage). The Pennine Way passes the centre. The local town of Hawes has a full range of shops. Harris House is an ideal base for Duke of Edinburgh's award expedition training or educational visits.

DETAILS

- **Open** - All year, 24 hours
- **Number of beds** - 32: 3x8, 2x3, 1x2
- **Booking** - Essential (20% deposit) but short notice bookings are often available.
- **Price per night** - £15 per person, min £150.
- **Public Transport** - Garsdale Station is 8 miles away, connected by infrequent buses. Hawes, a pleasant one and a half mile walk away, has more frequent buses.
- **Directions** - Turn north off A684 1 mile to the west of Hawes and proceed for ½ mile. Harris House is at the west end of the hamlet of Hardraw.

CONTACT: Warden
The Old School, Hardraw, near Hawes, Wensleydale, North Yorkshire, DL8 3LZ
Tel: 0161 226 2054
Harris.house@whgs-academy.org www.whgs-academy.org

MARSETT
BARN

Marsett Barn is a back to nature experience, an old barn in an old landscape. The barn is basic but full of character and charm and has been sympathetically restored to retain its special place in this dales setting.

On the ground floor there is an entrance area with living and dining space, a wood burning stove, a fully fitted kitchen, a drying area, and a toilet for people with disabilities.

Upstairs there are two sleeping areas, each with platform, to sleep 20 people. Also toilets with handbasins and showers.

Activities may be available at Low Mill Outdoor Centre from £125 per session. Contact the centre for more details.

DETAILS

- **Open** - All year,
- **Number of beds** - Sleeps approx 20 people
- **Booking** - Booking is essential
- **Price per night** - £9 per person (minimum of £36 per night) includes gas.
- **Public Transport** - The nearest bus stop is Bainbridge (4 miles) and nearest train station Garsdale (11 miles).
- **Directions** - From Marsett Green access is normally on foot or cycle. From the green, follow the track on left towards Stalling Busk. The Barn is in a field on the right, approximately ½ kilometre from the green.

CONTACT:
c/o Low Mill Outdoor Centre, Askrigg, Leyburn, North Yorkshire, DL8 3HZ
Tel: 01969 650432
info@lowmill.com www.lowmill.com

The Dales Bike Centre is the perfect venue for cycling and walking in the Yorkshire Dales, and is right on Wainwright's famous Coast-to-Coast walk, infamous Woodcocks off-road Coast-to-Coast mountain bike trip and the Yorkshire Dales Cycle Way. 4 Star rated Hostel accommodation, café, bike shop, bike workshop, bike hire, secure bike store, drying room and a wealth of advice about the Dales. We have 14 beds, in smart 2 and 4 bedded rooms, warmly decorated and with amazing views across the dale. Bedding is provided, and there is access to a kitchenette with free tea and coffee. After 5pm, the café lounge can be used, with plenty of outdoor reading material, free wifi internet, internet radio and 24 hour cake access! A hearty breakfast is included. Evening meals are available in pubs and restaurants in Reeth, a five-minute stroll away. Based in the tiny village of Fremington, in Swaledale, surrounded by the best biking in Yorkshire with a stunning landscape, crisscrossed by ancient lanes, moorland tracks and dry stone wall-lined roads.

DETAILS

- **Open** - All year, 24 hours
- **Number of beds** - 14. Old barn 1x4, 1x2; New barn 1x4, 2x2,
- **Booking** - Book by phone or email.
- **Price per night** - Bunk bed and breakfast £24. Single occupancy £35.
- **Public Transport** - Trains Darlington (25 miles). Buses X26 & X27 every 15 mins from Darlington to Richmond. Bus 30 from Richmond to Reeth (7 per day till 6.15pm).
- **Directions** - 20 mins from A1M: from Richmond take A6108 then B6270 signed to Reeth. Once through Grinton DBC is on left at end of a row of tall trees.

CONTACT:
Parks Barn, Fremington, Richmond DL11 6AW
Tel: 01748 884908
enquiries@dalesbikecentre.co.uk www.dalesbikecentre.co.uk

RICHMOND
CAMPING BARN

Richmond Camping Barn is converted from 3 former byres which are part of a Listed Traditional Dales Longhouse. It is situated at East Applegarth Farm, 3 miles west of the town of Richmond on the Coast to Coast walk. Grid ref NZ135017 OS Map 92. The farm borders the Yorkshire Dales National Park, with panoramic views over the lower valley of Swaledale and the River Swale.

The Barn is a great base for exploring the historic town of Richmond and The Yorkshire Dales National Park with all it has to offer. Sleeping accommodation is in two rooms on raised platforms with mattresses, pillows and lightweight sleeping bags. Heating and cooking facilities are available on a meter. Lighting is not metered and is included in the price. The shower is available on a seperate meter. Cutlery, crockery and pans are provided.

DETAILS

- **Open** - 1st March to 30th November. Access after 4pm and departure by 10.30am unless otherwise arranged.
- **Number of beds** - 12: 1 x 8, 1 x 4
- **Booking** - Book by phone or email
- **Price per night** - £7 per person. £84.00 sole use of barn.
- **Public Transport** - Nearest railway 15 miles away at Darlington.
Bus service 3 miles away at Richmond. Local taxi service is available.
- **Directions** - On the A6108 in Richmond at the Total petrol station (Victoria Road) turn right into Hurgill Road. Continue for 3miles. Farm entrance is on the left in a dip in the road 200 yds past the 2 radio masts on the right. The barn is at the end of the tarmac road ignoring the T-junction.

CONTACT: Mrs J Atkinson
East Applegarth Farm, Westfields, Richmond, North Yorkshire DL10 4SD
Tel: 01748 822940
rebekah.atkinson@virgin.net

Fell End, overlooking the unspoilt Howgill Fells, consists of two 18th-century buildings providing comfortable bunkhouse accommodation for people wishing to explore this beautiful area. Perfect for mixed groups, families and people with special needs or mobility difficulties. Walking, cycling, canoeing and caving nearby and the Lake District only 1 hour away. The Schoolhouse (white building) sleeps 8 people in bunks in the central area with an extra bed in an adjoining room. There is a fully equipped kitchen with a fridge, freezer, microwave and cooker. The bathroom has two toilets, one shower and 4 wash basins. The living room has a multi-fuel stove, which also heat the radiators. Greenslack has a further 2 bunks and 1 single bed plus a bathroom for people with mobility problems. Greenslack cannot be booked separately. Entry into both buildings is by a touch lock system. Dogs allowed under strict supervision. Fell End is owned by the Bendrigg Trust, a charity offering outdoor activities for disabled people. To discuss the facilities available please contact Lynne Irish.

DETAILS

- **Open** - All year, 24 hours
- **Number of beds** - 14: 1 x 8 : 1 x 5 : 1 x 1.
- **Booking** - Advance booking with 20% deposit
- **Price per night** - £9.50pp + VAT. Minimum booking: 6 for Schoolhouse only, 8 for both buildings.
- **Public Transport** - Trains at Kirkby Stephen (6 miles) on the Carlisle/Settle/Leeds line. Then take bus 564 Mon to Sat (4 per day). Tel 0871 200 2233 for times.
- **Directions** - GR:723983 (postcode CA17 4LN). Directions given on booking.

CONTACT: Lynne Irish
Bendrigg Trust, Old Hutton, Kendal LA8 0NR
Tel: 01539 723766, Fax: 01539 722446
Lynne@bendrigg.org.uk www.fellend-bunkhouse.org.uk

LONGRIGG
RESIDENTIAL CENTRE

Longrigg Residential Centre is within walking distance of Sedbergh, only 10 miles from Kendal and less than 10 minutes from the M6, an ideal location for exploring the Lakes and the Yorkshire Dales. The centre stands in its own grounds and overlooks the unspoilt splendour of the Howgill Fells. Perfect for mixed groups or families. Walking cycling, canoeing, and caving are nearby. The centre has recently been refurbished. It has two dormitories each sleeping 6 in the main building and a larger separate building sleeping 20 in dormitories of 2,4,6 and 8. There are ample shower and toilet facilities. Sleeping bags and pillowcase are required. The large kitchen is equipped for group catering. The lounge has easy chairs and gives access to the patio area. A separate games room has pool table TV and table football. There is a drying room and tumble dryer. The Centre holds an Adventure Activity Licence and can offer instruction and equipment. Entry is by a touch lock system. The centre is owned by an Education Authority and complies with relevant Health and Safety requirements.

DETAILS

- **Open** - All year, all day
- **Number of beds** - 32: 1x8, 3x6, 1x4, 1x2
- **Booking** - Book by phone or email
- **Price per night** - £14.50, minimum of 10 people.
- **Public Transport** - Trains at Oxenholme on the West Coast Line.
- **Directions** - Longrigg Centre is located near the village of Sedbergh which lies on the edge of the Yorkshire Dales and is just 30 minutes from the Lake District. Easy access via M6 junction 37.

CONTACT: Rob Gregory
Frostrow Lane, Sedbergh, Cumbria, LA10 5SW
Tel: 01539 621161
longrigg.centre@kencomp.net www.longrigg.org.uk

BENTS
CAMPING BARN

Bents Camping Barn was formerly a shepherds' cottage in the 1600s. You will need sleeping bags, walking boots and warm clothes. There are 2 sleeping rooms on the first floor with bunk beds. On the ground floor there is a kitchen with cooking area, a dining area with tables and benches and a WC with washbasins. Other facilities include electric lighting and power points throughout (£1 coin meter), crockery, cutlery, toaster, microwave, 3 electric cooking rings, 2 electric kettles, 2 electric convector heaters, parking.
The barn is accessible from the Coast to Coast path and there is good fell walking in the Howgill Fells, Wild Boar Fell and Crosby Garrett Common. Smardale Gill Nature Reserve and Sunbiggin Tarn are nearby. The area is ideal for mountain biking and the Settle to Carlisle Railway fives miles away at Kirkby Stephen. There is a shop 2 miles away.

DETAILS

- **Open** - All year, all day
- **Number of beds** - 12 to 14: 1x10, 1x6
- **Booking** - Booking is essential for groups in advance with full payment. Individuals are advised to phone first.
- **Price per night** - £7 (midweek), £8 (Fri, Sat and bank holidays) per person. Full barn £96 per night.
- **Public Transport** -   Train station at Kirkby Stephen (5 miles). Local buses to village of Newbiggin-on-Lune.
- **Directions** - GR MY 708 065 OS map 91. From Junction 38 of the M6 take the A685 to Newbiggin-on-Lune. Take Great Asby Road on left then first right through tall gate. Follow tarmac road past Tower House and follow signs to Bents Farm up track.

CONTACT: Dorothy Ousby
Newbiggin-on-Lune, Kirkby-Stephen, Cumbria, CA17 4NX
Tel: Booking 01946 758198 Dorothy 01768 371760
info@lakelandcampingbarns.co.uk www.bentscampingbarn.co.uk

KIRKBY STEPHEN
HOSTEL

UNDER NEW OWNERSHIP SINCE APRIL 2008. Kirkby Stephen Hostel is a former Methodist church with substantial additions. The old chapel now accommodates a large dining room and kitchens, with a lounge/reading room in the gallery. The bedrooms and dormitories are in a building at the rear, with ample lavatories and showers. The hostel features the original stained glass windows, pews, pulpit and organ.

Kirkby Stephen is a pleasant market town in the upper Eden valley, situated 15 miles from Kendal, 15 miles from Hawes and on Wainwright's coast to coast path and the W2W cycle path. It also enjoys easy access to Lady Anne's Walk, the Howgill Hills, the Dales National Park and the Lake District. The hostel stands prominently on the main street, with a range of restaurants, cafes, pubs, fish and chip shops and food shops on the doorstep. Paragliding is also available in Kirkby Stephen.
PLEASE CONTACT THIS HOSTEL BY PHONE OR POST.

DETAILS

- **Open** - All year, please arrive after 5pm
- **Number of beds** - 40: 1x8, 3x6, 2x4, 1x2, 1x2 ensuite
- **Booking** - Book by phone. Booking advised but not essential.
- **Price per night** - £18pp. Reductions for groups.
- **Public Transport** - One mile from Kirkby Stephen train station on the Leeds-Carlisle line. Regular buses from Penrith, Kendal and Appleby stop outside hostel.
- **Directions** - In the centre of town on main road. From M6 leave at junction 38 and follow signs towards Appleby.

CONTACT: Denise
Market Street, Kirkby Stephen, Yorkshire, CA17 4QQ
Tel: 0870 770 5904 or 01768 371793 or 07812 558525

New Ing Lodge is a friendly Bed and Breakfast and Hostel with nine letting rooms, directly on the Wainwrights Coast to Coast. It is the first accommodation in Shap on the walk from Patterdale. The two mixed dormitory rooms sleep 6 and 8 people and there are also private and family rooms. As well as a bed and a great atmosphere you have access to a kitchen with microwave, kettle, hob, toaster, fridge, and cooking utensils. The dormitory rooms come with the option of breakfast, cereal, toast, tea, coffee and fresh orange juice for £4 or £6 for a full English/vegetarian breakfast. Packed Lunches and evening meals are available on request. New Ing Lodge is ideal for individuals, families and groups. It is within three miles of Junction 39 on the M6 and close to the A6 which make it great for a break in a journey. It has a wild location on the edge of the Lake District National park, the Howgill Fells, the Pennine Fells and the Westmorland Way. Places for a day out include Shap Abbey (20min walk), Orton Chocolate Factory or the Rheghed Discovery Centre. Camping available

DETAILS

- **Open** - All year, all day, contact between 7am & 11pm
- **Number of beds** - 30:1x8,1x6,1x3,2x2(twin),2x2(dbl),1x1,1x4(family) + camping
- **Booking** - Not essential. As soon as possible in advance. Deposit 10%.
- **Price per night** - Dorms beds £14 per person without bedding, £16 with bedding. Discounts for larger groups, and longer stays – please request.
- **Public Transport** - By bus from Penrith station. Pick-up from station is possible.
- **Directions** - At the north end of Shap Village, just 20 metres off the A6 opposite the supermarket. Kendal 17 miles, Penrith 12 miles. M6 Junction 39 2 miles.

CONTACT: Scott or Jamie
New Ing Lodge, Shap, Penrith, Cumbria, CA10 3LX
Tel: 01931 716719 or 07792 222881
info@newinglodge.co.uk www.newinglodge.co.uk

Wythmoor Camping Barn is on the Walney to Wear coast to coast cycle route and a few hundred metres from the Dales Way long distance footpath. It enjoys great views of the Howgill fells and the distant mountains of the Central Lakes. Being only 4.5 miles from Kendal and less than 10 mins from the M6 this is an ideal location for exploring the Lake District and the Yorkshire Dales. The 19th century barn has hot water provided by solar panels, underfloor heating powered by ground source heat pump and mains electricity supplemented by wind turbine. The barn is generously sized for twelve people and includes facilities for wheelchair users, two separate heated shower rooms and a food preparation area with sinks and cooking slabs (bring your own camping stove). Kettle and microwave are provided. Local taxis available for transport to Kendal and Sedburgh. Holmescales Farm Outdoor Centre is close by.

DETAILS

- **Open** - All year, all day
- **Number of beds** - 12: 1x12 (10 single beds, 1 double)
- **Booking** - Book online, by phone or email. Booking not always required
- **Price per night** - £7 (midweek) £8 (Fri,Sat and bank holidays) per person.
- **Public Transport** - Oxenholme (6.5 miles) and Kendal (4.5 miles) have stations.
- **Directions** - Take Appleby Road (A685) from Kendal. After 2.5 miles turn right signed 'Docker' (single track). Opposite Docker Hall farm take left fork signed Lambrigg. Follow for 2 miles, barn is on left. From M6 Junction 37 take A684 towards Sedburgh; then direct left signed Lambrigg/Beck Foot. After 1.5 miles take left signed Lambrigg and Docker (single track). Barn is on right in half a mile.

CONTACT: Bruce Withington
Wythmoor Farm, Lambrigg, Kendal, LA8 0DH
Tel: Booking office 01946 758198, Farm mobile 07971 018567
info@lakelandcampingbarns.co.uk www.lakelandcampingbarns.co.uk

On the edge of the Lake District, the Walkers Hostel has 30 beds with between 2 and 9 beds to a room. Light breakfast which includes cereals, toast, fruit juice and tea or coffee is included in the price. We have a reasonably well stocked book shelf with guide books, maps and books of general interest. There is a no smoking policy in the house and grounds, a cycle lock-up, a drying room and an open fire. We enjoy the company of our guests. WiFi available. Ulverston is an old market town with plenty of good pubs. The Cumbria Way starts at Ulverston and there are street markets on Thursdays and Saturdays as well as other attractions. The lighthouse on Hoad Hill is a famous landmark and is adjacent to the Walkers Hostel, which is ideally suited for long and short walks. We are happy to give advice on how to get the most from your visit and scenery. Whole hostel booking enquiries welcome for walkers or corporate groups.

DETAILS

- **Open** - All year except a couple of days at Christmas., flexible hours.
- **Number of beds** - 30: 1x9, 1x8 1x6, 1x5 1x2
- **Booking** - Booking is advisable, not essential.
- **Price per night** - £17.50 per person.
- **Public Transport** - Ulverston has a good train service.   National Express Coaches and local Stage Coach buses also come to Ulverston - Enquires tel 0870 608 2608.
- **Directions** - From M6 Jn 36 take the A590. On the edge of Ulverston there is a roundabout. Turn left, and left again. From the bus or train station, walk towards town. Turn right down A590. We are just beyond the second roundabout.

CONTACT: Derek or Jocelynne Bigland
Oubas House, 1 Oubas Hill, Ulverston, Cumbria, LA12 7LB
Tel: 01229 480511
info@thewalkershostel.co.uk www.thewalkershostel.co.uk

DUDDON SANDS
HOSTEL

The purpose built Duddon Sands Hostel, overlooking the Duddon Estuary, stands in the grounds of The Ship, a cosy village inn built in 1691 and known for its friendly atmosphere, good ales and ghost story. The pub has a beautiful beer garden with estuary views, gas barbecue and a brazier which guests can use. In addition the pub garden features an indoor, all-weather solid fuel barbecue hut which seats 16 comfortably. The pub is open Thurs (Quiz Night), Fri and Sat evenings, and Sun on request for large groups. It does not serve bar meals but there are two other pubs in the village which do and several take-aways in nearby villages which will deliver. The pub has a kitchen and a cook can be arranged to provide a meal for large groups served in our bar or our dining/sitting room (with large screen TV). All bedding is provided (not towels) and a cot or cot sides are available. Bike wash / storage is available. Celebrate an event, reunions, stags / hens, staff trips, a big birthday or just Friday again!

DETAILS

- **Open** - All year, all day (phone to arrange arrival)
- **Number of beds** - 19 : 2x4, 1x8 + cot + 2-3 air beds (half price)
- **Booking** - Recommended, especially for large groups. A deposit required.
- **Price per night** - From £13 per person. Special rates 4 nights sole use Mon to Thurs £550, 3 nights sole use Fri to Sun £550.
- **Public Transport** - Train: request stop at Kirkby. Bus: Take X7 (Barrow-in-Furness to Millom) and get off at Moorland Stores in Kirkby, follow signs for hostel.
- **Directions** - At Moorland Stores crossroads on A595 in centre of Kirkby take turn for Sandside and Train Station. Hostel is at bottom of hill.

CONTACT:
The Ship Inn, Askewgate Brow, Kirkby-in-Furness, Cumbria, LA17 7TE
Tel: 01229 889454
theship1691@googlemail.com www.theship1691.co.uk

Fell End is a traditional 18th century Lakeland stone barn, located within its own grass courtyard approximately ½ mile from the farm. It is in the centre of a 500 acre estate in the western fells with easy access to some spectacular scenery, ideal for walkers, cyclists and wildlife enthusiasts. It is a short drive from Coniston (6 miles) and the Duddon Valley (5 miles). There are magnificent views, star-filled skies (a truly breathtaking sight) and the tranquil 'sound of silence'. Fell End Barn is lit by chandeliers and tea lights (provided) and heated by woodburing stove (a gas heater is also available for hire). There is no electricity and you will need to bring your own cooking and lighting equipment and bedding with mat. There are 2 picnic style tables, a wash basin and WC. Ideal for campfires or BBQs. Wood is available from the farm. Check the website www.lakelandcampingbarns.co.uk and book online..

DETAILS

- **Open** - All year, all day
- **Number of beds** - 12: 1x12
- **Booking** - Book online. Booking in advance is essential.
- **Price per night** - £7 (midweek) £8 (Fri,Sat and bank holidays) per person.
- **Public Transport** - Trains: Foxfield (3 miles). Buses: Grizebeck (3 miles).
- **Directions** - Leave M6 at J36, follow the A590 towards Barrow. Near Greenodd Estuary take A5092 signed to Broughton-in Furness. Follow this road until you reach Grizebeck. Just before Grizebeck garage take lane on right signposted 'Woodland'. Follow for 2 miles, over a cattle grid, until road becomes level. Take lane on left signed 'Woodland Hall' and follow for 1 mile.

CONTACT: Booking office / Jean
Thornthwaite Farm, Woodland, Broughton in Furness, Cumbria, LA20 6DF
Tel: Booking office 01946 758198, Farm 01229 716 340
info@lakelandcampingbarns.co.uk www.lakelandcampingbarns.co.uk

ROOKHOW
CENTRE

Perhaps the best situated small hostel in the Lake District. Peaceful, in 12 acres of its own woodland, but close to the heart of the Lakes, ten minutes from Coniston Water and Windermere, and on the edge of the famous Grizedale Forest Park with its trails and sculptures.   Superb area for walking, cycling and all outdoor activities. Also for quiet retreat, relaxation, study and artistic pursuits. The Rookhow Centre is within the former stables of the nearby historic Quaker meeting house which is also available for conferences and group sessions. Guests find the centre warm, comfortable and well equipped. It has electric heating and an optional wood burning stove. There are three sleeping areas, a self-catering kitchen/dining area and picnic tables and barbecue for warm days. There is a bonfire area within the centre's private woodand.

DETAILS

- **Open** - All year, all day
- **Number of beds** - 20: 1x9 : 1x8 : plus extra on bed settees. Also camping.
- **Booking** - Booking is essential (deposit).
- **Price per night** - From :- Adult £14.00, £7.00 for under 16's. Sole use from £160
- **Public Transport** - Trains at Grange-over-Sands (11 miles, approx £25 by taxi). A seasonal bus service sometimes operates to the hostel - check with the warden
- **Directions** - GR 332 896. From M6, Junction 36, follow A590, signs for Barrow. Leave A590 at Greenodd (A5092) junction and follow sign for Workington for ¼ mile. Take minor road to right signed Colton / Oxen Park. Continue through Oxen Park for a further 2 miles, Rookhow is on left. From Ambleside : to Hawkshead, then to Grizedale. Continue beyond Grizedale for 3.5 miles (Satterthwaite to Ulverston Road). Rookhow is on the right.

CONTACT: Warden
Rusland, Grizedale, Cumbria, South Lakeland, LA12 8LA
Tel: 01229 860231 Mob: 0794 350 8100
straughton@btinternet.com

HIGH WRAY
BASECAMP

Situated in the heart of South Lakeland in secluded woodland, 4 miles from the village of Ambleside, High Wray Basecamp provides an ideal base for groups wishing to explore and take part in activities in the Lake District Area. Local attractions include rambling, fell walking, climbing and water sports, with the Basecamp Warden being happy to assist with information on local walks and activities. The Longland Block has two separate fully centrally heated dormitories each sleeping 8, with a separate washing and living area/kitchen block. The comfortable living area is heated by a central wood burning stove and the kitchen has a commercial gas cooker, fridge freezer, microwave and utensils. The Acland block has two separate centrally heated dormitories sleeping 8 each, with toilet and shower room attached. The kitchen / lounge area is fitted with commercial gas cooker, fridges, microwave and utensils.

DETAILS

■ **Open** - All year, 24 hours
■ **Number of beds** - 16 + 20
■ **Booking** - Booking with deposit of £50
■ **Price per night** - Longland £9.25pp (Mon-Thur), £11pp (Fri-Sun). Acland £10pp (Mon-Thur), £12pp (Fri-Sun).
■ **Public Transport** - Nearest train station Windermere 8 miles. Local bus (505 'Coniston Rambler' Windermere - Hawkshead) stops 2 miles away at turning to Wray Castle (Cumbria travel-line 0870 6082608)
■ **Directions** - GR: 373 995 Take A593 from Ambleside towards Coniston, bear left onto the B5286 signed Hawkshead, fork left for High Wray village, signed Wray Castle. Basecamp is ¼ mile up dirt road on the left at the end of High Wray village.

CONTACT:
High Wray, Ambleside, Cumbria, LA22 0JE
Tel: 015394 34633
paul.kear@nationaltrust.org.uk

LAKE DISTRICT
BACKPACKERS

Situated in the heart of Windermere and central Lakeland, you will find our cosy, friendly hostel ideally situated for exploring the surrounding area.

We can advise you on routes for walks and cycle rides and provide you with maps. We are often asked to help organise abseiling, canoeing, sailing, windsurfing, even caving! There is easy access to the lake and fells from our door and we are adjacent to the main 555 bus route through Lakeland.

The hostel with its small dormitories provides you with every comfort but at a budget price. We are right next to a number of pubs, restaurants and take-aways and only minutes away from the rail and bus stations. Lockers are available and internet access and Sky keep you in touch! A well equipped kitchen and comfortable common room make your stay one to remember.

DETAILS

- **Open** - All year, 24 hours
- **Number of beds** - 20:- 1x7, 2 x 4, 1x 3, 1 x2
- **Booking** - Essential, 24 hours in advance.
- **Price per night** - £14.50 (£12.50 per night for 3 nts or more). Price includes self service continental breakfast and free tea/coffee.
- **Public Transport** - Windermere train station is 2 minutes walk. National Express coach stop 2 minutes walk.
- **Directions** - Turn left out of station, walk to information centre, hostel is opposite, next to Simpson and Parsons Insurance Company.

CONTACT: Paul
High Street, Windermere, Cumbria, LA23 1AF
Tel: 015394 46374, Fax: 015394 88611
fletcher_recruitment@yahoo.co.uk www.lakedistrictbackpackers.co.uk

MAGGS HOWE
CAMPING BARN
ENGLAND

Kentmere is a quiet, unspoilt valley within the Lake District National Park. It's a ramblers' paradise with woods, fields, lanes, a scattering of traditional lakeland farms and dwellings, and of course the fells with their walks so favoured by Wainwright. The Lakeland to Lindisfarne Long Distance path passes this way as well as the mountain bikers' and horse riders' Coast to Coast. Kentmere offers plenty of activities which include biking, riding and fishing, but most of all quiet enjoyment. A pleasant day's visit can be found at the market town of Kendal and Lake Windermere which are only 20 minutes away. The recently converted Barn has two sleeping areas, fully fitted kitchen, two showers and toilets. All you need is your sleeping bag, mattresses provided. Breakfasts and suppers are available next door at the B&B with notice.

DETAILS

- **Open** - All year, 24 hours
- **Number of beds** - 14: 1 x 6   1 x 8
- **Booking** - Recommended with 50% deposit for groups. Individuals can book but not essential
- **Price per night** - £10.00 per person or £100 sole use. There will be a surcharge for a single night booking on a Friday or Saturday night.
- **Public Transport** - Staveley 4 miles with train and bus service. Oxenholme train station is 10 miles. Kendal / Windermere National Express 8 miles.
- **Directions** - GR 462 041, MAP OS English Lakes South East. Green Quarter. Leave the A591 and come into Staveley, proceed to Kentmere for 4 miles, then take right fork to Green Quarter keeping right until you reach Maggs Howe.

CONTACT: Christine Hevey
Maggs Howe, Kentmere, Kendal, Cumbria, LA8 9JP
Tel: 01539 821689
enquiry@maggshowe.co.uk   www.maggshowe.co.uk

AMBLESIDE
BACKPACKERS

Get away to The English Lakes National Park, one of the most beautiful scenic areas in the UK. The hostel is in a marvellous location with fell and mountain walks, boating, scenic drives, cycle touring, mountain biking and outdoor activities practically from the doorstep. Set just 4 minutes walking from the centre of Ambleside it is also a great centre for visiting places made famous by Wordsworth, Ruskin and Beatrix Potter. Ambleside is excellent for shopping and eating out with many outdoor equipment shops, restaurants and pubs.

With 66 beds Ambleside Backpackers can accommodate groups and individuals in either single sex or mixed dorms. A large, traditional Lakeland cottage featuring a great lounge with a fire and piano, dining room, large well equipped kitchen for your use - not to mention central heating, showers and washing/drying facilities. Free light breakfast, tea/coffee and internet access. Good bus links to most fell walk starting places and lakes makes this hostel an ideal base.

DETAILS

- **Open** - Open most of the year,
- **Number of beds** - 66: 1x14, 1x12, 2x7, 2x6, 3x4, 1x2
- **Booking** - Recommended, essential for groups, deposit required.
- **Price per night** - £18pp. £16pp for three or more nights. Special winter breaks.
- **Public Transport** - Windermere train station 4 miles then 555 bus to Ambleside.
- **Directions** - From Ambleside bus stop: up hill to T junction, across road to Old Lake Rd, 200m up on left.– By road : A591 Windermere to Ambleside. At 2nd Hayes Garden Ctr. sign. turn right into Old Lake Rd. 300m on right.

CONTACT:
Ambleside BP's, Iveing Cottage, Old Lake Rd, Ambleside Cumbria, LA22 0DJ
Tel: 015394 32340
bookings@amblesidebackpackers.com www.amblesidebackpackers.com

RYDAL HALL
BUNKHOUSE

The Bunkhouse is situated in the centre of Rydal Hall estate, sheltered on three sides by the Fairfield Horseshoe and offering access to the best of Lakeland's activities. Facilities inside provide the necessities for groups of up to 36. There are 2 dormitories sleeping 14 and 18 in bunk beds and 2 leader rooms each sleeping 2. There is a large common room which can be used for dining or recreation. A welcoming log burner provides additional warmth to the ample heating powered by our nearby water turbine. The kitchen is fully furnished for cooking en-masse and there are 2 separate toilet facilities with showers. Laundry and drying facilities are close by and a games room with table tennis and pool is available on request. Users need to bring sleeping bags, pillow cases and extra blankets during winter. Rydal Hall also offers camping to organised groups and there is comfortable residential accommodation for up to 56 at the Hall in single, twin, double and family rooms.

DETAILS

- **Open** - All year, 24 hours
- **Number of beds** - Bunkhouse 36: 1x14, 1x18, 2x2
- **Price per night** - Sole use Nov-Mar £190, Apr - Oct and Xmas & New Year £285. 10% discount for youth groups + midweek. Individual bookings by arrangement.
- **Booking** - Required with deposit. No bookings by email please.
- **Public Transport** - Trains at Windermere. National Express at Ambleside. Local Stagecoach service (555) from Lancaster to Keswick stops 200 yards from Hall.
- **Directions** - GR 366 064. Take the A561 from Ambleside to Grasmere, Rydal is reached after 2 miles. By the church turn right and go up lane for 200m.

CONTACT:
Rydal Hall, Ambleside, Cumbria, LA22 9LX
Tel: 01539 432050, Fax: 01539 434887
mail@rydalhall.org www.rydalhall.org

Swirral Barn is one of a group of mine buildings situated at 1,000ft on the flank of the Helvellyn Mountain Range. It offers the basic necessities: hot water, toilet, tables, benches and a sleeping platform with mattresses. You will need to bring a stove and utensils if you wish to cook, a torch and a sleeping bag. The location is perfect for walking over the fells. Popular routes to Striding Edge and Swirral Edge pass the door, and there is quick access to Ullswater and the Eastern Fells. Enjoy a hike up Helvellyn and the surrounding peaks or, for less strenuous walking, try the scenic lake shore paths around Ullswater. Rowing, sailing and steam boats trips are available on Ullswater, where you can relax by the waterside. There are so many thing to do in this beautiful area. The barns facilities are: sleeping platform on the first floor, slate cooking area, cold tap and toilet, plus electric lighting. Nearest pub is only 1 mile away, with the nearest village store only 1.5 miles away.

DETAILS

- **Open** - All year, all day
- **Number of beds** - 8: 1x8
- **Booking** - Book online. Booking in advance is essential.
- **Price per night** - £7 (midweek) £8 (Fri, Sat and bank holidays) per person.
- **Public Transport** - Buses run every 2 hours from Penrith to Glenridding. It is just over 1 mile walk from bus stop to barn.
- **Directions** - From Pooley Bridge take A592 to Glenridding then to main car park. Follow the sign post to Helvellyn Youth Hostel. Swirrel Barn is 100 metres past the hostel on the left.

CONTACT: Jeanette
Striding Edge, Glenridding, Cumbria, CA11 0NR
Tel: Booking office 01946 758198, Farm mobile 07775 561512
info@lakelandcampingbarns.co.uk www.lakelandcampingbarns.co.uk

STICKLEBARN
BUNKHOUSE

The Sticklebarn is beautifully situated amidst some of the finest mountain scenery in England. It is at the foot of the famous Langdale Pikes and Dungeon Ghyll waterfalls and seven miles north west of Ambleside.

The bunkhouse has no common room or self-catering facilities but meals are provided in the pub. We provide a sheet, pillow and pillowcase. You must bring your own sleeping bag and towels.
Sorry no pets are allowed in the bunkhouse.

Live music every weekend from March to end of October.

Check out the weather via our webcam on the Langdale Website
www.langdaleweb.co.uk

DETAILS

- **Open** - February to November, all day
- **Number of beds** - winter 16, summer 12
- **Booking** - Pre-booking is advised for weekends and groups,50% deposit required.
- **Price per night** - £13 per person
- **Public Transport** - Bus service 516 to Great Langdale from Ambleside, ask for New Dungeon Ghyll Hotel, walk 2 mins (timetable 01946 632222).
- **Directions** - From the A591 Windermere to Keswick road at Ambleside take the A593 turn to Coniston / Torver. After two miles take the B5343 to Great Langdale via Chapel Stile. The Bunkhouse is adjacent to the Sticklebarn Tavern.

CONTACT:
Sticklebarn Tavern, Great Langdale, LA22 9JU
Tel: 015394 37356
sticklebarn@aol.com

"A truly magical experience" is how some of our guests have described staying in one of our Bell Tents. Situated right in the heart of the Lake District National Park on quiet western shore of Lake Windermere you couldn't ask for a more idyllic location. Surrounded by some of the most spectacular scenery the Lake District has to offer, come and experience 'living in the round' for yourselves and enjoy a unique holiday in a unique environment. Bell tents are for people who want something different from their holiday. For families, friends, lovers of the outdoors, romantics, those in search of adventure and anyone who wants a little bit of luxury but still wants to feel close to nature.

DETAILS

■ **Open** - From 1st April 2010 to 1st November 2010, all day
■ **Number of beds** - Each bell tent sleeps a maximum of 4 people
■ **Booking** - Please call Richard or John on to enquire about availability or to make a booking. Alternatively please see our website.
■ **Price per night** - School holidays / Bank Holidays: Weekdays (Mon–Fri) £245, Weekend (Fri–Mon) £245, Whole Week (Mon-Sun) £390. Off peak: Weekdays £225, Weekend £225, Whole Week £345. All prices are per bell tent.
■ **Public Transport** - From Ambleside take the 505 Coniston Rambler bus towards Hawkshead - ask to be let off at the Low Wray turn off, it's about 15 minutes walk from here. For more information: http://www.cumbria.gov.uk
■ **Directions** - Take the A593 from Ambleside, turn left at Clappersgate onto the B5286. Turn left at the sign for Wray. The site is less than one mile on the left.

CONTACT:
Low Wray Bell Tents, National Trust Campsite, Low Wray, Nr Ambleside, Cumbria, LA22 0JA
Tel: Richard Coulter 07884 315298 or John Maddy 07813 334865
yurts@realitybiteslearning.co.uk www.long-valley-yurts.co.uk

GRASMERE
ENGLAND INDEPENDENT HOSTEL

This small deluxe hostel is situated on a farm right at the heart of the Lakes. See the best of Lakeland right from our doorstep. Give the car a holiday. Take the Wordsworth walk around Grasmere and Rydal Lake, or do a mountain classic, climb Helvellyn or Fairfield from our door. The Coast to Coast footpath goes right through the farm. Over 101 other local attractions and activities, including a good pub with fine bar meals just 300 yds down the road. Our English Tourism Council 4 star graded hostel has en-suite bedrooms with made up beds (sheets & duvets), lockers, bedside lights, a coin operated sauna, commercial laundry, drying room, dining room, 2 self-catering kitchens with microwaves, fridges, toasters etc. A stunning common room with large TV, a lockable bike / luggage store and private parking. We are resident proprietors. Cleanliness and friendliness assured. Totally non-smoking. Individuals, families and groups all welcome. Please always check availability by phone.

DETAILS

- **Open** - All year (winter, subject to minimum numbers), 8am to 10pm, (keys issued)
- **Number of beds** - 24: 1 x 3 : 1 x 4 : 1 x 5 : 2 x 6.
- **Booking** - Advisable, credit card confirms bed.
- **Price per night** - From £19.50pp (bedding inc). Groups please apply.
- **Public Transport** - Train to Windermere (11 miles from hostel), catch 555 bus from Windermere or Keswick, ask for Travellers Rest Pub. There is also a National Express coach that runs between London and Grasmere daily.
- **Directions** - GR 336 094. 1.25 miles north of village. Stay on main A591 right to our drive, 400m north of Travellers Rest Pub on the right hand side.

CONTACT: Mr Bev Dennison
Broadrayne Farm, Keswick Road, Grasmere, Cumbria, LA22 9RU
Tel: 015394 35055
Bev@grasmerehostel.co.uk www.grasmerehostel.co.uk

FISHER-GILL
CAMPING BARN

Situated in Thirlmere at the foot of the Helvellyn range of mountains, close to Sticks Pass and spectacular Fisher-gill waterfall, with numerous walks, hill and rock climbing from the barn. It's an ideal place for touring the Lake District being just off the A591 road with local and national bus stops at the end of the lane.

Accommodation consists of two rooms: a kitchen/diner with fridge, 4 ring calor gas stove, kettle, toaster, tables and chairs, and all pots, pans etc; and a sleeping area consisting of 10 bunk beds with mattresses, pillows, blankets and duvets (sleeping bags/liners are required). Both rooms have a woodburning stove with a daily allowance of wood included (extra is available from the farm). There's also a shower cubicle (metered), toilet, wash basin and a small seating area. Outside there is ample parking with a small patio area with barbeque, tables and chairs. A pub serving meals is nearby (approx 1/4 mile). Keswick is 5 miles, Grasmere 7 miles. Open all year. Pets by arrangement.

DETAILS

- **Open** - All year, all day
- **Number of beds** - 10
- **Booking** - Advanced booking recommended.
- **Price per night** - £11 to £12 pp. Sole use £110-£120.
- **Public Transport** - Local and national buses stop at the end of the lane on the A591
- **Directions** - Travelling on the A591 SE from Keswick, after about 5 miles take 1st lane on left after junction with B5322. Barn is after about 100m.

CONTACT: Mrs Jean Hodgson
Stybeck Farm, Thirlmere, Keswick, Cumbria CA12 4TN
Tel: 017687 73232 or 017687 74391
stybeckfarm@farming.co.uk www.stybeckfarm.co.uk

CAMPING BARN
ENGLAND

St John's-in-the-Vale Camping Barn is adapted from an 18th Century stable and hayloft, in an idyllic setting overlooking St John's Beck on a peaceful hill farm, with stunning views to Blencathra, Helvellyn and Castle Rock.

The Barn has a sleeping area upstairs (mattress provided) with a sitting and dining area below. Seperate toilet, shower and cooking area (bring your own equipment) are within the building. A wood-burning fire provides a focal point and warmth! There is a BBQ and seating area outside, magical on a star-filled night as we have no light pollution.

Low Bridge End Farm has a tea garden - all home baking. Breakfasts and packed lunches can be ordered in advance from the farm. To get the full picture see our virtual tour, complete details then book online at.
www.lakelandcampingbarns.co.uk

DETAILS

- **Open** - All year, 24 hours
- **Number of beds** - 8 : 1x8
- **Booking** - Advised in advance. Credit card booking available on (01946) 758198.
- **Price per night** - £7 (midweek) £8 (Fri, Sat and bank holidays) per person.
- **Public Transport** - Trains terminate at Windermere. From there take a 555 bus towards Keswick. Get off at Thirlmere Dam Road End (Smaithwaite). Climb over ladder stile and we are ½ mile north along a footpath.
- **Directions** - Leave M6 at junction 40. Take A66 towards Keswick for 14 miles. Turn left onto B5322 St Johns in the Vale Road. 3 miles along the road on the right.

CONTACT: Graham or Sarah
Low Bridge End Farm, St Johns-in-the-Vale, Keswick, CA12 4TS
Tel: 017687 79242 (Bookings 01946 758198)
info@campingbarn.com www.campingbarn.com

CAUSEWAY FOOT
CAMPING BARN

Causeway Foot Farm Camping Barn is on a small family-run sheep and dairy farm set in the magnificent scenery of the Naddle Valley, just outside Keswick. The two-storey building enjoys a detached location with good access and parking. The ground floor has a well equipped fitted kitchen containing dual-fuel cooker, fridge, microwave, tumble drier, sink with hot and cold water and a range of pots, pans and cutlery. There are 3 dining tables with seating plus electric heaters. The upper floor has 16 bunkbeds with mattresses and pillows There is a toilet/shower block 50 metres from the barn. The farm also has a 3 bedroomed bungalow and three holiday caravans.

With glorious views over the Lakeland fells of Skiddaw, Latrigg, Blencathra and Helvellyn, this is a popular location for those wishing to relax, whilst also making an excellent and convenient base for walkers and families.

The barn has been assessed and approved as an Accredited Camping Barn by Quality In Tourism.

DETAILS

- **Open** - All year, 24 hours
- **Number of beds** - 16
- **Booking** - Deposit, balance on arrival.
- **Price per night** - Sole use of whole barn:- Fri or Sat £100, Sun-Thur £60 per night. Price includes gas, electricity by £1 meter.
- **Public Transport** - Trains at Penrith (16 miles). Hourly buses Penrith to Keswick.
- **Directions** - On the A591 between Keswick and Windermere, about 2.5 miles from Keswick opposite a lay-by and phone box.

CONTACT: Greg Nicholson
Causeway Foot Farm, Naddle, Keswick, Cumbria, CA12 4TF
Tel: 017687 72290
jackie@causewayfoot.co.uk www.causewayfoot.co.uk

Denton House is a purpose built hostel and outdoor centre in the heart of the Lake District. The hostel is designed for group use so has plenty of hot water for showers, central heating throughout, a commercial kitchen, a large dining room and solid bunkbeds! Denton House welcomes individuals too with facilities designed to be homely as well as functional.

Denton House Outdoor Centre can provide traditional activities for groups of all ages. The centre is particularly suitable for those wanting to explore the great outdoors; we have storage for kayaks and bikes and there's access / egress to the River Greta just across the road. Qualified instructors are available to provide advice as well as to run trips and help organise expeditions. Denton House is primarily an adult hostel; under 16s are welcome in supervised groups or in exclusive use dorms with parents. Dogs welcome in some rooms if pre-booked. Due to the large number of school, youth and military groups, corporate teambuilds and celebration weekends, early booking is advised.

DETAILS

- **Open** - All year, 24 hours
- **Number of beds** - 56: 1x4 : 2x6 : 1x8 : 2x10 : 1x12.
- **Booking** - Preferred (25% deposit for groups)
- **Price per night** - £14 midweek, £15 weekends
- **Public Transport** - Nearest train station Penrith, buses hourly to Keswick.
- **Directions** - From centre out of town towards Windermere, keep the park on your left (approx 10mins). We are on the right after post sorting office.

CONTACT:
Penrith Road, Keswick, Cumbria, CA12 4JW
Tel: 017687 75351
sales@vividevents.co.uk   www.vividevents.co.uk

SKIDDAW HOUSE

ENGLAND

At 1550 feet, Skiddaw House is the highest YHA affiliated hostel in Britain. A former shooting lodge and shepherd's bothy on the Cumbria Way, it is an ideal base for exploring the little used and quiet northern fells. This is a remote and isolated place in which to reflect on the wilderness, with no sign of the 21st Century in any direction. With no electricity, phones ringing or TV to distract from the vista of a clear unpolluted starry night. This is simple accommodation with log and coal fires the only heating. No noise pollution from traffic as the nearest road is 3½ miles away, yet only an hour or so's walk from civilisation. Walkers and cyclists are advised to bring a map and torch. Campers welcome.

DETAILS

■ **Open** - 1st March (to be confirmed) to 31st Oct. Groups only Nov-Dec, , mornings till 10am, 5pm to 11pm
■ **Number of beds** - 21: 1x7, 2x5, 1x4
■ **Booking** - Book in advance for groups of 5 or more, by email, text, phone or post (postal service is slow). 50% deposit required for advance bookings.
■ **Price per night** - £16 (over 21), £12.50 (16-21), £8.50 (under 16).
YHA members £1.50 - £3 discount. Camping £8.50. Credit / debit cards not accepted.
■ **Public Transport** - Nearest trains and National express coaches at Penrith. From Penrith take X4 or X5 bus towards Keswick and Workington. Alight at the Horse and Farrier (Threlkeld). From Carlisle take 554 bus to Keswick (only 3 per day). Alight at Castle Inn (Bassenthwaite) and then walk 6 miles.
■ **Directions** - No access for cars, nearest tarmac road 3½ miles. Vehicles can be left at Fell Car Park by Blencathra Centre above Threlkeld, at Lattrigg Car Park (end of Gale Rd near Applethwaite) or at Whitewater Dash Falls south of Bassenthwaite.

CONTACT: Martin or Marie
Bassenthwaite, Keswick, Cumbria, CA12 4QX
Tel: 07747 174293
skiddawhouse@yahoo.co.uk www.skiddawhouse.co.uk

Hudscales Camping Barn is part of a group of traditional farm buildings, situated at 1000ft on the northern-most flank of the Lakeland Fells. It overlooks the villages of Caldbeck and Hesket Newmarket and is in an ideal position for exploring the northern fells. It is situated right on the Cumbria Way.

Sleeping accommodation is on the ground floor along with a separate cooking and eating area. You will need to bring sleeping bags and mats. If you wish to cook bring a camping stove and all utensils / crockery. There is a separate toilet and washbasin and a metered shower.

A woodburning stove is provided for added comfort (logs extra) and there is electric lighting plus metered power points.
Check the website www.lakelandcampingbarns.co.uk and book on line.

DETAILS

- **Open** - All year, all day
- **Number of beds** - 12: 1x12
- **Booking** - Book online. Bookings preferred but not essential.
- **Price per night** - £7 (midweek) £8 (Fri,Sat and bank holidays) per person.
- **Public Transport** - Penrith station 12 miles. Carlisle station 15 miles. No buses from Penrith. Limited service from Carlisle. Taxi fare from Carlisle approx £20.
- **Directions** - Leave M6 at J41 and take B5305 for Wigton. After approx 9 miles take left turn for Hesket Newmarket. Drive to top end of village and take left turn for Fellside. Hudscales Camping Barn is approx 1 mile on left up a lane.

CONTACT: Booking office / William or Judith
Hudscales, Hesket Newmarket, Wigton, Cumbria, CA7 8JZ
Tel: Booking office 01946 758198, Farm 016974 78637
wr.cowx@btconnect.com www.lakelandcampingbarns.co.uk

CATBELLS
CAMPING BARN

Catbells Camping Barn is part of a traditional set of farm buildings dating back to the 14th century.   The barn is on the slopes of Catbells in the tranquil Newlands Valley, with magnificent views over the Lake District. The Cumberland Way passes through the farmyard. Keswick is only 4 miles away and both Borrowdale and Buttermere are in walking distance. The camping barn is on the ground floor and has sleeping accommodation for 12, with mattresses provided. Bring your own sleeping bags. The barn is heated with a multi-fuel stove (not suitable for cooking) and coal can be bought at the farm. In the adjacent building is a toilet and a cooking area suitable for a camping stove. Bring your own stove, cutlery, crockery and cooking utensils.   It is possible to walk to a pub which serves food.   Breakfast can be provided with notice.

DETAILS

- **Open** - All year, 24 hours
- **Number of beds** - 12: 1x12
- **Booking** - Advisable, groups require deposit.
- **Price per night** - £7 (midweek) £8 (Fri,Sat and bank holidays) per person.
- **Public Transport** - Trains at Penrith (20 miles). Regular buses (meet the trains) from Penrith to Keswick.   Summer bus from Keswick to Buttermere stops ¾ mile from Barn. Summer ferry from Keswick to Hawes End (3/4 mile from barn).
- **Directions** - GR 245211 Leave the M6 at Junction 40 and follow the A66 past Keswick. At Portinscale turn left, follow the Buttermere road for 3 miles. Turn sharp left at Stair, follow the sign for Skelgill, up the road for 1/2 mile and right into farmyard. Please follow these directions and not those from 'sat-nav'.

CONTACT: Mrs Grave
Low Skelgill, Newlands, Keswick, Cumbria, CA12 5UE
Tel: 01946 758198 or 0709 2031363
info@lakelandcampingbarns.co.uk www.lakelandcampingbarns.co.uk

Dinah Hoggus Camping Barn is situated on the old Packhorse route to Watendlath. It is right on the Cumbria Way and Coast to Coast routes. The sleeping area is on the first floor and 12 mattresses are provided. There is a cooking and eating area on the ground floor with tables and benches. There is mains electricity and water, a small electric ring cooker, microwave oven, electric kettle, toaster, clothes dryer and electric heaters. The toilet/shower room is at the end of the building and has a hot electric shower and washbasin. Electricity is charged extra. Meter reading at start and end of stay.

The pub is 300yds away and village shop 200yds.

Check the website www.lakelandcampingbarns.co.uk and book on line.

DETAILS

■ **Open** - All year, all day
■ **Number of beds** - 12
■ **Booking** - Book online
■ **Price per night** - £7 (midweek) £8 (Fri, Sat and bank holidays) per person.
■ **Public Transport** - The local bus service out of Keswick stops at Hazel Bank Lane End (Rosthwaite), just 100yds from the barn.
■ **Directions** - The camping barn is situated on the outskirts of the village of Rosthwaite in Borrowdale. Take the B5289 road out of Keswick up the Borrowdale Valley for approx 6 miles. When you see the Rosthwaite village sign take first left (Hazel Bank Lane) over the hump bridge and into the left. Park beside the barn.

CONTACT:
Thorneythwaite Farm, Borrowdale, Keswick, Cumbria, CA12 5XQ
Tel: Booking office 01946 758198, Farm 017687 77237
info@lakelandcampingbarns.co.uk www.lakelandcampingbarns.co.uk

MURT BARN
CAMPING BARN

Murt is a traditional farm, dating from 1728, situated in the Wasdale valley. The camping barn is a converted stone hayloft and byre, attached to the farmhouse, with stunning views to the Scafell Massif and the surrounding fells. Sleeping accommodation and cooking area are on the first floor, reached by an internal wooden staircase. The shower, toilet and washing up facilities are downstairs. Electricity is metered (£1 coins) and provides light, water heater, hot shower, electric heater and a power point. Car parking is adjacent to the barn. You need to bring a sleeping bag/mat and stove and eating utensils if you wish to self cater. Murt is 3/4 mile from Wastwater and is an ideal base for high fell walks including Scafell Pike, Mosedale Horseshoe, Great Gable etc. There is direct access to footpaths and bridle-ways. For those interested in flora and fauna, the Wasdale valley has great variety, and coastal dune walks, Muncaster Castle and Ravensglass (for the Eskdale railway) are all only a stones throw away. There are 2 pubs in the village, 10 minutes walk from the Barn.

DETAILS

- **Open** - All year, arrive after 4pm.
- **Number of beds** - 8: 1x8
- **Booking** - Booking recommended. Book online.
- **Price per night** - £7pp, £8 pp(Fri, Sat and BHs). Sole use wknds and BHs £56 .
- **Public Transport** - Seascale station, then taxi to Wasdale.
- **Directions** -   From the A595, follow signs to Santon Bridge and Wasdale. After approx. 2 miles, bear sharp left over bridge, and sharp right immediately afterwards. At junction turn right, to Wasdale Head, and Murt is the 2nd gate on left.

CONTACT:
Murt, Nether Wasdale, Seascale, Cumbria, CA20 1ET
Tel: Booking office 01946 758198
info@lakelandcampingbarns.co.uk www.wasdaleweb.co.uk

CAMPING BARN

Cragg Barn Camping Barn is a traditional stone-built barn with stunning views of Buttermere fells. It has a kitchen and seating area with a sink and cold running water. There is a hot shower on a meter and a toilet and washbasin with hot and cold water. The sleeping area has 8 mattresses, bring your own sleeping bag. You need a stove and eating utensils if you wish to self cater. Cragg Barn is a great base for walkers of all abilities. It is also ideal for climbing, fishing and wildlife/bird-watching. There are many local tourist attractions within a short drive. Cragg House Farm also has a holiday cottage sleeping 2.
Check the websites www.buttermerecottage.co.uk or
www.lakelandcampingbarns.co.uk and book on line.

DETAILS
- **Open** - All year, all day, late arrivals by arrangement.
- **Number of beds** - 8: 1 x 8
- **Booking** - Booking essential at least 24 hrs in advance. Book online.
- **Price per night** - £7 (midweek) £8 (Fri,Sat and bank holidays) per person.
- **Public Transport** - Train stations at Penrith / Workington. Bus links from Penrith station and Workington town centre to Keswick. Bus runs seasonally from Keswick.
- **Directions** - GR NY 173 171. From Keswick follow signs to Borrowdale, continue through Rosthwaite, Seatoller and over Honister Pass. Continue past Buttermere lake into Buttermere village. Keep on main road. Cragg House Farm is on the left on the brow of the hill before you get to NT carpark. In icy conditions approach from Cockermouth town centre and continue through Lorton. Turn left to Buttermere following road signs. Cragg Farm is 1st on the right past the Buttermere village sign.

CONTACT:
Cragg House Farm, Buttermere, Cockermouth, Cumbria, CA13 9XA
Tel: Camping Barn 01946 758198. Holiday Cottage 017687 70204
info@lakelandcampingbarns.co.uk www.buttermerecottage.co.uk

Towards the head of Ennerdale valley, one of the most beautiful, least spoilt and quietest valleys in the Lake District, sitting at the foot of Pillar and Red Pike you will find Low Gillerthwaite. An ideal base for fell walking, classic rock climbs, bird and wildlife watching, mountain biking, orienteering (we have our own permanent beginners course), canoeing (instruction available for groups) and environmental studies.

Originally a 15th-century farmhouse, the Centre has group self-catering facilities, drying room, a library of environmental books, a group lecture room and two lounges with log burning fires. Due to its remoteness the Centre generates its own electricity. Vehicle access is by forest track and a BT payphone is on site (most mobiles do not work here). Low Gillerthwaite is an ideal base for clubs, extended family groups, school and youth groups. More information can be found on our website.

DETAILS

- **Open** - All year, except Christmas and Boxing Day, 24 hours
- **Number of beds** - 40: 2x4 : 1x8 : 1x10 : 1x14
- **Booking** - Always phone to check availability
- **Price per night** - From £9.50 per person (children and students), £13 (adults), camping is £4.00.
- **Public Transport** - Whitehaven Station 12 miles. Buses to Ennerdale Bridge from Cleator Moor or Cockermouth (5miles).
- **Directions** - GR NY 139 141. From Ennerdale Bridge take road east, via Croasdale, 3.5 miles to Ennerdale Forest. Continue on forest track 3 miles. Hostel is the first building below the RH road, 200m before the YHA.

CONTACT:
Ennerdale, Cleator, CA23 3AX
Tel: 01946 861229
Warden@lgfc.org.uk www.lgfc.org.uk

CAMPING BARN

Lying in the picturesque Loweswater Valley, Swallow Barn is part of a traditional set of buildings dating back to 1670 on a working beef and sheep farm. The barn accommodates 18 people on mattresses in 4 sleeping areas. There is a cooking and eating area with tables and chairs, 2 coin-operated showers and 2 toilets.

Swallow Barn is an excellent base for exploring the western fells with both high and low level walks and spectacular views, or you can enjoy the peace and tranquillity of the valley. Boat hire and fishing permits are available from the farm. The coast to coast cycle route is right on the doorstep. The Kirkstyle Pub provides excellent food, just over a mile away and the market town of Cockermouth is only 8 miles.
Check the website www.lakelandcampingbarns.co.uk and book online.

DETAILS

- **Open** - All year, all day
- **Number of beds** - 18: 1x9, 3x3
- **Booking** - Book online in advance, especially for school and bank holidays.
- **Price per night** - £7 (midweek) £8 (Fri, Sat and bank holidays) per person.
- **Public Transport** - The nearest train station is Penrith with a bus to Cockermouth, then a taxi costing approximately £25.
- **Directions** - Leave the M6 at junct. 40 and follow the A66 to the Egremont turn off at Cockermouth. Follow the A5086, Egremont road for 6 miles. Turn left at Mockerkin and follow road to Loweswater. Farm is just past the Grange Hotel on the left .

CONTACT:
Waterend Farm, Loweswater, Cockermouth, Cumbria, CA13 0SU
Tel: Booking office 01946 758198, Farm 01946 861465
info@lakelandcampingbarns.co.uk www.lakelandcampingbarns.co.uk

TARN FLATT
CAMPING BARN

Tarn Flatt Camping Barn is a traditional sandstone barn on St Bees Head overlooking the Scottish coastline and the Isle of Man. It is on a working farm which also includes a lighthouse, RSPB bird reserve on 100 metre cliffs and access to Fleswick Bay - a secluded shingle cove. There is canoeing and fishing in the area and the rock climbing and boulders at the base of the cliff are superb.   There are several local circular walks with panoramic views of the coast and the fells and easy access to the quieter western Lakeland fells and lakes. The award-winning historic Georgian town and harbour of Whitehaven is only 3 miles away and St Bees (the starting point of the Coast to Coast walk) is 2 miles via the coastal path. The barn has a raised wooden sleeping area on the ground floor. There is electric light, a cooking slab (please bring your own stove and utensils) and an open fire (wood available from the farm). Toilets, wash-basin and showers are in adjacent buildings. Meals are available by arrangement. Children welcome. Dogs are accepted in sole use only.

DETAILS

- **Open** - All year, 24 hours
- **Number of beds** - 12 bed spaces.
- **Booking** - Booking in advance is advised.
- **Price per night** - £7 (midweek) £8 (Fri, Sat and bank holidays) per person.
- **Public Transport** - Trains at Whitehaven (4 miles) and St Bees (3 miles). Buses also at Whitehaven.
- **Directions** - GR 947 146. With Sandwith village green on right, pass row of houses and turn right, at phone box take private road for 1 mile.

CONTACT: Janice Telfer
Tarn Flatt Hall, Sandwith, Whitehaven, Cumbria, CA28 9UX
Tel: Detail 01946 692162, Booking 01946 758198
stay@tarnflattfarm.co.uk www.tarnflattfarm.co.uk

HILLSIDE FARM
BUNKBARN
ENGLAND

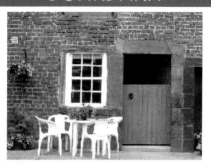

Hillside Farm is a Georgian farmstead in a conservation area just steps away from Hadrian's Wall.   It is located in the small village of Boustead Hill, near the Solway Coast Area of Outstanding Natural Beauty and RSPB nature reserve.   The farm has stunning views over the Solway Firth Marshes towards Scotland. Hadrian's Wall National Trail and Hadrian's Cycleway pass right by. Hillside farm is a working farm and the fourth generation of a farming family welcomes you to stay in the bunkbarn or in the B&B rooms in the farmhouse. The Bunkbarn is a recent conversion of the farm's Georgian stable block. It has cooking slabs, cutlery and crockery and a 2 ring gas stove. There are hot showers and towels and sleeping bags can be hired if required. There is no heating in the barn. You can arrange delivery of shopping via the farmhouse and with notice you can eat a full english breakfast at the farmhouse. Walking, cycling and family groups are most welcome.

DETAILS

- **Open** - All year, all day
- **Number of beds** - 12
- **Booking** - Book by phone.
- **Price per night** - £8 per person. £1 shower. £6 full English breakfast.
- **Public Transport** -
- **Directions** -   From M6 junction 43 follow signs for A595 past the castle, turn at small rundabout onto B5307. After 1 mile turn right following signs for Burgh-by-Sands. Pass through town and cross the cattle grid onto Marsh Road. Take next left into village of Boustead Hill, then 2nd turning on left under arches into farmyard.

CONTACT: Mrs Sandra Rudd
Hillside Farm, Boustead Hill, Burgh-by-Sands, Carlisle, Cumbria, CA5 6AA
Tel: 01228 576398
ruddshillside1@btinternet.com www.hadrianswalkbnb.co.uk

GREENHEAD
HOSTEL

Greenhead Hostel is a converted Methodist Chapel in the village of Greenhead on Hadrian's Wall. It is ideal for those walking the Pennine Way as well as The Wall and in a great location for those exploring the nearby Roman heritage sites. The church was built in 1886 to serve the village miners and gave its last service in 1972. It has been a YHA hostel since 1978. Greenhead Hostel has a self catering kitchen and guests lounge. There are 40 beds in four rooms of six beds and two rooms of eight beds. These can be booked as family rooms, by groups or by individuals by the bed. Evening meals, breakfast and packed lunches available. The hostel is operated by Greenhead Hotel (over the road) with a welcoming Hotel Bar and Restaurant. Now VisitEngland approved

DETAILS

- **Open** - All year, 8 - 10am, 7 - 10pm, hostel closes 11pm
- **Number of beds** - 40: 2x8, 2x6 + family rooms
- **Booking** - Book by phone or email.
- **Price per night** - Adult: £15, Under 18 £10.   Reductions for large groups or full rooms. Sole use of hostel £400.
- **Public Transport** - Trains: Haltwhistle 3 miles, Carlisle 19 miles, Newcastle 45 miles. Bus: May to Sept service Stagecoach AD 122 from Newcastle to Bowness On Solway. Also Arriva 685 Carlisle-Newcastle which passes Haltwhistle station and runs hourly all year.
- **Directions** - From Carlisle take the A69 to Newcastle, turn off for Greenhead (19 miles), turn right at the T- junction and the hostel is on the left opposite the Greenhead Hotel. From Newcastle take the A69 to Carlisle, turn right at the sign for Greenhead, follow instructions above.

CONTACT: Sue and Dave
Greenhead Hotel, Greenhead, Brampton, Cumbria, CA8 7HG
Tel: 01697 747411
daveandsuegreenhead@btconnect.com http://Greenhead-hotel.co.uk

Gibbs Hill Farm Hostel is a new conversion of a barn on a traditional working hill farm near Oncebrewed on Hadrians Wall. The hostel is designed to reduce energy consumption and is centrally heated throughout. There are 3 bunkrooms, 2 shower rooms, 2 toilets, a well equipped kitchen, comfortable sitting and dining area and a large deck where guests may enjoy the evening sun. The hostel has a drying room, lockers, laundry facilities and safe cycle storage. Ideal for families who may take a whole room with private facilities. Study groups welcome and evening meals can be provided. Situated near Hadrians Wall it is an excellent base for exploring the Roman sites, Hadrians Wall Trail and Northumberland National Park. Basic items of food may be purchased and meals can be ordered in the evening for the next day. Continental breakfast is £4, packed lunches £5.

DETAILS

- **Open** - All year, flexible, but no check in after 9pm
- **Number of beds** - 18: 3x6
- **Booking** - Advisable, groups require full payment 4 weeks before arrival.
- **Price per night** - £15 adult, £10 child (under 12), including bedding.
- **Public Transport** - Trains at Haltwhistle 6 miles. Regular Bus Service along A69 between Newcastle and Carlisle, and in summer the Hadrians Wall Bus runs between Newcastle and Carlisle. Alight at Once Brewed Information Centre and walk north to farm. Last bus 5.30pm from Haltwhistle.
- **Directions** - From the A69, turn north at Bardon Mill, signed 'Once Brewed'. Follow the signs towards 'Housesteads'. At the B6318, turn right and then immediately left towards 'Steel Rigg'. Follow for 1 mile, turn right to 'Gibbs Hill'.

CONTACT: Valerie Gibson
Gibbs Hill Farm, Bardon Mill, Nr Hexham, Northumberland, NE47 7AP
Tel: 01434 344030, Fax: 01434 344030
val@gibbshillfarm.co.uk www.gibbshillfarm.co.uk

ALBATROSS
BACKPACKERS IN!

Fly high with the award winning Albatross! This clean and modern backpackers hostel is located in Newcastle's City Centre. In walking distance are sporting, musical and conference venues, art galleries, historical attractions, food markets and public transport facilities. So come discover the North East, and get ready for Newcastle's highly acclaimed night life. The Albatross provides rooms of 12, 10, 8, 6, 5, 4 or 2 beds and has a total capacity of 177 beds. The overnight price includes: bedding; 24hr reception; fully fitted self-catering kitchen with tea, coffee and toast; free WiFi access and computer terminals; pool table; satellite TV; 150-year old cellar; outside sitting/ barbeque area; free first come first served car parking; free baggage storage; laundry facilities; CCTV; and electronic key card system. The Albatross has been awarded for Outstanding Customer Service and voted by Hostelworld customers as " No 1 Hostel in England".

DETAILS

- **Open** - All year, 24 hours
- **Number of beds** - 177
- **Booking** - Recommended. Photo ID at check-in (passport or driving licence).
- **Price per night** - From £16.50pp (dorm) to £22.50pp (2 bed room)
- **Public Transport** - Five minutes walk from central train, bus and metro stations.
- **Directions** - Central Station / Megabus drop off point: from main entrance, head right, take the first street on your left (Grainger St), you'll find us on your left 200m uphill. From National Express coach station: head down Scotswood Rd to Central Station. From Airport: take Metro to Central Station (20 mins travel). From Port (Ferry): buses travel between the port and Central Station and take 20 mins.

CONTACT: Reception
51 Grainger Street, Newcastle Upon Tyne, NE1 5JE
Tel: 0191 2331330, Fax: 0191 2603389
info@albatrossnewcastle.co.uk www.albatrossnewcastle.com

HOUGHTON NORTH
ENGLAND FARM ACCOMMODATION

Houghton North Farm, partly built with stones from Hadrian's Wall, has been in the Laws Family for five generations. It is situated in the beautiful Northumberland countryside right on the Heritage trail and 15 miles from the start of the Hadrian's Wall Trail. Within the region walkers can enjoy marked woodland trails, rugged moorland and hills, and some of the most beautiful deserted beaches in the UK. The newly built spacious accommodation can take a group of up to 23 and is also ideal for individuals and families. It is a 4Star Hostel with Visit Britain. The bunk style rooms (some en-suite) are located around the central courtyard and include the use of a self-catering kitchen where a light breakfast is served. There is also a well appointed TV lounge with log fire and internet access, barbecue, secure cycle storage and parking. Long-term parking, baggage transfer and packed lunches are available on request. Within 10 mins walk are pubs, a restaurant and shops in Heddon-on-the-Wall.

DETAILS

- **Open** - All year, All day
- **Number of beds** - 22: 1x5, 3x4, 1x3, 1x2
- **Booking** - Book with a non refundable deposit of £10 per person per night
- **Price per night** - From £25 (adult), £15 (under 12) inc breakfast. Group discounts.
- **Public Transport** - Trains at Wylam (2 miles) and Newcastle (7 miles). The 685 Newcastle-Carlisle bus stops right outside the farm. Baggage transfer is available.
- **Directions** - From Newcastle take the Heddon turn off the A69 to the B6528, farm is 1/4 mile outside of the village of Heddon. From Carlisle take Horsley junction and continue approx 3 miles beyond Horsley. Farm on the left at the top of a hill

CONTACT: Mrs Paula Laws
Houghton North Farm, Heddon-on-the-Wall, Northumberland, NE15 0EZ
Tel: 01661 854364
wjlaws@btconnect.com www.houghtonnorthfarm.co.uk

Demesne Farm Bunkhouse is a self-catering unit which was converted in 2004 from a barn on a working hill farm. The farm is situated on the Pennine Way, Route 68 cycle route, Reivers cycle route and is within 100 metres of the centre of the North Tyne village of Bellingham on the edge of the Northumberland National Park. The bunkhouse provides an ideal base for exploring Northumberland, Hadrian's Wall, Kielder Water and many climbing crags. It accommodates 15 and is perfect for smaller groups, individuals and families. The bedrooms are fitted with hand crafted oak man-sized bunk beds, high quality mattresses, pillows and curtains with cushion flooring. The communal living area with potbelly stove and fitted kitchen includes cooker, microwave, fridge, kettle, toaster, crockery, cutlery, cooking utensils, farmhouse tables, chairs and easy chairs. It has 2 bathrooms with hot showers, basins, toilets and under floor heating. In the courtyard there is ample parking, bike lock up, drying room and a gravelled area with picnic tables. Complete bed linen is included.

DETAILS

- **Open** - All year, flexible, but no check in after 9pm
- **Number of beds** - 15: 1 x 8, 1 x 4, 1 x 3
- **Booking** - Please book in advance.
- **Price per night** - £16 per person (including linen).
- **Public Transport** - Trains at Hexham (17 miles), regular bus service from Hexham to Bellingham. Bellingham bus stop 100 metres from Bunkhouse. By car: Newcastle 45 mins, Scottish Border 20 mins, Kielder Water 10 mins.
- **Directions** - 100 metres from centre of village, located next to Northern Garage.

CONTACT: Robert Telfer
Demesne Farm, Bellingham, Hexham, Northumberland, NE48 2BS
Tel: 01434 220258 Mobile 07967 396345
stay@demesnefarmcampsite.co.uk www.demesnefarmcampsite.co.uk

FOREST VIEW
WALKERS HOSTEL

Forest View is set in the hamlet of Byrness on the edge of Keilder Forest and Northumberland National Park. An ideal stopover on the A68 England to Scotland route.

The Pennine Way runs just a few hundred yards from the hostel. The building has just undergone a major refurbishment with new beds, curtains and carpets. The central heating is supplied by an eco-friendly wood pellet boiler and the hot water by solar panels. The log burning stoves in the quiet room and dining room keep the hostel cosy all year round. The beds are arranged in 2, 3 & 4 bedded rooms and bed linen is supplied. Secure storage is provided for up to 10 bikes.

There is a large selection of bottled beers and wines, meals can be provided or guests can use the well equipped self catering kitchen.

DETAILS

- **Open** - All year, check in from 4pm - check out by 10.30 am.
- **Number of beds** - 20: 2x4, 2x3, 3x2
- **Booking** - Booking is recommended
- **Price per night** - Adult £17, Under 16s £15
- **Public Transport** - Nearest rail station Newcastle-Upon-Tyne 40 miles then National Express to lay-by 200yds from hostel.
- **Directions** - Forest View is just off the A68, 4 miles from the Scottish Border, 16 miles south of Jedburgh and 10 miles north of Otterburn. The National Express bus drops off 200yds from the Hostel.

CONTACT: Colin or Joyce
7 Otterburn Green, Byrness Village, Northumberland, NE19 1TS
Tel: 01830 520425
joycetaylor1703@hotmail.co.uk www.forestviewbyrness.co.uk

HARESHAW HOSTEL
BELLINGHAM
ENGLAND

Hareshaw Hostel (previously YHA Bellingham) is set in its own grounds with plenty of parking and a large picnic area. The partitioned dormitories have 8 single beds for males and 6 single beds for females. Each dorm has showers and toilets. There is a well stocked kitchen with cooker, fridge, microwave, crockery, pans, cutlery and a communal area with armchairs and tables and chairs. A family flat is available in a separate building with 4 beds, toilet & shower. All guests have the use of a drying room. Bellingham is on the Pennine Way route and there are many beautiful walks and historic buildings to discover. Close by is an 18 hole golf course, plenty of wildlife and fishing. Further afield is Kielder Water, the Roman wall and its many forts, the Scottish Borders and the lovely North East coast. The surrounding villages have many very fine pubs to relax in and enjoy a meal and a drink. There is a Chinese restaurant/take away and pubs in the centre of the village.

DETAILS

- **Open** - All year, all day
- **Number of beds** - 18: 1 x 8 male, 1 x 6 female, 1 x family flat of 4 beds
- **Booking** - Booking is essential. More details at time of enquiry.
- **Price per night** - £10 per person
- **Public Transport** - Trains at Hexham (17 miles) from Newcastle and Carlisle. There is a bus service from Hexham to Bellingham each day.
- **Directions** - The hostel is located close to the centre of the village on the West Woodburn road. When arriving in Bellingham turn right at the newsagents, go past police station on right and take left fork in road signed West Woodburn, go up hill and past entrance to housing estate. Hostel is third entrance on left.

CONTACT: Susan Liddle
Hareshaw Hostel, Woodburn Road, Bellingham, Hexham, NE48 2ED
Tel: 07980 047821 or 07860 932857
susanliddle@hotmail.com

JOINERS SHOP
BUNKHOUSE
ENGLAND

The Joiners Shop Bunkhouse is an attractive 17th-century building retaining much of its historical charm and character. It is situated in a quiet hamlet only 7 miles from Alnwick, the seat of the Duke of Northumberland, 5 miles from the beautiful Northumberland Coast and 10 miles from Wooler and the Cheviot Hills. The area offers opportunities for walking, climbing, mountain biking, golfing, all water sports or simply sightseeing.

The Joiners Shop Bunkhouse has full cooking facilities and a dining area along with a log fire and cosy sitting area. The 18 large pine beds are in heated dormitories of twos and threes. Indoor space is available for bikes and other equipment and there is ample parking.
Dogs welcome. NB There are dogs on site!

DETAILS

- **Open** - All year, all day
- **Number of beds** - 18
- **Booking** - Advised for weekends and holidays.
- **Price per night** - £12 per person.
- **Public Transport** - There are train stations at Chathill (1.5 miles) limited service and Alnmouth (10 miles). There are National Express services at Alnwick (7 miles) and Berwick (24 miles). The local bus company is called ARRIVA and the nearest stop is Brownieside on the A1 (1.5 miles).
- **Directions** - GR 183 254 Seven miles north of Alnwick on the A1 to Brownieside. Turn off A1 at sign for Preston Tower, hostel is 1.5 miles on the left

CONTACT: Wal Wallace
Preston, Chathill, Northumberland, NE67 5ES
Tel: 01665 589245 or 07745 373729
bunkhouse.wal@btinternet.com www.bunkhousenorthumberland.co.uk

TACKROOM
BUNKHOUSE

The Tackroom Bunkhouse is situated on a mixed working farm between the seaside villages of Beadnell and Seahouses, yards from a beautiful sandy beach on the spectacular Northumberland Coast. The area is ideal for walking, watersports, climbing, cycling, diving or just sightseeing. Accommodating 12, the bunkhouse is ideal for smaller groups, individuals and couples. The two bedrooms are each fitted with 6 man sized bunk-beds and a locker for each visitor. Sleeping bags are essential.

The communal area has a mini kitchen with hob, microwave, fridge, toaster etc, a dining table to seat 12 and colour TV. All crockery, cutlery and cooking utensils are supplied but there is no oven.

Adjoining the bunkhouse is a shared shower/toilet block complete with washing machine and tumble drier. Also available is a lock-up and off road parking. The Tackroom Bunkhouse is heated.

DETAILS

- **Open** - All year, flexible, but no check-in after 10pm.
- **Number of beds** - 12: 2 x 6.
- **Booking** - Recommended but not essential
- **Price per night** - £12 per person or £120 sole use.
- **Public Transport** - Nearest train station is Berwick upon Tweed. There are intermittent local buses to Seahouses and Beadnell, passing ½ mile away from the hostel.
- **Directions** - From A1 take the B1340, follow road to Beadnell (signed Seahouses/Beadnell). Annstead farm is approx ½ mile past Beadnell on the left.

CONTACT: Sue Mellor
Annstead Farm, Beadnell, Northumberland, NE67 5BT
Tel: 01665 720387, Fax: 01665 721494
stay@annstead.co.uk www.annstead.co.uk

Chatton Park Bunkhouse started life as a Smithy and has been converted into self-catering accommodation. It is situated on a mixed working farm which nestles around the river Till, half a mile from Chatton village. Eight miles from the coast and five miles from the Cheviot Hills, Chatton Park is an ideal base for exploring Northumberland's vast empty beaches, heather clad hills & historic castles. Walking, watersports, climbing, fishing, golf and cycling are all available nearby.

Accommodating 12, the bunkhouse is perfect for smaller groups, families & individuals. The 2 bedrooms are fitted with large custom made bunks and can be rented separately as secure units. Bedding can be provided at a small extra fee. The living area has a fully equipped kitchen & seating around the original blacksmith's fire. Wash & drying room with hot showers. Secure storage, ample parking. Room for camping. DIY livery. Dog kennels provided.

DETAILS

- **Open** - All year, flexible but no check in after 9pm
- **Number of beds** - 12: 2x6
- **Booking** - Booking recommended but not essential
- **Price per night** - £12 - £15 pp. Group bookings negotiable
- **Public Transport** - Nearest train station Berwick upon Tweed. Buses to Chatton from Alnwick / Berwick.
- **Directions** - From A1 take B6348 to Chatton. 4 miles at bottom of hill on right is Chatton Park Farm

CONTACT: Jane or Duncan
Chatton Park Farm, Chatton, Alnwick, Northumberland, NE66 5RA
Tel: 01668 215247
ord@chattonpk.fsnet.co.uk www.chattonparkfarm.co.uk

BLUEBELL FARM
BUNKBARN

Bluebell Farm Bunkbarn is situated on a family-owned caravan park and campsite. The Bunkbarn sleeps 14, and there is also a wooden ark which sleeps 4 and five self-catering cottages. The bunkbarn has a family room for 6 and an 8 bed dorm. The bunks are equipped with blankets and pillows. Linen and towels can be hired or bring your own sleeping bag. There is a fully equipped self-catering kitchen and a bike store. Hot showers, electricity and gas are all included in the price.

Bluebell Farm is in the centre of the village within walking distance of shops and pubs. It is ideally located for exploring Nothumberland's Heritage Coast Route to the east, the Cheviot Hills National Park to the west and the historic Scottish Borders. Many outdoor pursuits are available including golf, climbing, canoeing, diving, horse riding, fishing, cycling and walking. Dogs welcome by arrangement. Duke of Edinburgh groups welcome. Exclusive use available.

DETAILS

- **Open** - All year, check in by 9 pm, departure by 10 am.
- **Number of beds** - 14 : 1 x 8, 1 x 6
- **Booking** - Not essential
- **Price per night** - Adults £10, under 14s £5. Linen and towel hire £5 per person.
- **Public Transport** - Trains at Berwick upon Tweed. Buses from Berwick to Belford. National Express coaches stop in Belford. Local bus from Newcastle.
- **Directions** - From the A1 take B1342 into the village. Turn onto B6349 signposted for Wooler. Bluebell Farm is first main driveway on right, almost opposite the Co-op.

CONTACT: Phyl
Bluebell Farm Caravan Park, Belford, Northumberland, NE70 7QE
Tel: 01668 213362
corillas@tiscali.co.uk www.bluebellfarmbelford.co.uk

THE HIDEAWAY
HOSTEL

Centuries old, The Hideaway is conveniently situated in the heart of picturesque Old Berwick, yet is amazingly secluded, set behind high stone walls. Admire the magnificent stone fireplace as you toast yourself by the multi fuel stove. Enjoy a barbecue on the verandah or in the tiny but delightful courtyard garden as you relax in the cool summer night air, heavy with the scent of honeysuckle and jasmine. Shared facilities include a well equipped kitchen, sitting room with TV and dining room.

Berwick is an ideal base for exploring Northumberland, Lindisfarne and the Scottish Borders. It is also close to an amazing number of cycle routes. We have excellent secure cycle storage and drying facilities.
Well behaved dogs ONLY by prior arrangement. No smoking.

DETAILS

- **Open** - All year, all day. BUT PLEASE NOTE check in 4 - 10pm.
- **Number of beds** - 11: 1x3, 4x2 (1 twin ensuite, 2 double, 1 double ensuite)
- **Booking** - Booking advisable. 33% deposit.
- **Price per night** - £18-£25pp. Price includes Continental Breakfast and bedding! Single supp £5. Towel Hire £1
- **Public Transport** - 10 mins walk from Berwick Station and long distance buses.
- **Directions** - Look for Church Street by the Guildhall. The Hideaway can be found between "The Sporran" giftshop and "Hair at 11". Look for the cycle logos in the passageway through the wrought iron gate! For a detailed location map, go to Google Maps, and type Hideaway plus our postcode.

CONTACT: J Morton
1 The Courtyard, Church Street, Berwick-upon-Tweed, TD15 1EE
Tel: 01289 308737, Mobile 07989 468008
patmosphere@yahoo.co.uk

BERWICK-ON-TWEED
BACKPACKERS
ENGLAND

Berwick-on-Tweed Backpackers has the perfect location inside the Elizabethan walls of this ancient market town and only a short walk from the bus and train stations. Berwick is an ideal stop-off on the train and road route from London to Edinburgh. Stop for a last taste of England just 50 miles from Scotland's capital or stay longer and explore the bracing Northumberland Coast.

Berwick-on-Tweed Backpackers is in a quiet courtyard and has an informal come and go as you please atmosphere. The hostel has self-catering facilities and there is a covered area for dry secure storage of bicycles. The hostel is next to Berwick Quayside, the Maltings Art Centre, Barrels Ale House, Brilliant Bikes and the Green Shop.
Four Star Tourist Board Graded

DETAILS

- **Open** - All year, 11am to 7pm - summer. 4pm to 7pm - winter.
- **Number of beds** - 20: Lots of twins and doubles
- **Booking** - Advisable in summer but not essential
- **Price per night** - from £16.95 to £29.95 inc continental breakfast
- **Public Transport** - Berwick-on-Tweed railway station is 10 minutes walk away and the bus station is 5 minutes walk away.
- **Directions** - In Berwick town centre, follow the main street towards the town hall. Take first right turn after the town hall, down Hide Hill, turn first right at the bottom of the hill into Bridge Street. The hostel is half way along Bridge Street on the right opposite the bookshop.

CONTACT: Angela Chappell
56 Bridge Street, Berwick-on-Tweed, Northumberland, TD15 1AQ
Tel: 01289 331481
bkbackpacker@aol.com   www.berwickbackpackers.co.uk

MAUGHOLD VENTURE CENTRE BUNKHOUSE

Maughold Venture Centre Bunkhouse is built of Manx stone, overlooking farmland with views in the distance to the sea. It offers self-catering facilities with the option of purchasing meals from the neighbouring adventure centre if required (subject to availability). All bedrooms are en-suite with full central heating. Facilities include a basic but functional games room and kitchen. The number of beds in each room can be altered to suit your requirements.

The local beach of Port e Vullen, 10 mins walk away, is popular with our visitors and the Bunkhouse is adjacent to the Venture Centre where you may arrange sessions of kayaking, abseiling, air rifle shooting, archery, gorge walking, dinghy sailing, power boating and team events. We have our own stop, Lewaigue Halt, on the Manx Electric Railway giving access to Douglas, Ramsay and to mountain walks and tranquil glens. Ideal for groups, families and individuals.

DETAILS

- **Open** - February to November, 24 hours
- **Number of beds** - 52 2x2 : 1x6 : 4x8 : 1x10
- **Booking** - Telephone reservation essential
- **Price per night** - £10-£15 per person
- **Public Transport** - No 3 Bus or Manx Electric Railway from Douglas or Ramsey. Get off bus at Dreemskerry (5 mins walk); get off railway at Lewaigue Halt (nearby). Taxi from Ramsey £5. Taxi from Douglas £25.
- **Directions** - GR 469922. From Douglas take the A2 coast road. When the road begins to descend into Ramsey the Venture Centre is signposted on the right hand side. Follow the signs - it is the first building on the left.

CONTACT: Simon Read
The Venture Centre, Maughold, Isle of Man, IM7 1AW
Tel: 01624 814240
Contact@adventure-centre.co.uk www.adventure-centre.co.uk

King William's College is the only independent school in the Isle of Man and is located on Castletown Bay in the south of the island. The Isle of Man has lots to offer, including an interesting transport system, great beaches, mountainous heathland, historic sites, charming villages and numerous walks.

Junior House, formerly used for junior boarding, is set in the expansive College grounds and provides a mix of accommodation options ranging from twin rooms to dormitories. There is a lounge, laundry room, TV room, drying room and a limited kitchen area.

Junior House is an ideal location for all the attractions in the south of the island and the facilities are well matched to those looking for outdoor activity holidays. Catering can be provided at most times although guests should check at the time of booking. Junior House is relaxed, clean and well maintained.

DETAILS

- **Open** - All year (except Christmas and New Year), all day
- **Number of beds** - 60: 1x14 : 2x12 : 1x 8: 7x2
- **Booking** - Groups, TT races book with deposit.
- **Price per night** - From £15.50 per person. Breakfast extra.
- **Public Transport** - The airport is located next to the College. Ferries dock at Douglas from Liverpool, Heysham, Dublin and Belfast.
- **Directions** - From Douglas follow signs to Castletown and the Airport. Bus stop is located opposite the entrance to King William's College.

CONTACT: Ruth Watterson
King William's College, Castletown, Isle of Man, IM9 1TP
Tel: 01624 820470 / 820400, Fax: 01624 820402
rooms@kwc.sch.im www.kwc.sch.im

| 0 | miles | 25 |
| 0 | kilometres | 40 |

Aberystwyth 262
265

New Quay

252   A487

Cardigan   Lampeter

244   246
247

239
Fishguard   231

242
240

Carmarthen

Haverfordwest   A40
St Clears
232

Milford Haven   234,236
238   237

Pembroke   283
Tenby   Llanelli

230

KEY

45 - **Hostel page number**

45 - **Page Number of group
only accommodation**

266,268

Machynlleth

A487

A470

Newtown

E
N
G
L
A
N
D

264

A44

261

258

256

A470

Rhayader

Tregaron

248   250

260

Llandrindod Wells

255

Llanwrtyd Wells

253

Builth Wells

254

A438

Llandovery

A40

Brecon

228
227

226

A4067

225

229

Abergavenny

A465

Tredegar   224

A40   222

**Merthyr
Tydfil**

A470

Neath

Swansea

Port Talbot

Pontypridd

Newport

M4

216-221

Cardiff

South Wales

0   miles   25
0   kilometres   40

Holyhead

Colwyn Ba

Llandudno   288
Conwy
286

290   A55

A55

A470

Bangor

Caernarfon   283

291   A5

292

A487   293

Betws-y-coed

284

282   281

294

298

299   296

Ffestiniog

Porthmadog

Criccieth

Pwllheli

300   272

A470

A496

Dollgellau

Barmouth   270   271

269

266,268

Machynlleth

Aberdyfi

97

KEY

45 - **Hostel number**

45 - **Number of group only accommodation**

Rhyl

Flint

A55

Queensferry

A494

Ruthin

279
278

Wrexham

Corwen   A5   276

A494   Llangollen

Bala
273,274

A458

Welshpool

A470

Newtown

E N G L A N D

North Wales

NOSDA STUDIO
HOSTEL

NosDa means "Good night" in Welsh and that is exactly what we promise. NosDa Studio Hostel is a hostel / hotel hybrid, a new concept of stylish budget accommodation. There's a choice of secure mixed and single sex dormitories and also a number of private rooms, each with their own pod style bathrooms, mini kitchens, TVs and even balconies. "NosDa is redefining the hostelling genre"- Lonely Planet. Uniquely situated along the banks of the river Taff, NosDa occupies a newly refurbished 19th century building with superb views of the iconic Millennium Stadium. Our lively bar has a selection of Welsh beers, ciders and spirits and the affordable menu lets you taste some delicious local produce. There is an in house gym and nightclub, and if that wears you out why not chill in our new funky TV lounge? With the castle, stadium and train station all within sight, NosDa Studio Hostel is the most centrally located hostel with a view to die for and the facilities to match!

DETAILS

- **Open** - All year, 24 hours
- **Number of beds** - 138: 4 x 4, 6 x 6, 2 x 8, 1 x 10 + 52 beds in private rooms.
- **Booking** - Essential for groups, advisable for individuals. Book online.
- **Price per night** - From £17.50, Double / twin from £40
- **Public Transport** - Train, coach and bus stations 5 minutes walk from the hostel.
- **Directions** - By car: From the M4, take junction 32 and follow signs for city centre. Approaching the centre follow the road around the castle then straight ahead over the bridge crossing the river Taff. Take the next left into Lower Cathedral Road, then 1st left into Despenser Street. By foot from Cardiff Central Station, turn left across the river and follow the embankment upstream, with the stadium opposite. Look ahead.

CONTACT: Reception
53-59, Despenser Street, Riverside, Cardiff, CF11 6AG
Tel: 029 2037 8866
info@nosda.co.uk www.nosda.co.uk

Cardiff University is situated in the heart of the city and close to all its tourist attractions. Accommodation is available during the summer vacation periods (June – September inclusive) at a number of venues, all within walking distance of the city centre.

There is a range of options including self-catering and bed and breakfast. All rooms are en suite and provided with bed linen, towels and tea / coffee making facilities. All rooms are single occupancy with a fully equipped kitchen per flat.

Cardiff University provides an ideal accommodation venue providing high quality comfortable accommodation.

DETAILS

- **Open** - 18th June - 17th September 2010, reception open 8am-10pm
- **Number of beds** - 1200+ single occupancy en suite
- **Booking** - Telephone or email
- **Price per night** - Self catering £26.95 per person per night or £162.70 per week. Bed & Breakfast (if available) £35.50 per person per night.
- **Public Transport** - Cardiff Central Station: trains, coaches, connections to airports. Buses from city centre.
- **Directions** - From junction 29 of M4, follow the A48(M)/A48, signpost Cardiff East and South, to the A470, signpost City Centre, into the Cathays area of the city.

CONTACT: Cardiff University Conference Office
Southgate House, PO Box 533, Cardiff, CF14 3X2
Tel: 029 2087 4702 / 4616, Fax: 029 2087 4990
Groupaccom@cardiff.ac.uk www.Cardiff.ac.uk/CSERV

RIVER HOUSE
HOSTEL

This is an award-winning family run 4 star hostel in the heart of Cardiff, voted number 1 in the Hostelworld list of best hostels 2008. Opened in 2007 to rave reviews, the brother and sister team have made sure this will be the best hostel experience you will come across on your travels. With fabulous views of the world famous Millennium Stadium and River Taff and with the central train and bus stations just 5 mins walk away, what's stopping you?

Facilities include well equipped kitchen, cosy TV lounge, decked garden with barbecue, free lockers and free wireless broadband. Bikes, irons, and hairdryers available for hire. Linen, duvets and breakfast are included in the price and the beds are made up for you.

Treat yourself to a quality stay at budget prices.

DETAILS

- **Open** - All year, 24 hours
- **Number of beds** - 50: 2 bed private rooms, 4 bed dorms and 6 bed dorms.
- **Booking** - Book by phone or online.
- **Price per night** - From £17.50 pp. Private (twin) rooms from £40 for two people. All prices include breakfast.
- **Public Transport** - Cardiff Central coach and train stations, with regular services to UK cities and airports 5 minutes walk away.
- **Directions** - From Central train station turn left and cross river on Tudor Street. Once over the river Fitzhamon Embankment is first turn on right.

CONTACT: Reception
59 Fitzhamon Embankment, Riverside, Cardiff, CF11 6AN
Tel: 02920 399 810
info@riverhousebackpackers.com www.riverhousebackpackers.com

Cardiff Backpacker Caerdydd, the original independent hostel, has recently been redesigned to become perfect group accommodation. With a choice of different sized dormitories and a number of private rooms we cater perfectly for schools, colleges, sports teams or large groups of friends looking to visit Cardiff. With secure access throughout, a superb self catering kitchen and a bar available on request your group of 20+ poeple can have sole occupancy of the building with no need to keep the noise down.

During the weekend we are open to individuals (over 18's only) and with just 40 beds we are small enough to feel cosy and friendly whilst large enough to accommodate a good mix of people from all over the world. Our bar is a great place to get to know your fellow travellers and have a few drinks before hitting town which is only a 10 minute walk away. All the staff are well travelled and would love to offer tips on the coolest things to do whilst in Cardiff and share travelling tales with you!

DETAILS

- **Open** - All year, 24 hours
- **Number of beds** - 39 , 1 x 4, 1 x 5, 1 x 6, 2 x 8, 4 x 2
- **Booking** - Booking recommended and essential (with deposit) for groups.
- **Price per night** - From £15 per person, including light breakfast.
- **Public Transport** - Train, coach and bus stations 5 to 10 minutes walk away.
- **Directions** - From Cardiff Central Station, turn left crossing the River Taff. Follow river upstream, turn left past NosDa Studio Hostel. Hostel on roundabout ahead.

CONTACT:
98 Neville Street, Riverside, Cardiff, CF11 6LS
Tel: 029 20 345577
info@cardiffbackpacker.com www.cardiffbackpacker.com

RICKYARD
BUNKHOUSE

Welcome to Rickyard Bunkhouse set amidst idyllic countryside and well away form the hustle and bustle. Offa's Dyke footpath passes the entrance and we are within 25 mins of Wye Valley, Symonds Yat, and the Forest of Dean. Many outdoor pursuits can be enjoyed, canoeing, rafting, potholing, quad biking, rock climbing, paint balling to name but a few. The river Trothy borders our land, kingfishers and otters enjoy the peace and tranquillity of the Trothy valley. Buzzards circle high above, easily recognised by their distinctive call. The Bunkhouse holds 20 easily, has an excellent, very well equipped kitchen, separate dining/relaxing area with TV, background heating and sleeping accommodation split into several areas. It is totally self contained, ideal for re-unions, groups and families. Please come and enjoy our tranquil surroundings (we don't welcome loud music or wild parties). There is a large secure area for camping where children can safely play and ample parking with hard standing. Luggage transfer, breakfasts and packed lunches can be arranged. Bedding can be supplied. Exclusive use available, please enquire.

DETAILS

- **Open** - All year, all day
- **Number of beds** - 20: + camping
- **Booking** - Deposit required, no credit cards. Notice not always required.
- **Price per night** - £14pp. Private en-suite room for 6 persons £16pp. Can be booked for sole use. Tents £5pp.
- **Public Transport** - Trains at Abergavenny (11m). Buses Monmouth (3m).
- **Directions** - Next to the Hendre Farm House on the same side of the road.

CONTACT: Graham Edwards
Wonastow, Monmouth, NP25 4DJ
Tel: 01600 740128
rickyardbunkhouse@googlemail.com   www.rickyardbunkhouse.co.uk

MIDDLE NINFA
BUNKHOUSE/COTTAGE

Middle Ninfa Farm, situated in the Brecon Beacons on the edge of the Blaenavon Industrial Landscape World Heritage Site, offers bunkhouse/cottage accommodation, camping and hands-on training in coracle making and willow sculpture. The farm has fine views over the Usk Valley, of the Skirrid and rural Monmouthshire. The Bunkhouse provides comfortable self-catering accommodation for up to 6 people. The rustic charm of the old stone building has been retained whilst ensuring modern comforts. The ground floor has a lounge / dining area with double divan and TV, a well-equipped kitchen and a toilet/shower room. Upstairs (Mezzanine Floor) there are 4 single beds, accessed by a spiral staircase. Guests should bring food, sleeping bags, towels & pillowcases. Home grown fruit, veg and local produce available.
Sauna available. Walking and Cycling Welcome.
Green Dragon Level 2 environmental award.

DETAILS

- **Open** - All year, all day
- **Number of beds** - 6: 1x4, 1x2 [double]
- **Booking** - Book by phone or email
- **Price per night** - Sun to Thur £10pp or £50 sole use. Fri, Sat and Bank Holidays £12pp or £60 sole use. Sole use per week £220-£300. Camping £3pp.
- **Public Transport** - The nearest bus is at Llanfoist (1.5 miles). The train station is at Abergavenny (3.5 miles). Taxis from the station cost approximately £7
- **Directions** - Approx. 2 miles from A465 (Hereford/Neath), A40 (Brecon/Monmouth and M50) and A4042 (Newport, M4). See website for map. The farm is reached by a steep winding road from Llanfoist, crossing the Monmouthshire and Brecon Canal.

CONTACT: Richard and Rohan Lewis
Middle Ninfa Farm, Llanellen, Abergavenny, NP7 9LE
Tel: 01873 854662
richard@middleninfa.co.uk www.middleninfa.co.uk

Wern Watkin Bunkhouse is located in the Brecon Beacons National Park, high up on Mynnedd Llangattock. It is also known as YHA Llangattock Mountain. There is direct access on foot to the mountainside and a flat mountain road to a National Cycle Route. The Bunkhouse is a converted stone barn with bunks for 30 people in 7 mainly en-suite bedrooms. The massive dining room and seating area opens out onto ancient woodlands. There is under-floor heating throughout, excellent drying facilities and ample hot water. The location is ideal for caving, rock climbing, canoeing, abseiling, orienteering, pony trekking and mountain biking. Outdoor pursuit training can be arranged from local qualified instructors. The bunkhouse is within easy walking distance of Llangattock cave complex (one of Europe's most elaborate cave systems) as well as climbing crags and open moorland. A short drive away are the rest of Brecon Beacons, the scenic Wye and Usk river valleys and a wealth of industrial heritage at the World Heritage site of Blaenavon. Catering can be provided for groups.

DETAILS

- **Open** - All year, all day
- **Number of beds** - 30: 4x6, 1x4, 2x2. All rooms but one en-suite
- **Booking** - Availability shown online. 10% deposit, balance two weeks in advance.
- **Price per night** - Sole use £450 week nights, £600 weekend nights. Smaller groups by negotiation £16pp weeknights, £18.50 pp weekend.
- **Public Transport** - Trains Abergavenny (8miles). Nearest buses Crickhowell.
- **Directions** - Access can be either from Crickhowell or Brynmawr on small mountain roads. Detailed instructions will be sent with your booking.

CONTACT: Andrew Fryer
Wern Watkin, Hillside, Llangattock, Crickhowell, NP8 1LG
Tel: 01873 812307
enquiries@wernwatkin.co.uk   www.wernwatkin.co.uk

THE WAIN HOUSE

WALES

This old stone barn continues the tradition of 900 years when Llanthony Priory provided shelter and accommodation. Surrounded by the Black Mountains in the Brecon Beacons National Park, this spectacular setting is a superb base for walking, riding, pony trekking and other mountain activities.

Sixteen bunks are split into three separate areas for sleeping; there is a fully equipped kitchen, hot water for showers, heating throughout and a wood burning stove in the eating area. Small or large groups are welcome, but there is a minimum charge at weekends. Two pubs offer real beer and bar food.

Just 50 minutes from the M4 Severn Bridge and 1 hour from the M5 / M50 Junction, this must be one of the easiest bunkbarns to reach from the motorways - and yet you feel you are miles from anywhere.

DETAILS

- **Open** - All year, 24 hours no restrictions
- **Number of beds** - 16: 1 x 8 : 1 x 4 : 1 x 6
- **Booking** - Booking and deposit required.
- **Price per night** - £11.00 per person.
Minimum charge of £260 at weekends (2 nights).
- **Public Transport** - Abergavenny railway station 12 miles.
- **Directions** - GR SO 288 278 Map on website. Turn west off A465 Abergavenny to Hereford road at Llanvihangel Crucorney (5 miles north of Abergavenny). Llanthony is 6 miles along country lane - follow signs to Priory. On cycle route 42.

CONTACT:
Court Farm, Llanthony, Abergavenny, Monmouthshire, NP7 7NN
Tel: 01873 890359
courtfarm@llanthony.co.uk www.llanthony.co.uk

The Upper Cantref Farm Bunkhouses are on a working farm situated in the heart of the Brecon Beacons National Park within walking distance of the main peaks and four miles from the town of Brecon. Two farm buildings have been converted to top quality bunkhouse accommodation.

The large bunkhouse accommodates groups up to 24 people.

On the ground floor 6 bedrooms and 4 shower / toilet rooms are provided whilst on the 1st floor a fully equipped kitchen / dining area combines with a large common room. There is disabled access throughout lower floor.

The smaller bunkhouse accommodates up to 10 people. This building is single story and contains 3 bedrooms, 2 showers / toilet rooms and a fully equipped kitchen and eating area.

Both bunkhouses are fully heated and have plenty of hot water at all times and the use of coin operated tumble dryer. The bunkhouses may be used independently or together. We also offer pony / horse riding on site.

DETAILS

- **Open** - All year, By arrangement
- **Number of beds** - Large 24: 2x6, 2x4,1x2, 1x2 ensuite. Small 10: 2x4,1x2.
- **Booking** - Advanced booking with deposit
- **Price per night** - From £13.50 pp. See website for details.
- **Public Transport** - Trains: Abergavenny 20 miles. Buses: Brecon 4 miles.
- **Directions** - GR 057 258. From Brecon take the A40 east, after 2 miles turn left onto B4558, see Cantref Riding Centre sign, follow brown & white signs.

CONTACT:
Cantref, Brecon, Powys. LD3 8LR
Tel: 01874 665223
info@cantref.com www.cantref.com

CANAL BARN
BUNKHOUSE

Nestling between the river Usk and the Canal, Canal Barn Bunkhouse has a superb setting and yet is near Brecon town centre.   The Bunkhouse is at the centre of activity in the Brecon Beacons National Park with easy access to the numerous exciting outdoor activities available in this beautiful part of Wales. Brecon town has a range of pubs, restaurants, takeaways and entertainments to satisfy most tastes and pockets, and all nearby in a safe walking distance.

Sleeping up to 24 people, the Bunkhouse offers award winning environmentally friendly, competitively priced, group accommodation of exceptional quality. Specifically designed as a base for your outdoor activities club, the Bunkhouse is equipped to a very high standard indeed and is an excellent venue for team building and residential training courses, D of E training or the place for an action packed get together with friends and family.

DETAILS

- **Open** - All year, all day
- **Number of beds** - 24 (in 6 rooms)
- **Booking** - Booking essential (minimum group of 6 people)
- **Price per night** - From £13.50
- **Public Transport** - Train/bus to Merthyr Tydfil or Abergavenny, then bus to Brecon.
- **Directions** - GR 052 279. On the canal towpath close to Brecon town centre. Vehicular access is via the canal bridge next to the Morrison Petrol Station on the nearby Abergavenny to Brecon road (B4601).

CONTACT: Ralph or Liz
Ty Camlas, Canal Bank, Brecon, Powys, LD3 7HH
Tel: 01874 625361
ihg@canal-barn.co.uk www.canal-barn.co.uk

Clyngwyn Bunkhouse is situated in the Brecon Beacons, in the heart of waterfall country, very near to the caves and waterfalls of Ystradfellte and close to the famous Sgwd Yr Eira waterfalls. The terrain is ideal for mountain biking, gorge walking, canyoning, caving, abseiling, climbing, quad biking, photography and painting. Clyngwyn Bunkhouse is perfect for groups of friends or family. It sleeps up to 19 with camping available to larger groups and 3 double B&B rooms in the farm house. There is a fully equipped kitchen, central heating, drying area, lounge with TV, DVD and a seperate dinning area seating 20. Relax in the evenings and enjoy the mountain views by a fire or BBQ . There are four acres of land for ball games and team building and a separate function room for hire. The villages of Ystradfellte and Pontneddfechan (2½ miles by mini bus taxi) have pubs with restaurants.. Four star graded by Visitwales.

DETAILS

- **Open** - All year, all day
- **Number of beds** - 19: 1x11, 2x4
- **Booking** - Booking essential. Only groups can book the bunkhouse at weekends. Credit / Debit cards not accepted
- **Price per night** - Weekdays: sole use for up to 15 people £180pn,up to 19 people £228pn,£17pp for small groups. Weekends up to 15 people £210pn, or up to 19 £265pn. Small extra charge for bedding or bring your own. B&B in Farmhouse £25pp.
- **Public Transport** - Trains Neath or Merthyr (11 miles). Minibus can be arranged.
- **Directions** - From A465 leave at Glenneath drive-through and take signs for Pontneddfechan. Then 2.5 miles up Ystradfellte road, turn right down small track.

CONTACT: Julie Hurst
Clyngwyn Farm, Ystradfellte Rd, Pontneddfechan, Powys, SA11 5US
Tel: 01639 722930
enquiries@bunkhouse-south-wales.co.uk www.bunkhouse-south-wales.co.uk

HARDINGSDOWN
BUNKHOUSE

Hardingsdown Bunkhouse is a tastefully restored stone barn situated on an organic farm. It provides comfortable self-catering accommodation for families or groups. The ground floor consists of a fully equipped kitchen, 2 shower/toilet rooms, a living room with 2 single sofa-beds and comfy chairs. Off the living room is a bedroom with a bunkbed sleeping 2 people. A spiral staircase leads upstairs where there are 3 bedrooms sleeping 5, 3 and 2 in bunks and single beds. A separate drying room is available for outdoor gear and a lock-up for storing bikes, surfboards, canoes etc. There is ample parking and a patio area which catches the evening sun. The Gower has national nature reserves, outstanding coastal scenery, family beaches, castles and ancient monuments. Llangennith beach is one of the best surfing beaches in the south west and Mewslade Bay and Fall Bay are used by climbers. Walkers and bikers can use the local network of footpaths and bridleways. Shops and pubs nearby.

DETAILS

- **Open** - All year, 24 hours
- **Number of beds** - 14: 1x5, 1x3, 3x2
- **Booking** - Non-returnable deposit of 30%, balance 1 month before arrival.
- **Price per night** - Sole use £200pn (weekends & bank holidays), £170pn (midweek). Whole week £1100. Smaller groups sharing the bunkhouse with other users, £15 per person.
- **Public Transport** - Regular bus (No116) from Swansea 0870 6082608.
- **Directions** - Turn left off the B4295 ½ mile after Burry Green (by bus shelter and post box). Follow lane till it changes into a rough track and turn right into Lower Hardingsdown Farm. Bunkhouse is on left of farmyard.

CONTACT: Allison or Andrew Tyrrell
Lower Hardingsdown Farm, Llangennith, Gower, Swansea, SA3 1HT
Tel: 01792 386222
bunkhousegower@tiscali.co.uk www.bunkhousegower.co.uk

Gilfach Wen Barn has been converted to provide competitively priced self-catering accommodation for individuals, extended families or groups on a working farm adjacent to Brechfa Forest. Graded as a 4 star bunkhouse it sleeps up to 32 in 7 bedrooms and has a large kitchen/dining room, lounge and drying room. There is a downstairs bedroom and shower room for disabled visitors. The facilities are purpose designed to be walker, cyclist and equestrian friendly for those taking advantage of the benefits of being adjacent to Brechfa Forest - the largest man-made forest in Europe.

Gilfach Wen Barn is a perfect venue for a holiday or weekend away – if you do not want to drive you need never leave the valley. The barn is fully equipped and the village is within walking distance (1mile).
This is a stunningly beautiful area close to Brecon Beacons National Park, in the foothills of the Cambrian Mountains but only a short drive to Cefn Sidan Sands - an award winning 7 mile long beach.

DETAILS

- **Open** - Open all year, all day
- **Number of beds** - 32: 3x6, 1x5, 1x4,1x3,1x2 in 10 double beds and 12 singles.
- **Booking** - Advance booking required.
- **Price per night** - £15 per person. Sole use £325 per night.
- **Public Transport** - Trains and coaches at Carmarthen. Daily bus from Carmarthen to Brechfa passes gate. Bus stop at Horeb crossroads but may drop at gate,
- **Directions** - GR SN 513 292 On the B4310 between Horeb and Brechfa.

CONTACT: Jillie
Gilfach Wen, Brechfa, Carmarthenshire, SA32 7QL
Tel: 07970 629726
GilfachWenBarn@aol.com www.brechfa-bunkhouse.com

PANTYRATHRO
INTERNATIONAL HOSTEL

Llansteffan is a beautiful quaint village set at the tip of the Towi River and Carmarthen Bay. The sandy beaches nestled below the castle offer swimming and relaxation. The virtually traffic free country lanes make this area ideal for cycling. For the walker Carmarthenshire offers coastal walks and country walks. Carmarthen (Wales' oldest city) and ancestral home to Merlin of King Arthur's Legends, offers most social and cultural activities. The Pantyrathro International Hostel provides dorm and double room accommodation and also 3 new ensuite units of 6, 8 and 12 beds. Facilities include self-catering kitchen, dining area, TV lounge and showers. Our two Mexican bars offer pool, darts, TV, weekly drink specials and food (eat-in or take-out). Horse riding, cycle hire and excursions for trekking, canoeing and surfing offered. Take a day trip or relax on the beaches or have a drink in our bars - something for everyone.

DETAILS

- **Open** - March to Jan, 24 hours
- **Number of beds** - 51: 1 x 12, 1 x 8, 2 x 6, 4 x 4, 1 x 3
- **Booking** - Booking recommended. 50% depost required in advance for groups.
- **Price per night** - £14pp dorm, £15pp ensuite. Group discounts.
- **Public Transport** - Carmarthen has both coach and train stations serving South Wales, SW England and London. Local bus runs 6 times a day to Llansteffan. Ask driver to let you off at Pantyrathro.
- **Directions** - Pantyrathro is 6 miles from Carmarthen on the B4312, midway between Llangain and Llansteffan. Two miles from Llangain you will see the hostel signposted, turn right and follow signs to top of lane.

CONTACT: Ken Knuckles
Pantyrathro Country Inn, Llansteffan, Carmarthen, SA33 5AJ
Tel: 01267 241014, Fax: 01267 241014
kenknuckles@hotmail.com www.backpackershostelwales.co.uk

Tenby is a picturesque town surrounded by award winning beaches and town walls. A great destination for walkers, backpackers and families.
Tenby Backpackers is an Old Rectory and more recently a 3 star hotel. It has a stunning location overlooking Tenby's South Beach, golf course and Caldey Island. There are double, twin and family rooms and three group rooms sleeping 8,6 and 6. Bedding is provided and the ocean can be seen from all rooms. There is a cafe on site as well as a licenced bar. Tenby town centre is only 5 minutes walk, with interesting shops, many pubs and restaurants as well as Internet Café 25. See the photos on our website.

DETAILS

■ **Open** - All year, anytime (please arrange times for late arrivals)
■ **Number of beds** - 36: 1x8, 2x6, 4x4, doubles, twins and family rooms.
■ **Booking** - Booking not essential but advised. Deposit of £5 to £10pp required by post, balance payable in cash on arrival.
■ **Price per night** - Various rates from £15pp (for multi occupancy room and 3+ nights) to £23pp (for a single room for 1 night). Group rate £17pp (based on shared rooms for 2+ nights).
■ **Public Transport** - 5 mins walk from train and bus stations,head for South Beach.
■ **Directions** - Follow A40 from Carmarthen. Enter Tenby off the double mini roundabout up the hill under the viaduct. Follow signs for South Beach and brown tourist signs for 'Kinloch Court'. Tenby Backpackers is a stand alone stone building overlooking the beach.

CONTACT: Gethin
Kinlock Court, Battery Road, Queens Parade,
Tenby, Pembrokeshire, SA70 7EG
Tel: 07810 325525 / 07977 543396
bookings@tenbyweekends.co.uk www.kinlochcourthotel.co.uk

PENQUOIT
CENTRE

The Penquoit Centre is a welcoming courtyard of historic longhouses converted into hostel accommodation for groups of 10 to 25 people. The land on which the centre stands includes a range of fields, ancient woodland, direct access to the Cresswell river and the Pembrokeshire National Park. The land is rich in birdlife, river, sea and wildfowl and within easy reach of over 20 beautiful beaches, the Preselli Hills, castles, Tenby and Caldy, riding and canoeing.

The hostel consists of 2 dormitories (one on the ground floor), communal showers and toilets. There are 2 private rooms, a large dining room with wood burning stove and a long room ideal for group activities, workshops and creativity. The kitchen is fully equipped and the centre is centrally heated. The Centre is ideal for family and friend get-togethers, art, yoga, drama, healing and plant and wildlife enthusiasts.

DETAILS

- **Open** - All year, all day
- **Number of beds** - 25+: 1 x 10, 1 x 15, plus 2 private rooms.
- **Booking** - Booking essential, deposit 25%.
- **Price per night** - £10 per person
- **Public Transport** - Trains and National Express stop at Kilgetty or Tenby (7miles). Irish Ferry and Pembroke (6 miles). We can collect if necessary
- **Directions** - M4 to Carmarthen, A40 towards Haverfordwest. At Canaston Bridge (just after Robeston Wathem) take A4075 for Pembroke. At Cresselly (6 miles) turn right, then right again at T junction. After small bridge turn left uphill towards Lawrenny, the Centre is on right (½ mile).

CONTACT: Joan Carlisle
Lawrenny, Kilgetty, Pembrokeshire, SA68 OPL
Tel: 01646 651666
joan@penquoit.plus.com

LAWRENNY
MILLENNIUM HOSTEL

The Lawrenny Hostel is a refurbished Victorian school situated in an attractive village and just a short stroll from ancient woodlands and the shores of the beautiful Cleddau Estuary. The hostel is centrally heated thoughout, it has a modern kitchen / dining area, a good-sized common room and access to a large hall for activities (hire separate). There are 4 small dorms and one room with a double bed and bunks which is ideal for families or a couple. There are 2 showers, 3 WCs and all rooms have wash hand basins. The kitchen area is equipped with a large oven, 3 four-ring hobs, 2 microwaves, 2 large toasters, 2 fridges and a freezer. There is a good drying room, a large car park, cycle shelter and a patio with picnic tables.
Community shop in village is open 7 days a week.
Pub and tearoom within walking distance.

DETAILS

- **Open** - All year, from 5pm.
- **Number of beds** - 23. 1x3, 2x4, 1x8, 1xdouble/family. All can be family rooms.
- **Booking** - Required with deposit of 50%. No deposit for late bookings.
- **Price per night** - Adults £14, under 18 £9, under 3 years free. Family room £42 (for four) or £35 (if used as a private room for two). Sole use of whole hostel by group £225 per night .
- **Public Transport** - Coachs/trains at Kilgetty (8m). Get 381 bus (Tenby to Pembroke Dock) at Kilgetty, ask for Cresswell Quay, 2.5miles (40 mn walk) to hostel.
- **Directions** - From A40 St Clears to Haverfordwest take A4075 signed Tenby and Oakwood Leisure Park. Just past turning to Oakwood, turn right and follow signs to Lawrenny. Bear right in front of church. Car park is on left behind Village Hall.

CONTACT: Laura Lort-Phillips
Lawrenny Hostel, Lawrenny, Pembrokeshire, SA68 0PW
Tel: 01646 651270
hostel@lawrennyvillage.co.uk www.lawrennyvillage.co.uk/hostel

Set in the heart of Britain's only Coastal National Park, the Pembrokeshire Adventure Centre is the perfect place to begin exploring this captivating edge of Wales! The modern and comfortable Bunkhouses overlook the stunning Cleddau Estuary and can sleep up to 80. Accommodation is in 4 blocks each with self catering facilities, lounge area and 2/3 bathrooms. Guests have use of all onsite facilities including sports pitch, conference rooms and drying room.

Bedding is included and we can provide catering for larger groups. At the Adventure Centre you can try an array of land and water based activities from coasteering to rock climbing! We welcome all ages from 8-80 on a tailor made adventure – families, experts and beginners, no-one is left out! We also provide programs for schools, youth groups, team building and adventure training. Pembrokeshire's famous beaches like Barafundle Bay are under 30 minutes away. Alternatively try some local attractions like Oakwood or the Celtic Village at Castell Henllys! Feel free to ask us any questions, we are happy to help! The centre is situated in Pembroke Dock with excellent rail, road and ferry links.

DETAILS

- **Open** - All year, all day
- **Number of beds** - 80: 2 houses of 6 x 4 beds; 2 other floors of 8 x 2 beds.
- **Booking** - Booking is essential
- **Price per night** - From £15pp. Group discounts available.
- **Public Transport** - Pembroke Dock train station 1 mile, Irish ferry port 2 miles.
- **Directions** - From Pembroke, head north on A4139, then onto A477. On A477 take 3rd right, just before the bridge. Turn right at roundabout, the Centre is 1/2 mile.

CONTACT:
Cleddau Reach, Pembroke Dock, Pembrokeshire, SA72 6UJ
Tel: 01646 622013
pac@princes-trust.org.uk www.pembrokeshire-activity-centre.co.uk

Upper Neeston Lodges are energy-efficient barn conversions on a family run sheep farm. Close to the Milford Haven Waterway in the Pembrokeshire Coast Park they are ideal for divers, climbers and walkers. There are two independent units, one accommodating 10 people and one accommodating 8. Shared between the units are a laundry / drying room, wash-down area, secure storage areas and ample parking. THE COWSHED is single storey with disabled access. It has a large sitting room and kitchen/dining area, and two bedrooms, each with a large en-suite shower room and sleeping 6 and 4 in bunks. THE BARN has two storeys with an upstairs sitting room and kitchen / dining area. The bedrooms are downstairs sleeping 6 and 2 in bunks, each with en-suite shower room. Each unit has a TV, CD player and wood burning stove, both have access to garden/patio areas. Graded as a 5 Star bunkhouse by the WTB.

DETAILS

- **Open** - All year, check in from 4pm. Check out before 10.30am
- **Number of beds** - Cowshed 10: 1x6,1x4   Barn 8: 1x6,1x2
- **Booking** - Provisional booking taken by phone and confirmed by deposit.
- **Price per night** - £15pp (includes bed linen). Minimum of 6 people guarantees exclusive use of a lodge. Minimum of 2 nights stay on weekends (3 nights on Bank Holidays).
- **Public Transport** - Trains and coaches at Milford Haven. Buses at Herbrandston (approx 1/4 mile). Puffin coastal shuttle passes the farm. www.traveline-cymru.org.uk
- **Directions** - Follow A4076 through Milford Haven to roundabout by Docks. Take first exit (signed Hakin). Follow for 2 miles, look for first farm on left (next to layby).

CONTACT: Sean or Mandy Tilling
Upper Neeston Farm, Dale Road, Herbrandston, Milford Haven, SA73 3RY
Tel: 01646 690750
mail@upperneeston.co.uk www.upperneeston.co.uk

Hamilton Backpackers Lodge is an excellent overnight stop on the stunning Pembrokeshire Coast Path. It is also an ideal overnight stay five minutes from the ferries to Rosslare in Ireland. Pembrokeshire has a wealth of natural beauty and local history and many beautiful secluded beaches.

The Backpackers Lodge is a very comfortable and friendly hostel with small dormitories and double rooms, all centrally heated. There is a dining room and TV lounge with Sky. The garden at the back of the hostel has a hammock, barbecue and picnic tables. We provide free tea, coffee and light breakfast. There is parking close by and the hostel is in the centre of town near to a number of pubs serving good meals. There is no curfew. Smoking is permitted only in the garden patio. To find out more see website.

DETAILS

■ **Open** - All year, 24 hours
■ **Number of beds** - 10: 2 x 4, 1 x 2
■ **Booking** - Booking advised to confirm beds. 50% deposit required from groups.
■ **Price per night** - £16pp in dorms, £20pp in double ensuite
■ **Public Transport** - Fishguard ferry port has a train station and ferries to Rosslare in Ireland. The port is 1 mile from the hostel (approx taxi fare £7). National Express coaches call at Haverfordwest (15 miles). For local buses in Pembrokeshire phone Richard Bros (01239) 613756.
■ **Directions** - From Haverfordwest (A40) to Fishguard Square, across first right by tourist office, 50 yds on left. From Cardigan A487 (North Wales Road) up hill and first left. From harbour 1 mile to Fishguard Square, left, first right, 50 yards on left.

CONTACT: Steve Roberts
23 Hamilton Street, Fishguard, Pembrokeshire, SA65 9HL
Tel: 01348 874797 / 07813 687570
hamiltonbackpackers@yahoo.co.uk www.hamiltonbackpackers.co.uk

CAERHAFOD
LODGE

Ideally situated between the famous cathedral city of St Davids and the Irish ferry port of Fishguard, the Lodge overlooks the spectacular Pembrokeshire coastline. It is within easy walking distance of the well known Sloop Inn at Porthgain and the internationally renowned Coastal Path. The Celtic Trail cycle route passes the bottom of our drive making it an ideal stopover for cyclists. The Lodge is a good base for all outdoor activities. Boat trips around Ramsey Island or to Grassholm to see the gannets can be arranged, as well as surfboard, wetsuit and cycle hire. The lodge is centrally heated and sleeps 23 in 5 separate rooms (4,4,4,5,6) all en-suite with great showers! There is a modern fully equipped kitchen/diner with patio, picnic tables and glorious sunsets. There is also a sitting room for cosy evenings, on-site washing/drying room and secure storage area. Dogs welcome by prior arrangement. Smoking outdoors. Wales Tourist Board 4 star. Bike hire.

DETAILS

- **Open** - All year, 24 hours
- **Number of beds** - 23: 3x4 : 1x5 : 1x6.
- **Booking** - Advised in high season. 50% deposit.
- **Price per night** - Adult £16, Under 16 £12.50. Group rates available.
- **Public Transport** - Trains at Fishguard (9m) and Haverfordwest (15m). Fishguard/Rosslare ferry. National Express Haverfordwest. 413 Bus St Davids-Fishguard 50yds from Lodge. Seasonal coastal shuttle service for walkers.
- **Directions** - GR Landranger 157, SM 827 317. A40 from Haverfordwest, left at Letterston (B4331) to Mathry. Left onto A487 to St Davids, right in Croesgoch for Llanrhian, at crossroads right for Trefin. After ½ mile turn into our drive.

CONTACT: Carolyn Rees.
Llanrhian, St Davids, Haverfordwest, Pembrokeshire, SA62 5BD
Tel: 01348 837859
Caerhafod@aol.com www.caerhafod.co.uk

OLD SCHOOL HOSTEL
FORMERLY YHA TREFIN
WALES

Escape to this wonderful, wild and rugged corner of the Pembrokeshire Coast National Park. We are in the centre of Trefin, an attractive village just a quarter of a mile from the famous coastal path and only 15 minutes from the cathedral city of St Davids and the popular beach at Whitesands Bay. The village has a pub and café. Stunning wild beaches and small harbour villages can be reached in a few minutes by car, or visited as part of a days circular walk. Our friendly characterful 4 Star hostel offers comfortable accommodation at prices that are hard to beat. Shared rooms are from £12 per person and we also offer singles, twins and doubles from only £15 per person. Family rooms sleeping 3 to 6 are available from £37 peak season. We also offer the option of an organic breakfast if desired. Our electricity is supplied from renewable energy, we offer 'eco' discounts and plant a tree for every booking. Help create a forest for the future – come and stay!

DETAILS

- **Open** - All year, check in from 5pm. All day access once checked in.
- **Number of beds** - 25: 1x6, 2x5, 1x4, 1x3, 1x2
- **Booking** - Advance booking recommended
- **Price per night** - £12/£13 shared rooms, private rooms from £15 per person, family rooms from £37, exclusive use of hostel £225 per night.
- **Public Transport** - Train to Fishguard then bus 413 to Trefin. Or train/ National Express to Haverfordwest, bus 411 via St Davids to Trefin. For times phone Traveline 0870 6082608.
- **Directions** - From the A40 turn left onto the B4331 at Letterston then left onto the A487. After 2.5 miles turn right just after the Square and Compass pub for Trefin.

CONTACT: Sue or Chris
Ffordd-yr-Afon, Trefin, Haverfordwest, Pembrokeshire, SA62 5AU
Tel: 01348 831800
oldschoolhostel@btconnect.com www.theoldschoolhostel.co.uk

TYCANOL FARM
CAMPING BARN

Tycanol Farm offers accommodation for four in a camping barn close to the beautiful Pembrokeshire coast. For larger groups there is a camp site for tents and caravans which overlooks the whole of Newport Bay. The campsite showers and toilets are available for users of the barn and camping and the hot water is free. There are no meals provided on the site but the camping barn has limited self-catering facilities and there are pubs and restaurants within a 10 minute walk. Laundry facilities are available on the site and there is also access to a drying room. There are many activities to enjoy in the surrounding area. Pony trekking and a golf club are within a mile of the site. The area is also ideal for canoeing and sailing. The site is a five minute walk to the coastal path and ten minutes to Newport itself. There is also a nature trail which contains badger setts. Free barbecue every night at 6.30pm. Everybody greeted with a warm welcome PLEASE CONTACT THIS HOSTEL BY PHONE OR POST.

DETAILS

- **Open** - All year, 24 hours
- **Number of beds** - 4 in the barn plus camping.
- **Booking** - Booking not always necessary.
- **Price per night** - £12pp per night (camping barn), £7pp per night (camping).
- **Public Transport** - Nearest train station is at Fishguard (7 miles away). Nearest National Express coaches are at Haverfordwest (18 miles away). Local buses pass the farm drive every hour; call 01239 613756.
- **Directions** - Tycanol Farm is near the beach a mile outside of Newport, Pembrokeshire on the A487 towards Fishguard. Turn right at milk-stand signpost.

CONTACT: Hugh Harries
Tycanol Farm, Newport, Pembrokeshire, SA42 0ST
Tel: 01239 820264

NANT Y POBTY
HOSTEL

The hostel is a basic but nice old stone building on a small working farm in the hills near the West Wales coast. Our closest beach is about 7 miles away. The hostel has two floors, the top floor splitting into two rooms of 8 or two family rooms. The sleeping is basic on comfortable camp beds. There is a fully equipped kitchen, nice sized lounge, log burning stove and TV. There are 2 toilet shower rooms and a small drying room. We are close to one of the 7 top Welsh mountain bike areas (Brechfa Forest). Also as Adventure Beyond we offer a number of packages for stag and hen groups, schools, etc for team building or just a laugh. Activities (subject to availability) include canoeing, kayaking, raft building, climbing, fishing, farm fun, assault course, clay shooting, zorb ball, hill walking, orienteering courses, coasteering and surfing.

DETAILS

- **Open** - All year, all day
- **Number of beds** - 10: 2x8, 1x2 (family rooms on request)
- **Booking** - Booking is essential, deposit required if booking more then 1 week.
- **Price per night** - £10pp (bring your own bedding)
- **Public Transport** - Train and bus stations at Carmarthen. Bus stop at Croeslan.
- **Directions** - From Carmarthen follow the A485. At Windy Corner Garage take left turn A4459 to Pencader. After Pencader take the next left (at top of hill) to Llandysul. Follow the road over the river on the A486 to the village of Croeslan. Take the left turn to Maesllyn, a very small road. Follow the road down a large hill and up the other side. At the village of Coed-y-Bryn there will be a dead end road in front of you. Go down to the yard and you are there.

CONTACT: Jethro, Glenis or Stuart
Nant Y Pobty Farm, Coed Y Bryn, Llandysul, Ceradigion, SA44 5LQ
Tel: 01239 858852, Mob 07787 123761
fun@AdventureBeyond.co.uk www.adventurebeyond.co.uk

The Long Barn is a traditional stone barn providing comfortable and warm bunkhouse accommodation. It is situated on a working organic farm in beautiful countryside with views over the Teifi Valley. The stunning Ceredigion Coast and the Cambrian Mountains are both an easy drive away and the busy small town of Llandysul (1.5 miles) has all essential supplies.

The barn's location is ideal for exploring, studying or simply admiring the Welsh countryside. Activities enjoyed by guests in the surrounding area include fishing, swimming, climbing, abseiling, canoeing, farm walks and cycling.

The barn is open all year, having adequate heating with a lovely warm Rayburn, log fire, roof insulation and double glazing throughout.

DETAILS

- **Open** - All year, all day
- **Number of beds** - 34
- **Booking** - Essential, deposit required
- **Price per night** - £10pp (adult). Discount of 10% for groups of 20 or more.
- **Public Transport** - Carmarthen (16 miles) has a train station and National Express service. Llandysul (1.5 miles away) has a local bus service, phone 0871 2002233 for details.
- **Directions** - OS map 146, GR 437 417. In Llandysul, at the top of the main street, take right hand lane. Turn sharp right down hill. After 100 yds turn sharp left. Another ½ mile turn first right. Continue for 1 mile and Long Barn is on your right.

CONTACT: Tom or Eva
Penrhiw, Capel Dewi, Llandysul, Ceredigion, SA44 4PG
Tel: 01559 363200, Fax: 01559 363200
cowcher@thelongbarn.co.uk www.thelongbarn.co.uk

TY'N CORNEL
TYNCORNEL HOSTEL

Ty'n Cornel Hostel is an isolated old farmhouse in the hills, with a cosy open fire. Favoured by walkers, cyclists, bird-watchers and lovers of solitude it is in the beautiful Doethie valley on the Cambrian Way long distance footpath. There are comfortable wooden bunk beds and good self-catering facilities.

You can enjoy the wild open moorlands of the Elenydd uplands. Other attractions include the Cors Caron National Nature Reserve, red kite feeding station, the Welsh Gold Centre at Tregaron, Teifi Pools, Llyn Brianne reservoir, Dolaucothi Roman gold mines, Strata Florida Abbey and Llanerchaeron country house (National Trust).

DETAILS

■ **Open** - All year, 24 hours. Reception 5pm -11pm, 7am -10am
■ **Number of beds** - 16: 2x8
■ **Booking** - Booking advisable; essential mid November to mid March. Book online at www.yha.org.uk. or ring YHA booking office on 0870 770 8868. For bookings within a week of your stay, ring 01980 629259.
■ **Price per night** - £12 per adult, £9 (under 18s). Block bookings negotiable.
■ **Public Transport** - Trains: Aberystwyth 28m; Llanwrtyd Wells 16m, Cynghordy 12m. Coach: x40 (Cardiff – Aberystwyth) Lampeter 15 m. Bus: 585 (Lampeter – Tregaron) Llanddewi-Brefi 7m.
■ **Directions** - Road from Llanddewi-Brefi, near Tregaron: follow hostel signs SE 7m (last mile track) Bridle path N. up Doethie valley on the Cambrian Way (Llandovery 15 m) or byway 2m NW from Soar y Mynydd chapel.

CONTACT: YHA booking office or www.yha.org.uk
Llanddewi Brefi, Tregaron, Ceredigion, SY25 6PH
Tel: YHA booking 0870 770 8868 or (within two days of stay) 01980 629259,
Fax: 0870 7706081
tyncornel@yha.org.uk www.elenydd-hostels.co.uk

DOLGOCH
HOSTEL

Come and experience the peace of this unique location in the remote Tywi valley. A stay in this 17th century farmhouse will take you into an era before electricity, with gas for lighting and a large open fire for heat. Dolgoch is a traditional simple hostel now owned by the Elenydd Wilderness Trust. It has hot showers, a self catering kitchen/dining room and 21 beds in 3 dormitories. Recently refurbished to include new toilets and showers and less able accommodation. Upgraded track. The Lôn Las Cymru (Welsh National Cycle Route) and the Cambrian Way pass nearby and there are many other mountain tracks to explore on foot, by mountain bike or pony. The location is also ideal for bird-watchers and lovers of solitude. The hostel is close to an old drovers' track which leads over the scenic Cambrian mountains for 5 miles to the equally remote and simple Ty'n Cornel Hostel. Why not stay a night in each hostel and follow in the treads of the old drovers?

DETAILS

- **Open** - All year, 24 hours, Reception 5pm -11pm, 7am -10am
- **Number of beds** - 21: (in 3 rooms)
- **Booking** - Booking information is available on the YHA website: yha.org.uk
- **Price per night** - £12 per adult, £9 (under 18). Campers £6.
- **Public Transport** - Train to Aberystwyth, Carmarthen or Llanwrtyd Wells. Bus X40: Cardiff/Carmarthen to Lampeter/Aberystwyth, Bus 585: Lampeter/Aberystwyth to Tregaron. Postbus 287: Llandovery to Rhandirmwyn.
- **Directions** - SN 806 562. You can walk to Dolgoch over the hills from Tregaron or take the winding Abergwesyn mountain road. The hostel is ¾ mile south of the bridge, along an unsurfaced track.

CONTACT: YHA Booking Office or Chris Mason
Dolgoch, Tregaron, Ceredigion, SY25 6NR
Tel: 0870 770 8868. For bookings within 5 days call 01782 253274
dolgoch@yha.org.uk www.elenydd-hostels.co.uk

PIGGERY POKE
HOSTEL

Piggery Poke is on the public footpath that loops from the Ceredigion Coast Path between Mwnt and Parcllyn. Local cycle routes link the road at the top of the entrance drive to long distance cycle routes Lôn Teifi (within 4 miles) and the Celtic Trail. See also Sustrans Route 82. Piggery Poke comprises a 3 dormitory unit designed to accommodate up to 16 people; 8 in dormitory 1, 5 in dormitory 2, and 3 in dormitory 3. Each dormitory has en-suite facilities and the dining room seats 16 at one sitting. There is a drying room on the ground floor and wireless broadband. Ample parking is provided, there is a large garden area with sea views and barbeque, and there is also a secure cycle store. A courtesy collection and delivery service is usually available from points within 15 miles along the coast for walkers and cyclists and / or their cycles and luggage.

DETAILS

■ **Open** - 1st March to 9th January, 4pm to 10pm and 7.30am to 10am
■ **Number of beds** - 16: 1 x 8, 1 x 5, 1 x 3
■ **Booking** - Book by phone.
■ **Price per night** - £15 - £18 per person.
■ **Public Transport** - Trains at Aberystwyth and Carmarthen. From Aberystwyth station take the X50bus to Blaenannerch or 550 bus to Felinwynt, via Aberporth. From Carmarthen station take the 460 or 461 bus to Cardigan (Finch Square) then change to the 550 bus to Aberystwyth via Aberporth, alighting at Felinwynt.
■ **Directions** - Piggery Poke hostel is part of Cardigan Coastal Cottages which is at Ffrwdwenith Isaf, Felinwynt, half-way between Mwnt and Aberporth, 4 miles along the coast north of Cardigan. Lat: 52.13108, Long: -4.58939

CONTACT: Paul or Angela
Ffrwdwenith Isaf, Felinwynt, Cardigan, SA43 1RW
Tel: 01239 811777
hostel@cardigan.cc www.cardigan.cc

STONECROFT
LODGE

Stonecroft Lodge, our self-catering guest house, is situated in Llanwrtyd Wells, 'The Smallest Town in Britain '.   Surrounded by the green fields, mountains and glorious countryside of mid-Wales, Llanwrtyd is renowned Red Kite country and is the centre for mountain biking, walking, pony trekking etc.   The town hosts many annual events such as the Man v Horse Marathon, World Bog Snorkelling Championships and the mid-Wales Beer Festival.

The Hostel offers a warm welcome and a comfortable stay.   We are Wales Tourist Board Star Graded and have private or shared rooms with fully made up beds.   There is a fully equipped kitchen, TV, video, free laundry and drying facilities, central heating, large riverside garden and ample parking.   The Hostel adjoins our Good Beer Guide pub, Stonecroft Inn (where great food is available), and is truly your 'home away from home', offering the best of everything for your stay.

DETAILS

- **Open** - All year, all day - phone on arrival
- **Number of beds** - 27: 1 x 1 : 3 x 4 : 1 x 6 : 4 x (dbl + 1 sgl)
- **Booking** - Welcome, 50% deposit.
- **Price per night** - £16. Discounts for 3+ nights. Phone for exclusive-use rates.
- **Public Transport** - Llanwrtyd Wells station on the Heart of Wales line is a few minutes walk from the hostel.
- **Directions** - GR 878 468. From Llanwrtyd town centre (A483) take Dolecoed Road towards Abergwesyn. Hostel is 100 yds on left. Check in at Stonecroft Inn.

CONTACT: Jane Brown
Dolecoed Road, Llanwrtyd Wells, Powys, LD5 4RA
Tel: 01591 610327, Fax: 01591 610304
party@stonecroft.co.uk www.stonecroft.co.uk

TRERICKET MILL
BUNKHOUSE

Across the stream from Trericket Corn Mill this stone bunkhouse in an old cider orchard overlooks the River Wye. It is particularly suitable for small groups and individuals with two rooms sleeping four people each and an additional en-suite bunkroom for two in the mill. The bunkhouse is clean and cosy; heating, hot water and showers are all inclusive. Limited self-catering facilities are provided in a covered outdoor kitchen. Alternatively breakfasts and packed lunches can be provided and good pub meals are available locally. There are heated drying and common rooms in the mill and camping is also available.

Trericket Mill is situated on the Wye Valley Walk and National Cycle Route 8. An ideal stop-over for walkers, cyclists and for others wishing to relax in the beautiful countryside of mid Wales. Canoeing, pony trekking, gliding, mountain bikes, rope centre and white water rafting all available locally.

DETAILS

- **Open** - All year, 24 hour access
- **Number of beds** - 10: 2 x 4, 1 x 2 en-suite, plus 6 veggie B&B beds
- **Booking** - Advanced booking advised.
- **Price per night** - From £12.50 per person
- **Public Transport** - Train stations at Builth Wells (10 miles) Hereford (30 miles) Merthyr Tydfil (30 miles). Daily bus service - ask to be dropped at Trericket Mill. National Express coaches drop off at Hereford and Brecon (13 miles). For travel information: www.traveline-cymru.info
- **Directions** - GR SO 112 414. We are set back from the A470 Brecon to Builth Wells road between the villages of Llyswen and Erwood.

CONTACT: Alistair / Nicky Legge
Erwood, Builth Wells, Powys, LD2 3TQ
Tel: 01982 560312
mail@trericket.co.uk www.trericket.co.uk

Maesbryncoch Barn is set in a peaceful spot near Builth Wells with lovely views of Mid Wales Hills. Ideal for families and small groups to get away from it all. The open-plan living, sleeping and kitchen area has 6 fold out beds (pillow and pillowcase provided), heater, large dining table, cooking facilities, fridge/freezer and sink unit. Separate washroom with shower (free hot water) and WCs. BBQ and picnic bench outside, also storage for bikes and a pony paddock. The local area is excellent for walking, mountain biking, riding, canoeing, fishing and paragliding. Less than 2 miles from the Wye Valley, 3 miles from Royal Welsh Showground and 3½ miles from Builth Wells with shops, pubs, theatre, cinema, leisure centre and golf course. Nearest pub serving food is 2½ miles away in Hundred House village. We can provide breakfast and supper with a little notice. Bring your own sleeping bags or order a bedding and towel pack for your stay. Visit Wales rated 2star bunkhouse. Member of ABO. Sorry, no dogs.

DETAILS

- **Open** - Open 1st March to 31st October, all day
- **Number of beds** - 6: 1x6
- **Booking** - By email or phone
- **Price per night** - Sliding scale from £10pp for 6 people sharing, up to £15pp for single. Bedding and towel pack £5pp. Min. 4 people for Royal Welsh Show week.
- **Public Transport** - Nearest trains at Builth Road (4½ miles). Daily buses to Builth from Newtown, Brecon, Cardiff, Abergavenny, Aberystwyth. Pick up from Builth /Builth Road may be possible or local taxi. More info: 0871 200 2233, www.traveline.org.uk
- **Directions** - Just to the south of the A481, 3½ miles from Builth Wells, half way between Llanelwedd and Hundred House. Grid reference SO079527.

CONTACT: Louise and Tim
Maesbryncoch, Llanfaredd, Builth Wells, Powys, LD2 3TE
Tel: 01982 551116 or 07709 202355
louise.mbc@virgin.net www.maesbryncochbarn.co.uk

BEILI NEUADD
BUNKHOUSE

Beili Neuadd Bunkhouse is a converted 18th-century stone barn beautifully positioned in quiet, secluded countryside with delightful views, its own paddocks, stream, pools and woodland. The centrally heated barn sleeps 16 in 3 en-suite bunkrooms and includes a fully equipped kitchen/dining room, drying room and facilities for wheelchair users. The bunks have a standard mattress, bed linen is included, towels can be hired. Accommodation for 4 is also available in the adjacent Chalet and there is space to camp in the paddock behind. There are picnic tables and BBQ in the paddock and ample parking in the yard. The barn is 2.5 miles from the small market town of Rhayader - the gateway to the Elan Valley reservoirs, known as The Lakeland of Wales. It is adjacent to the Upper Wye Valley and the Cambrian Mountains.This spectacular countryside offers a wide range of activities including cycling, mountain biking, fishing, pony trekking, canoeing and of course bird watching and walking.

DETAILS

- **Open** - All year, all day access.
- **Number of beds** - 16: 2 x 6, 1 x 4. Chalet: 1 double, 2 singles
- **Booking** - Booking preferred (with deposit).
- **Price per night** - £15 per person. £200 sole occupancy.
- **Public Transport** -   Nearest trains at Llandrindod Wells -12 miles. Some buses from Rhayader. Taxi from Rhayader about £4. Assistance with transport available.
- **Directions** - OS Explorer 200/OS147 GR 994698. Take the A44 east bound from Rhayader town centre (clock). After 0.4 miles turn left on unclassified road signposted Abbey Cwm-hir with Beili Neuadd sign. Take 1st left after 1.5 miles. Beili Neuadd is 2nd farm on right after 0.4 miles.

CONTACT: Gillian and Richard Marks
Beili Neuadd, Rhayader, Powys, LD6 5NS
Tel: 01597 810211
rhayaderbreaks@yahoo.co.uk www.midwalesfarmstay.co.uk

Mid Wales Bunkhouse at Woodhouse Farm provides affordable accommodation for groups or individuals. Set in the most wonderful countryside, midway between Rhayader and Llanidloes it is convenient for the Elan Valley, Wye Valley, Trans Cambrian Trail and Glyndwrs Way. The area is ideal for walking, mountain biking, cycling, horse riding, bird watching and trekking and is also favoured by 4x4 offroad owners. The accommodation will sleep up to 20. There is a kitchen available for self catering or we can prepare meals for you (order by 4pm). There is a garden area and where the River Marteg passes through the farm a Private Nature Reserve is being established with the Radnorshire Wildlife Trust. Otters and many bird species have been spotted here. Camping and tipi hire available. Please let us know if arriving after 7pm

DETAILS

- **Open** - All year, 24 hours. New arrivals after 3pm, depart before 11am.
- **Number of beds** - 20
- **Booking** - Booking online, by email or phone with deposit, and full payment 8 weeks before arrival. If arriving at short notice please phone to check availability.
- **Price per night** - £10pp, £50 for private 6-bed room, £175 sole use (20 people).
- **Public Transport** - Trains at Llandrindod Wells / Newtown. Daily NE coach to Llanidloes. Buses from Llandrindod to Rhayader and limited service to St. Harmon and Pant Y Dwr. We can usually collect from Llandrindod, Llanidloes or Newtown.
- **Directions** - From the clock tower in Rhayader take A44/A470 towards Llangurig for about 100 metres then B4518 towards St Harmon. Follow for about 5 miles. At the Mid Wales Inn turn right, signed Bwylch-Y-Sarnau. After a mile turn right, just before a garage. Bunkhouse on right in half a mile. SatNav use is not advised. GR SN998750.

CONTACT: John or Steph
Woodhouse Farm, St Harmon, Rhayader, LD6 5LY
Tel: 01597 870081
john-steph@woodhouse-farm.org.uk www.bunkhousemidwales.co.uk

NEW INN
BUNKHOUSE

Stay at the 16th century New Inn on the River Wye and discover the forgotten countryside of mid-Wales. The New Inn has a bunkhouse ideal for parties of walkers and cyclists as well as double, twin and family B&B rooms. The bunkhouse has its own entrance and a large lobby which can be used for boots and waterproofs. Secure storage is available for cycles and motor-cycles. The bunkhouse is self contained with toilets and showers.

There are no self catering facilities but the Inn specialises in serving imaginative home-cooked locally grown food. A Welsh breakfast of home-made sausages and dry cured bacon is available for £5. Explore the surrounding countryside, inhabited by red Kites, or relax in the secluded beer garden. There is plenty of parking and a large function room for parties.

DETAILS

- **Open** - All year, all day, Pub closed 3pm - 5pm some days.
- **Number of beds** - Bunkhouse 10: 1x6, 1x4; B&B 11: family rooms, double & twin
- **Booking** - Book by phone or email.
- **Price per night** - £10 pp (Bunkhouse), £60 sole use of 6 bed room, £40 sole use of 4 bed room. Breakfast £5pp. Ensuite B&B in Inn £60 double/twin. Family rooms also available from £80.
- **Public Transport** - Trains at Llandrindod Wells 5 miles away. Infrequent bus service.
- **Directions** - Newbridge-on-Wye is on the A470 between Builth Wells and Rhayader. Travelling north on the A470 take a right turn in Newbridge and the New Inn is on the right.

CONTACT: Debbie and Dave
New Inn, Newbridge-on-Wye, Llandrindod Wells, Powys, LD1 6HY
Tel: 01597 860211
dave@pigsfolly.orangehome.co.uk www.pigsfolly.co.uk/bunkhouse.htm

Set in the beautiful mid-Wales countryside on the Glendwrs Way the Bunkhouse is an ideal location for exploring or unwinding. Built to the highest standards, newly opened in July 2008 and with 4 star tourist board rating it provides high quality accommodation for groups or individuals. It can also be booked for conferences and seminars. There is a well equipped kitchen and a large communal area with fabulous elevated views over the mid-Wales countryside. The bunkbeds are large with comfortable mattresses. Pillows and pillowcases are included, sheets and duvet can be hired for £5 per set. Attractions close by include sailing, golf course, outdoor pursuit centre, shooting range, motorbike school and the picturesque market town of LLanidloes (1 mile) with many places to eat and drink. You will need to bring your own soap and towels. Boots and dirty footwear must be kept in the drying room so please bring footwear for indoors. Bike hire, and taxis for walkers and cyclists to / from routes available.

DETAILS

- **Open** - All year, 24 hours. Arrival and departure times by arrangement.
- **Number of beds** - 23 in 2 dormitories and 1 family room.
- **Booking** - Booking is required (with non-refundable deposit) by phone, email or booking form on plasnewyddbunkhouse.co.uk.
- **Price per night** - Sole use £403 per night. Smaller groups from £18 per person. Individuals £22 pp.
- **Public Transport** - Caersws train station (7 miles), Llanidloes bus station (1 mile). Pick ups can be arranged from these points if required.
- **Directions** - From Llanidloes take the Gorn Road and Plasnewydd is signposted on the left hand side after about 2 miles.

CONTACT: Susan
Gorn Rd, Llanidloes, Powys, SY18 6LA
Tel: 01686 412431 or 07977 508 648
susanvaughan@aol.com www.plasnewyddbunkhouse.co.uk

PLAS DOLAU

Plas Dolau is set in quiet countryside just 3 miles from the popular coastal town of Aberystwyth. Ideal for exploring West Wales, walking, cycling, riding, fishing and golf etc. The holiday centre includes a warm country mansion (WTB 4 star hostel) with mainly dormitory style accommodation and an adjoining Scandinavian style farmhouse (WTB 3 star guesthouse) set in 22 acres.

Plas Dolau includes meeting rooms, dining rooms, games room, outdoors areas and walks. The centre can accommodate groups of up to 45 people. Various options for accommodation, provision of food, cooking facilities, etc are available. We are ideally suited for youth groups, field courses, retreats, house parties and many other groups or individuals.
Phone to discuss your requirements.

DETAILS

- **Open** - All year, 24 hours
- **Number of beds** - 45: + cots etc. Plus 16 in farmhouse.
- **Booking** - Recommended.
- **Price per night** - Ranges from £17.50 (including basic breakfast) to £30 (private room, en-suite with full breakfast). From £550 per night for the whole mansion.
- **Public Transport** - Nearest train station is in Aberystwyth. Taxi from the station will cost around £5. National Express coaches and local buses (525 and 526) will set down at the end of the hostel drive.
- **Directions** - GR 623 813, OS map 135. On the A44, 3 miles from Aberystwyth, 1 mile from Llanbadarn railway bridge, 0.6 miles from turning to Bow Street. Sign on roadside says 'Y Gelli', B+B. Reception in 'Y Gelli'.

CONTACT:
Lovesgrove, Aberystwyth, Ceredigion, SY23 3HP
Tel: 01970 617834
pat.twigg@virgin.net www.dolau-holidays.co.uk

MAESNANT
CENTRE

Maesnant is set in the remote hillsides of the Plynlimon mountain, an ideal location for hillwalking and mountain biking.   The Centre is designed for use by youth groups, but family and other groups are welcome.   Inside the centre there are 3 bunk rooms, two wash rooms (each with shower, WCs etc), kitchen and a large common room with dining facilities.

Accommodation in the Centre is limited to 16 persons, though camping is possible in the 12 acres of grounds.   Maesnant is hired out on a self-catering basis. Groups under 16 years of age must include 2 adults. There are many attractions in the area: Devils Bridge waterfalls and steam powered railway, Llywernog Mine Museum, Bwlch Nant Yr Arian Forest Centre and the Powergen Rheidol Hydro Electric Power Scheme visitor centre.

DETAILS

- **Open** - March to November, no restrictions
- **Number of beds** - 16: 2 x 6 : 1 x 4
- **Booking** - Telephone booking essential. Deposit (£30) required 4 weeks in advance.
- **Price per night** - £5 pp
- **Public Transport** - Nearest mainline railway station Aberystwyth, bus services to Ponterwyd.
- **Directions** - A44 from Aberystwyth to Ponterwyd, take scenic route to Nan y Moch via mountain road, (east end of village by 30mph sign). After 6 cattle grids and before 7th take a right turn, Maesnant is then 1.5 miles, at the end of the road.

CONTACT: Julie Bellchambers
Maesnant, Ponterwyd, Aberystwyth, Ceredigion, SY23 3AG
Tel: 07747 017371
info@maesnant.org.uk www.maesnant.org.uk

Maes-y-Mor offers superior accommodation at a budget price. Ideally situated near the town centre, 80m from the beach and 40m from the bus station. Accommodation at the hostel is room-only. There is a large kitchen diner with fridge freezer, hob oven, microwave and toaster enabling guests to prepare their own food. Bedrooms have TV, tea/coffee making facilities and beds of a superior quality to ensure a good nights sleep. Towels are provided. Halls and landings are themed in welsh history pictures. There is a car parking area at rear and secure shed for bikes. Free WiFi Internet.

Aberystwyth is an ideal base for north and south Wales. Visit Devil's Bridge with its dramatic waterfalls or Vale of Rheidol narrow guage railway, The National Library of Wales, the Castle and the Harbour. Aberystwyth is a university town so there is plenty of night life. We offer a personal and helpful service.
Croeso Cymraeg Cynnes i bawb / a warm welsh welcome to all!

DETAILS

- **Open** - All year, 8am to 10pm
- **Number of beds** - 20: 8 x 2, 1 x 4 (en-suite)
- **Booking** - Booking advisable
- **Price per night** - £20 per person, en-suite £22 per person. Single £22.
- **Public Transport** - Bus and train stations are within approximately 400 mts.
- **Directions** - From bus and train stations follow Terrace Road in a straight line towards beach. Turn right at Tourist Board Shop, you will find us approx 30 mts along next to the cinema.

CONTACT: Gordon or Mererid
25 Bath Street, Aberystwyth, Ceredigion, SY23 2NN
Tel: 01970 639270 or 07966 502715
maesymor@hotmail.co.uk www.maesymor.co.uk

BRAICH GOCH
BUNKHOUSE & INN

The Braich Goch is a 16th-century coaching inn situated 3 miles from Cadair Idris. There are stunning views of the Dulas valley and Dyfi Forest. The Braich has been specifically set up with outdoor enthusiasts in mind. Facilities include drying room, secure bike storage and large well equipped self-catering kitchen. There are 6 bedrooms, 4 en-suite and a further two bathrooms.

The location is ideal for walking, mountain biking, cycling, climbing and canoeing at all levels as well as bird watching or simply chilling out. Dyfi Forest mountain bike trails are on the doorstep. The Braich is also a pub with pool table, darts and other games to keep you entertained in the evening! Also available are activity packages with qualified instructors suitable for all levels. In the area are King Arthur's Labyrinth and Corris Craft Centre, Centre for Alternative Technology, Coed-y-Brenin Forest Park and the coast. Wales Tourist Board 4 stars. Walkers & Cyclists Welcome Awards.

DETAILS

- **Open** - All year, all hours by arrangement
- **Number of beds** - 26: 5 x 4 : 1 x 6
- **Booking** - Essential for groups. 20% deposit, balance 4 weeks before arrival.
- **Price per night** - From £16pp
- **Public Transport** - Nearest train station to Corris is Machynlleth. Bus stop outside the 'Braich Goch' Inn. Taxis can be hired from Machynlleth.
- **Directions** - GR 754 075 On A487 between Machynlleth and Dolgellau at Corris turning. 2.5 miles north of Centre for Alternative Technology.

CONTACT: Ann or Andy
Corris, Machynlleth, Powys, SY20 9RD
Tel: 01654 761229 mobile 07881 626734
AnnBottrill@aol.com www.braichgoch.co.uk

CORRIS
HOSTEL

Nestled in the foothills of Cadair Idris, this award winning hostel enjoys splendid views over the Dyfi Valley. Corris Hostel is renowned as a spiritual haven with its caring, easy going atmosphere, friendly staff, cosy wood fires and collection of books, games and artefacts. Outdoors the evolving landscaped gardens provide a serene, relaxing environment.

Environmental awareness is promoted through the hostel's vegetarian focus, recycling, composting, gardens and energy efficiency. Visitors can find more about Green lifestyle at the nearby Centre for Alternative Technology (celebrated worldwide as Europe's leading Eco-Centre). Down river are national Biosphere nature reserves and miles of golden beaches at Aberdyfi. A wide range of countryside and environmental activities are available with workshops run by local people.

DETAILS

- **Open** - All year, all day access.
- **Number of beds** - 42/44
- **Booking** - Phone to check.
- **Price per night** - Adult £15, child £12, Breakfast £3.50.
- **Public Transport** - Buses 30, X32, 34 and Trawscambria pass Machynlleth train station on the Cambrian Coast line with connection to Aberystwyth and Birmingham.
- **Directions** - GR 753 080. We are in the mountain village of Corris 6 miles north of Machynlleth. At Braich Goch turn off A487 into Corris. At Slaters Arms pub turn left, hostel is 150m uphill beyond a small carpark.

CONTACT: Michael or Debbie
Old School, Corris, Machynlleth, Powys, SY20 9TQ
Tel: 01654 761686
mail@corrishostel.co.uk www.corrishostel.co.uk

Ty'n y Berth is a former school at the foot of Cadair Idris on the southern edge of the Snowdonia National Park. Surrounded by mountains, valleys and crystal clear rivers, yet only 12 miles from the coast, it's a great location for outdoor activities and family holidays. The spacious accommodation sleeps up to 36. The main room is divided into dining and lounge areas; there is a commercial kitchen with large oven, hob and microwave; plenty of toilets & showers; drying room; pay phone; lockable storage for boats & bikes and parking for 10 cars.

Corris is within walking distance and has two pubs: the Slaters Arms, which does bar meals, and the Braich Goch Inn, which regularly has live music. Courses are also available in climbing, mountain walking, abseiling, gorge scrambling, mine exploration, ropes courses, orienteering, and team building. Accommodation for a further 35 is available at the Bryn Coedwig Centre (also run by Wide Horizons), four miles from Tyn Y Berth in the village of Aberllefenni.

DETAILS

■ **Open** - All year , all day
■ **Number of beds** - 36: 1x8, 3x6, 1x4, 1x2, 1xdbl, 2x1
■ **Booking** - Book by phone or email.
■ **Price per night** - Sole use £380, 12-14 beds £130, 10 beds £120.
■ **Public Transport** - Trains run from London to Machynlleth with a change at Birmingham New Street.
■ **Directions** - On entering Corris Uchaf from north on A487. you will enter a 30 mph speed limit. Ty'n y Berth is the old school on the right, just inside the 30mph signs.

CONTACT: Jane or Dave
Corris Uchaf, Machynlleth, Powys, SY20 9RH
Tel: 01654 761678
tynyberth@widehorizons.org.uk www.widehorizons.org.uk/tyb

This self-catering bunkhouse is ideal for groups but also open to individuals.
Caban Cader Idris is a listed building in a secluded wooded valley within
walking distance of Cader Idris and the Mawddach Estuary in Eryri (Snowdonia
National Park). It is in an ideal setting for field work and outdoor pursuits with
wonderful unspoilt mountain, valley and estuary walks from the doorstep.
Local activities include climbing, hill walking, pony trekking, biking, canoeing,
rafting and fishing. The area is also ideal for the study of geology, geography,
local history, industrial archaeology and ornithology (RSPB woods adjoin
grounds). Nearby are slate mines, narrow gauge railways and beaches.
There is a large kitchen / dining room, two dorms sleeping 6 and 10, a lounge
(with 3 beds), toilets, hot showers and a drying room.
It is heated and open all seasons. Camping by arrangement.

DETAILS

■ **Open** - All year, no restrictions
■ **Number of beds** - 19
■ **Booking** - Booking is essential. Always phone before arrival. £20 per night
deposit. Last minute enquiries welcome from individuals or groups.
■ **Price per night** - Sole use:- £100 midweek, £125 Fri, Sat, Bank Holidays and New
Year. Reduced rates for whole week bookings. Individuals £10 pp when available.
■ **Public Transport** - Nearest train station is Morfa Mawddach (4 miles). Nearest
bus stop is Abergwynant (¼ mile). For local bus info call 01341 422614.
■ **Directions** - GR 682 169. From Dolgellau take the A493 to Fairbourne. 1 mile after
Penmaenpool turn left just before Abergwynant Bridge. Bunkhouse 300yds on left

CONTACT: Dafydd Rhys
Islawrdref, Dolgellau, Gwynedd, LL40 1TS
Tel: 01766 762588, Mobile 07887 954301
dafydd.rhys@virgin.net

HyB Bunkhouse is situated on Heol y Bont (Bridge St) in the old market town of Dolgellau, mid-Wales, nestling at the foot of Cader Idris. It is centrally located above the design-led gift shop Medi, and has free private parking for up to six cars at the rear of the premises. Seconds from pubs and restaurants, launderette and bike repairers, it backs onto the Mawddach trail and the Marian playing fields, on the banks of the river Wnion and only 10 mins drive to Coed y Brenin mountain biking centre. This quirky listed building has lovely original features such as oak floors, beams and panelling and consists of four bunk rooms, sleeping 16 in total. Each room has a mini-kitchen for basic self catering with fridge, hob, toaster and kettle. One room is en-suite, and there are also two other lovely modern bathrooms. Communal lounge on the ground floor. Bring your own bedding. HYB has wireless internet connection for laptops.

DETAILS

- **Open** - All year, all day
- **Number of beds** - 16: 4 x4
- **Booking** - Please phone or email.
- **Price per night** - £18 per person
- **Public Transport** - Buses stop at Eldon square (1 minute walk) and links with main train stations at Machynlleth and Barmouth for connections to the Midlands and London
- **Directions** - HYB is above Medi - the last shop before the main bridge on the one way system out of Eldon square. By car, turn into Y Marian car park and take a sharp left behind the public loos into HyB car park through the double wooden gates.

CONTACT:
2-3 Heol y Bont (Bridge St), Dolgellau, Gwynedd, LL40 1AU
Tel: 01341 421755
medi-hyb@tiscalli.com   www.medi-gifts.com

CROWN LODGE
GROUP ACCOMMODATION

Crown Lodge, in Snowdonia National Park, sleeps 19 and is ideal for groups who require twin and single bedrooms. It is owned by Coleg Harlech WEA and is often used for educational purposes. It offers good basic no-frills accommodation (VisitWales 2 star) with ample parking and views over the miles of sandy beach at Tremadog Bay. There is a kitchen for self catering and meals can be provided with prior notice. All bedding is provided but bring your own towels.

The area is a haven for anyone who enjoys walking, climbing, sailing, fishing, pony trekking or cycling. Crown Lodge is within ¼ mile of Harlech town centre with its pubs, cafes, small shops, Harlech Castle and Theatr Ardudwy. The prestigious Royal St David's links golf course, considered to be the most difficult par 69 in the world, is nearby.

DETAILS

- **Open** - All year, key provided
- **Number of beds** - 19: 8 x 2, 3 x 1
- **Booking** - Booking is essential, non-refundable deposit of £60 required, full payment due 6 weeks prior to start date.
- **Price per night** - Sole use of property £470 - £2,100 per week – shorter periods available on request
- **Public Transport** - Harlech train station ¼ mile, limited bus service passes the property.
- **Directions** - Please apply for directions when booking.

CONTACT: Valmai Owen
Ffordd Isaf, Harlech, Gwynedd, LL46 2PR
Tel: 01766 781927
accom@fc.harlech.ac.uk   www.harlech-holidays.com

BALA
BUNK HOUSE

The bunkhouse is a converted 200-year-old Welsh stone building. It carries WTB two star approval and is set back from the road in over an acre of picturesque grounds with a river and stream. Modernised to provide accommodation for outdoor activity groups, it is light, airy and comfortable with night storage heating and drying facilities. There is a large lounge / dining area and bunk rooms for 2, 4 and 8 plus annexe for 6. Separate ladies' and gentlemen's toilets have washing areas and hot showers. Fully equipped self-catering kitchen. The Little Cottage, a large converted self-contained bunkroom sleeping 6, with kitchenette, shower and toilet/washing area, is ideal for smaller groups & families. Sheets & pillowcases are provided - bring a sleeping bag.

There is a splendid view of the Berwyn Hills; together with the Aran and Arenig hills they provide superb walking. Bala Lake and the National White Water Centre are brilliant for water sports. Good pubs, restaurants and shops in Bala.

DETAILS

- **Open** - All year, no restrictions
- **Number of beds** - 26 : 1x2 : 1x4 : 1x6 : 1x8. 1x6 self-contained
- **Booking** - Book if possible, ring or write with 20% deposit. Weekends are busy.
- **Price per night** - Single night £16 pp, two or more nights £15 pp.
- **Public Transport** - Trains at Wrexham (30 miles). National Express at Corwen (10 miles). Local buses call at Bala (1.6 miles from hostel). Call hostel for a taxi.
- **Directions** - GR 950 372. From England take M6, M54, A5 through Llangollen then A494 for Bala. We are on the A494 1.5 miles before Bala.

CONTACT: Guy and Jane Williams
Tomen Y Castell, Llanfor, Bala, Gwynedd, LL23 7HD
Tel: 01678 520738, Fax: 01678 520738
thehappyunion@btinternet.com www.balabunkhouse.co.uk

BALA
BACKPACKERS

For Outdoor Adventures within the Snowdonia National Park, Bala Backpackers is Hostel-Style Good-Value Self-Catering Accommodation offering 30 Comfy SINGLE BEDS, 3 Private TWIN ROOMS and a Double Holiday-Let, in 1800's Character Buildings, located in a quiet, sunny chapel square, in the bustling market town of Bala, Mid North Wales. It is clean, safe and nice for the price with a careful, old, arty, homely atmosphere, with hints of Luxury, now called Posh-Packing! From 2010 there are 4-Star Showers, Bedrooms, Wet-Room, Dining Facilities & Guest Kitchen. Catering is available. Bala boasts a five-mile-long Lake, a white-water river for raft rides, and nestles beneath three 900metre Peaks. The Lake-side, River and Leisure pursuits are 5 mins walk away. Plan your activities or just soak up the atmosphere by day or evening, in Town.

DETAILS

■ **Open** - All year by arrangement, reception 5pm-10pm and 8am-10am.12pm curfew
■ **Number of beds** - Hostel: 30: 2x2,4x4,2x5 + 3 Twin Rooms + Double Holiday-Let.
■ **Booking** - On-line or by phone or email.
■ **Price per night** - Hostel: 1st Night £15, 2nd Night £14, 3rd & All Nights £13.50. Weekly £90. Twin room: £45, £55 ensuite. Holiday-Let: £365/week. One-Night-Supplement for groups. All prices Include Bedding.
■ **Public Transport** - Trains: Wrexham (30 miles) or Barmouth (30miles). Bus no 94 every 2 hours Daily from Wrexham and Barmouth.
■ **Directions** - GR 926 358. Bala is on A494. Turn in the middle of Bala High Street, opposite the White Lion Royal Hotel, down Tegid Street to see HOSTEL Sign. Unload outside Hostel, but park round corner, in FREE overnight Pay & Display.

CONTACT: Stella Welch
32 Tegid Street, Bala, LL23 7EL
Tel: 01678 521700
info@Bala-Backpackers.co.uk www.Bala-Backpackers.co.uk

Lletty - Lodge
ala-Backpackers.co.uk

On-line Booking or Tel: 01678 521 700

LLANGOLLEN
HOSTEL

Llangollen's independent hostel is a Victorian town house with plenty of charm and character. In the centre of town, it is an ideal spot to explore the magnificent Vale of Llangollen, which offers walking, climbing, canoeing, paragliding, mountain biking and many other activities.
We provide comfortable and clean accommodation with twin / double rooms, family en-suite rooms, and great value 6 bed dorms.   Light breakfast is available, or you can prepare your own food in the fully equipped self-catering kitchen. There is a lounge with log-burner, book exchange and wi-fi, plus a dining room, drying room and secure bicycle and kayak storage. Llangollen offers a great choice of restaurants and traditional pubs and is home to many cultural events, including the Fringe music festival and the annual International Eisteddfod. Other attractions include Valle Crucis Abbey, Telford's aqueduct, steam railway, Dinas Bran Castle, plus miles of superb scenery.

DETAILS

- **Open** - All year, all day
- **Number of beds** - 32
- **Booking** - Internet, e-mail or phone.
- **Price per night** - £17 dorm and en-suite private room (if full) inc. light breakfast.
- **Public Transport** - Daily National Express from London. Trains Ruabon (5 miles) – buses all day (every 15 mins until 6pm).
- **Directions** - From the A5 heading west, the hostel is located 50 yards past the main set of traffic lights on the right. Parking is at the rear of the hostel on Market Street – at the main traffic lights, turn right then first left.

CONTACT:
Isallt, Berwyn Street, Llangollen, LL20 8NB
Tel: 01978 861773, Mob: 07783 401894
info@llangollenhostel.co.uk www.llangollenhostel.co.uk

www.llangollenhostel.co.uk

Llangollen Hostel
EN-SUITE
01978 861773

Croeso

FFYNNON WEN
BUNKHOUSE

Ffynnon Wen is a fully catered luxury bunkhouse in the Hiraethog region at the heart of North Wales. This stunning and unspoilt landscape of rolling heather moor, deep forest and quiet lakes is ideal for exploration on foot, water, mountain bike and horseback. There are many mountain bike trails for all levels and opportunities for kayaking or canoeing. Go fly-fishing on the still waters of Llyn Brenig, take part in falconry at Parc Pen y Bryn, watch sheepdog demonstrations at Ewephoria or enjoy tree top thrills on the High Rope Course. The bunkhouse has six bunk rooms with adjacent rooms for group leaders. There is a drying room so your gear will be just as cosy as you, and secure bike storage. The bunkhouse is fully catered so sit back and enjoy a well earned hot meal after your day's exertions. Quality meals made with quality local ingredients together with a handy packed lunch service. You can also book outdoor adventure activities including family packages and stag / hen groups.

DETAILS

- **Open** - All year, all day
- **Number of beds** - 36: 2x8, 2x6, 1x4, 2x2
- **Booking** - Book by phone or email. Always pre-book. 25% deposit required.
- **Price per night** - Mar-Oct £18.50 (£13.50 for U'18's), Nov-Feb £15.50 (£10.50 for U'18's). Discounts for groups of 10+. Sole use £650 (min of two nights).
- **Public Transport** - Bus stop in village (2 miles). Trains at Wrexham & Llandudno Junction. National Express in Llangollen.
- **Directions** - Turn off the A5 about half a mile before Cerrigydrudion onto the B4501 (signposted to Bala). The hostels is a mile up the road on the right.

CONTACT: Kate
Canolfan Ffynnon Wen, Ty Nant, Cerrigydrudion, Conwy, LL21 0RH
Tel: 01490 420349
info@ffynnonwenbunkhouse.co.uk www.ffynnonwenbunkhouse.co.uk

Tyddyn Bychan is an 18th-century traditional Welsh farmhouse complex, set in two and a half acres of private grounds surrounded on all sides by farmland with a large parking area well away from the road.
Situated in an excellent location for cycling, walking, climbing, fishing and numerous watersports including whitewater rafting.

The main bunkhouse sleeps 18 in two en-suite rooms. All the bunks are handmade and of a very high standard. The smaller bunkhouse sleeps 12 in two en-suite rooms and has its own kitchen and conservatory. All bedding, heating and electricity are included. We can provide delicious pre-booked, homemade food in the farmhouse and make up packed lunches. The bunkhouses are also very well equipped for self-catering with a well equipped kitchen / dining room.

DETAILS

- **Open** - All year, all day
- **Number of beds** - 30:- 1x10 1x8 2x6
- **Booking** - Booking is advisable
- **Price per night** - £12pp including bedding.
- **Public Transport** - Nearest train station is at Betws-y-Coed. Nearest National Express service at Llandudno. Phone 01492 575412 for details.
- **Directions** - GR 931 504. Turn off A5 at Cerrig y drudion. Take B4501 out of village for Llyn Brenig, take the turning on left for Cefn Brith. After about 2 miles you will see a phone box on left, chapel on right and the road widens for a layby. The gate for Tyddyn is on the left directly opposite junction on the right.

CONTACT: Lynda
Cefn Brith, Conwy, LL21 9TS
Tel: 01490 420680
lynda@tyddynbychan.co.uk www.tyddynbychan.co.uk

HENDRE ISAF
BASECAMP

Hendre Isaf is a 400-year-old converted farm building of stone and slate construction situated on the Ysbyty Estate. The 8,000 hectare estate takes in 51 hill farms, 31 cottages, forested valleys and high open moorland known as the Migneint. The Basecamp, set in a peaceful part of Snowdonia 6 miles from Betws-y-Coed, is available for private hire by groups and by negotiation is free for volunteers undertaking conservation work for the National Trust.

Local attractions include the dry ski slope and Plas y Brenin National Mountain Centre at Capel Curig, shops, leisure centre and swimming pool at Llanrwst, seaside resorts of Rhyl, Prestatyn and Llandudno. The centre may be able to accommodate one person with special mobility needs - telephone for details of access. No pets permitted.

DETAILS

■ **Open** - All year, 24 hours
■ **Number of beds** - 17 in two dormitories on two floors
■ **Booking** - Early booking recommended (March to October is very busy). A non returnable deposit of £100 paid with booking (cheques payable to the National Trust).
■ **Price per night** - £12pp (£15 bank holidays). Minimum of 8 people.
■ **Public Transport** - Trains at Betws-y-Coed (6 miles), Llandudno Junction (20 miles) and Llanrwst (10 miles); National Express bus station at Llandudno. Some local buses to Betws-y-Coed, but we advise bringing your own transport.
■ **Directions** - Situated 6 miles SE of Betws-y-Coed near the junction of the A5 and the B4407 (signposted Ysbyty Ifan and Ffestiniog). GR855511 (OS sheet 116).

CONTACT: Dilys Jones
National Trust Ysbyty Estate Office, Dinas, Betws-y-Coed, Conwy, LL24 0HF
Tel: 01690 713321 / 710636, Fax: 01690 710678
dilysw.jones@nationaltrust.org.uk

The Eagles is a traditional inn offering real ales and a very friendly atmosphere. Wales Tourist Board 4 star graded. The private accommodation (no sharing with strangers) consists of 6 rooms sleeping 4 and 2 rooms sleeping 2. All rooms are centrally heated and with tea and coffee making facilities; duvets, pillows and sheets are supplied. A guest lounge, a fully equipped guest kitchen, secure bike storage and drying room are available.

The Eagles is situated on the edge of the peaceful village of Penmachno, in a secluded valley 4 miles south of Betws-y-Coed, within the heart of the Snowdonia National Park. The world class Penmachno Mountain Bike Trail is half a mile away. Snowdon itself is about 15 miles away. Surrounded by mountain scenery, this is ideal accommodation for groups or individuals walking, climbing, cycling or canoeing.

Self-catering cottages are also available.

DETAILS

- **Open** - All year, totally flexible
- **Number of beds** - 28: 6 x 4 : 2 x 2.
- **Booking** - Recommended, essential for groups
- **Price per night** - £16pp. Groups of 10 plus £14.50pp. Whole bunkhouse £350.
- **Public Transport** - Betws-y-Coed station 3.5miles. Bus 64 from Betws-y-Coed to Penmachno. From Ireland or London and points between London to Holyhead main line change at Llandudno Junction for Betws-y-coed.
- **Directions** - From A5, 2 miles east of Betws-y-Coed, at Conwy Falls Café, turn onto B4406 to Penmachno, cross bridge and The Eagles is in front of you.

CONTACT: Gerry or Linda McMorrow
Penmachno, Betws-y-Coed, Conwy, LL24 0UG
Tel: 01690 760177
inn@eaglespenmachno.co.uk www.eaglespenmachno.co.uk

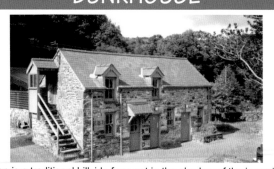

Bryn Tirion is a traditional hillside farm set in the shadow of the imposing tower of Dolwyddelan Castle, with magnificent views over the upper reaches of the Lledr Valley. The farm has a campsite, bed and breakfast accommodation and bunkhouse. The bunkhouse occupies the first floor of a traditional farm building and is a non smoking area. It consists of one room with a fully equipped kitchen area and 4 bunks (sleeps 8). A second unit of 2 bunks (sleeps 4) on the ground floor has its own kitchen. Both units have mattresses (bring your own sleeping bags). The toilet block (shared with the campsite) has hot showers, basins with hot & cold water, and shaving points. Situated at the foot of the mountain of Moel Siabod, Bryn Tirion is an ideal base for walking in the Snowdonia National Park. The farm is convenient for travelling to the popular village of Betws-y-Coed (6 miles), Llechwedd Slate Mines & Ffestiniog Railway at Blaenau Ffestiniog (5 miles), the Italianate village of Portmeirion (10 miles), Porthmadog (11 miles) and Bodnant Gardens (18 miles). The tranquil village of Dolwyddelan is a short stroll away with many paths to explore.
PLEASE CONTACT THIS HOSTEL BY PHONE OR POST.

DETAILS

- **Open** - All year, by arrangement
- **Number of beds** - 8: 1x8 and 4: 1x4
- **Booking** - Recommended (with deposit). CONTACT BY PHONE OR POST.
- **Price per night** - From £13pp. Camping £5pp, B&B from £32.50 to £35pp.
- **Public Transport** - Dolwyddelan train station ¾ mile away.
- **Directions** - On the A470, ¾ mile on the Ffestiniog side of Dolwyddelan at the foot of the prominent castle, and 6 miles from Betws-y-Coed.

CONTACT: Mrs Caroline Price
Bryn Tirion Farm, Dolwyddelan, Nr Betws-y-Coed, Sir Conwy, LL25 0JD
Tel: 01690 750366

Caban-Cysgu offers comfortable, purpose-built accommodation at the foot of the Carneddau in the Welsh-speaking village of Gerlan. Being a community-run bunkhouse, a warm welcome is guaranteed. This is an ideal location for walking in Snowdonia, and provides an obvious base for the '14 3000ft Peaks' long-distance challenge. Cyclists are welcome too, the hostel being within a mile of Sustrans route 'Lôn Las Ogwen'. Rock-climbing at Idwal is close at hand, as well as the Carneddau crags. The nearby Afon Ogwen provides a popular venue for canoeists.

For more leisurely pursuits, try visiting Coed Meurig, Penrhyn Castle or the Greenwood Centre. Shops, pubs and cafés in Bethesda are within walking distance.

DETAILS

- **Open** - All year, all day
- **Number of beds** - 16 : 1x5, 1x2, 1x1, 1x8
- **Booking** - Not essential, but recommended (with 20% non-returnable deposit).
- **Price per night** - From £12.50 - £15 (with concessions for group bookings and children).
- **Public Transport** - Bangor train station is 6 miles. Catch a bus from Bangor bus station to Gerlan (66), or Bethesda (fare £1.40). Taxi from Bangor approx. £10.
- **Directions** - GR 632665. Travelling south on the A5, turn left in the centre of Bethesda just before Spar. Bear right, go up the hill over 2 cross-roads. Caban-Cysgu is the old school on the left, about ½ mile from the A5.

CONTACT: Dewi Emyln, Manager
Ffordd Gerlan, Gerlan, Bethesda, Bangor, LL5 3TL
Tel: 01248 605573
dewi@cabancysgu-gerlan.co.uk www.cabancysgu-gerlan.co.uk

LLEDR
HOUSE

Nestled alongside the River Lledr in the heart of Snowdonia National Park, this former Quarry Manager's house is popular with travellers, walkers, schools, D of E and families. There is a large self-catering kitchen, dining room and television lounge, all centrally heated and with Wifi access. All bedding is provided in single, twin and family rooms plus a nine-bed dorm. We also offer a luxury self-contained cedar log cabin, sleeping 5, in the grounds.
Lledr House has a private riverside garden, bicycle shed and plenty of parking. It is surrounded by woodland walks and cycle trails. Betws-y-Coed (4 miles) and stunning Llyn Elsi are popular tourist sites. Within walking distance of a pub, one mile from a Spar shop (open daily until 9pm), and 25 minutes drive to Mount Snowdon. Just 2 miles from Moel Siabod.

DETAILS

- **Open** - All year (except Christmas week), check in from 5pm till 10.30pm.
- **Number of beds** - 31: 1x9, 2x4,1x6, 3x2, 2x1
- **Booking** - Bookings by phone or email held till 6pm. First nights deposit for larger groups.
- **Price per night** - £12.50 per person, £10 for children under 16. Sole use of hostel £295.
- **Public Transport** - Pont-y-Pant station on the Conwy Valley Line is ¾ mile away. On Sunday there are 2 buses a day instead of the train.
- **Directions** - On the A5 from Llangollen to Bangor turn left just before Betws-y-Coed onto the A470 (signposted Dolgellau). The hostel is 4 miles, just after the large playing field. Walking from Pont-y-Pant station, turn left and left again after stone road bridge.

CONTACT: Brian or Melanie Quilter
Pont-y-Pant, Dolwyddelan, North Wales, LL25 0DQ
Tel: 01690 750202. Mobile 07915 397705 or 07915 397660
Lledrhouse@aol.com www.ukyh.com

CONWY VALLEY
BACKPACKERS BARN

Conwy Valley Backpackers is situated on a peaceful working farm that has organic status, in the heart of the beautiful Conwy Valley with excellent access to Snowdonia. Centrally heated with fully equipped self-catering kitchen, log fires, hot showers and a fire alarm system. We have three separate dorms sleeping 4, 6 and 10, two of which have their own toilet facility. We can also provide secure bike / canoe storage, grazing for horses & tourist information.

Beside the barn is a small stream and guests may picnic and BBQ on the river bank. An ideal space for restoration, relaxation and retreat. Continental breakfast (£3.50) / packed lunch (£5) / and buffet suppers (£10) are available by arrangement. Local activities range from fishing and hiking to white water rafting and mountain biking, and there are some great pubs and eating places within walking distance. Groups are welcome. Dogs only by prior arrangement.

DETAILS

- **Open** - All year, all day
- **Number of beds** - 20: 1 x 4 : 1 x 6 : 1 x 10
- **Booking** - Not essential but recommended
- **Price per night** - From £15pp. Sole use from £250. £2.50pp bed linen hire.
- **Public Transport** - Train stations and coaches at Llandudno Junction and Conwy. Local bus 19 or 19a runs every 20 minutes from Conwy and Llandudno Junction, ask driver to drop you at Pyllau Gloewon farm gate.
- **Directions** - GR 769 697. Six miles south of Conwy on the B5106, look for Backpackers sign just before entering Tal-y-Bont.

CONTACT: Claudia or Helen
Pyllau Gloewon Farm, Tal-y-Bont, Conwy, Gwynedd, LL32 8YX
Tel: 01492 660504
claudia.bryan@btconnect.com www.conwyvalleybarn.com

LLANDUDNO
HOSTEL

James and Melissa would like to invite you to their charming Victorian 4 star hostel. We are a friendly hostel where individuals, families and groups (including schools) are welcome all year. Some of the guests comments: "friendliest hostel we've ever stayed in", "Wow isn't it clean", "these bathrooms are fabulous, as good as any hotel". Come and try us, we love to meet new people and look forward to getting to know you. Set in the heart of the Victorian seaside resort town of Llandudno, an ideal place to shop or explore the many varied local attractions. Excellent blue flag beaches, dry slope skiing, toboggan run, ten pin bowling, bronze age copper mine, traditional pier and many museums, fishing trips etc. Llandudno is within easy travelling distance to Snowdon, Bodnant Gardens and local castles. We are able to book local attractions for groups and secure some discounts.

DETAILS

- **Open** - All year. Telephone in winter prior to arrival , All day
- **Number of beds** - 46: 2x8 : 2x6 : 4x2 : 1x4 : 1 x family
- **Booking** - Essential April to July.
- **Price per night** - From £18 per person, £44 per private twin room, £48 per private twin en-suite. Group and family rates on request.
- **Public Transport** - Trains at Llandudno. Turn right as you exit station, cross road, turn left down Vaughan Street (towards the beach), left into Charlton Street.
- **Directions** - From the A55 take A470 and follow signs to Llandudno town centre, straight through all roundabouts, after Asda turn 3rd left into Vaughan Street (signed train station), then 1st right into Charlton Street. Hostel is No 14.

CONTACT: James
14 Charlton Street, Llandudno, LL30 2AA
Tel: 01492 877430
info@Llandudnohostel.co.uk   www.llandudnohostel.co.uk

OUTDOOR
ALTERNATIVE

Wonderfully situated in 7 acres of an Area of Outstanding Natural Beauty, 300m from a beach at the south end of Holy Island, Anglesey. Nearby Holyhead has rail links and ferries to Ireland. The centre is an excellent base for so much in the outdoors and is immediately adjacent to the Anglesey Coastal Path. There is spectacular geology, a range of habitats and species of marine life, birds and plants. There are prehistoric remains and good walking on a varied and accessible coast. Kayakers have classic sea tours, overfalls, playwaves, surf and rockhopping. Climbers have Gogarth nearby and Rhoscolyn offers all grades in an attractive setting. Divers can beach launch for wrecks and scenic marine life. Birdwatching is excellent. There are two self-contained units and camping with toilets and showers. We encourage careful energy use, composting & recycling. Walking distance to pub.

DETAILS

- **Open** - All year, 24 hour access
- **Number of beds** - 20: 2x2, 1x4, 2x6. 16: 1x3, 2x4,1x5.
- **Booking** - Essential
- **Price per night** - £16.35
- **Public Transport** - Trains at Holyhead (10km) (London direct 4.5 hrs) or Valley (5km). National Exp Valley (6km). Bus 23/25 Holyhead Rhoscolyn (1km) or 4 & 44 Holyhead-Four Mile Bridge (3km). Ferry: Holyhead - Dublin or Dun Laoghaire.
- **Directions** - GR SH 278 752. From A5 traffic lights at Y Fali/Valley take B4545 Trearddur. In 2km at Four Mile Bridge fork left at sign to Rhoscolyn 2miles. After 2km sharp left at camping symbols. In 800m fork right at large white gatepost.

CONTACT: Jacqui or Andy
Cerrig-yr-Adar, Rhoscolyn, Holyhead, Anglesey, LL65 2NQ
Tel: 01407 860469
enquiries@outdooralternative.co.uk www.outdooralternative.org

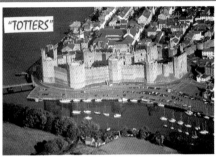

Totters is situated in the heart of the historic castle town of Caernarfon. Sheltered by the castle town wall, we are only 30 metres from the shores of the Menai Straits and get to see some fantastic sunsets. The town not only offers the visitor a huge selection of pubs and restaurants to choose from, but also acts as the perfect base for trips into the Snowdonia National Park. There is very good public transport in and out of the National Park.

The hostel is a 200-year-old, five floored town house, which is fully heated with all the comforts of home. We have a common room with TV and games, book exchange, dining room and a secure left luggage facility. The bedrooms sleep either 4 or 6 and can be arranged as mixed or single sex dorms. We also have what we call our 'Penthouse', a huge double en-suite with views over the Straits. This can be arranged as a family room

DETAILS

- **Open** - All year, all day access. Book in by 10pm.
- **Number of beds** - 30 : 4 x 6, 1 x4, 1 x 2 (en-suite)
- **Booking** - Booking is essential for groups in June, July, August and September.
- **Price per night** - £16pp. £47.50 for double en-suite. Discounts for groups.
- **Public Transport** - Bangor train station is 7 miles from the hostel. Catch a bus from outside the station to Caernarfon. National Express coaches drop off in Caernarfon 200m from the hostel.
- **Directions** - Coming by road:- follow signs for town centre, turn right 200m after the big Celtic Royal hotel, keep going and Totters is the last house on the left.

CONTACT: Bob/Henryette
Plas Porth Yr Aur, 2 High Street, Caernarfon, Gwynedd, LL55 1RN
Tel: 01286 672963, Mob 07979 830470
totters.hostel@googlemail.com www.totters.co.uk

YR HELFA
BUNKHOUSE

Yr Helfa is a traditional bunkhouse situated in the heart of the Snowdonia National Park. This former farmhouse has been carefully restored and will sleep up to 18 people in 3 comfortable rooms. It has underfloor heating, 3 shower rooms with toilet and sink and a coal fire in lounge. All bedding is supplied. Winner of the Green Snowdonia Project Low Carbon Award, it has a wind turbine, solar panels and a wood pellet boiler. Yr Helfa nestles directly at the foot of Moel Gynghorion with panoramic views from the Llanberis path around to Bwlch Masgwn (Telegraph Pass). It is in a mountain environment with direct access to a number of routes up Snowdon and yet only 20 minutes walk (1 mile) from Llanberis. The area is ideal for climbing, walking, fell running, horse riding and mountain biking. Award winning attractions include The Slate Museum, Electric Mountain, Dolbadarn Castle, Llanberis waterfall, Lake Railway and Snowdon Railway. Llanberis has several restaurants and plenty of pubs.

DETAILS

- **Open** - All year, all day
- **Number of beds** - 18: 3x6
- **Booking** - Availability and booking form on website. Book by post, 30% deposit.
- **Price per night** - Whole Bunkhouse - £150 per night, 7 nights £1,000. Shared occupancy - Smaller groups £12 per person per night, each room sleeps six.
- **Public Transport** - Trains at Bangor (10 miles). Buses from Llanberis to Caernarfon and Bangor every half hour.
- **Directions** - The bunkhouse is on the road to the beginning of the Llanberis Snowdon track. Carry on past the track and it is the first gate on your right. Park in the parking area then walk ten minutes down another track.

CONTACT: Jane O'Donnell
Grove House, 18 High Street, Llanberis, Gwynedd, LL55 4EN
Tel: 0790 0087692
yrhelfa@hotmail.co.uk   www.snowdonbunkhouse.co.uk

Pentre Bach provides alpine style bunkhouse accommodation, outdoor activities and a campsite. The camping barn has two floors. The ground floor has tables with benches and a cooking area with gas burners, 2 microwaves, fridge and freezer. Upstairs are alpine sleeping platforms with mattresses for 16. Toilets with washing facilities and showers, shared with the campsite, are just across the yard. Based between Waunfawr and Betws Garmon, Pentre Bach is surrounded by the superb scenery of Moel Eilio and Mynydd Mawr and has views towards Mount Snowdon. There are great walks from the barn or take a short car journey to the Nantlle ridge and the main footpaths up Snowdon (Ranger and Rhyd Ddu). Bach Ventures provide a variety of outdoor activities, whether you wish to be guided around the hills, try kayaking, climbing, or have an adventure gorge-scrambling.

DETAILS

- **Open** - All year, enquiries 9am until 10pm. Arrival after 4pm.
- **Number of beds** - 16: 1x16
- **Booking** - One night's deposit, balance payable on arrival. Short notice bookings accepted by phone or email.
- **Price per night** - £8.50 per person (inc gas / electric / showers). Sole use bookings negotiable according to group size.
- **Public Transport** - Train station at Bangor. S4 bus from Caernarfon to Beddgelert stops at the bottom of the drive on request.
- **Directions** - GR 531 579. At Pentre Bach just south of Waunfawr on the Caernarfon to Beddgelert road (A4085). Look for Camping Barn sign.

CONTACT: Karen Neil
Pentre Bach, Waunfawr, Caernarfon, Gwynedd, LL54 7AJ
Tel: 01286 650643
info@bachventures.co.uk www.bachventures.co.uk

CRAFLWYN
BASECAMP

The historic Craflwyn Estate dates back to 1200 AD. Having been part of a monastery, a family residence and a Victorian hunting lodge, it is now a fully resourced conference and activity centre. The bunkhouse, located in the old stables, accommodates 12 people and can be divided into 2 self-contained units of 7 and 5 beds. There is a dining / lounge area and a large kitchen.

Craflwyn is set in a stunning location at the foot of Snowdon, in the Nantgwynant valley, with dramatic views and a magical atmosphere. The village of Beddgelert can be reached on foot via a riverside footpath. The village has pubs, bistros, cafés, shops and an information centre. Snowdon and the legendary Dinas Emrys are both on the doorstep and a wide range of beaches, historic houses, gardens and archaeological sites are all within easy reach. The hall offers en-suite accommodation and sleeps 14 people.

DETAILS

- **Open** - All year, all day. Office hours 9am-5pm Mon-Fri.
- **Number of beds** - 12 (2 self-contained units of 7 and 5 beds)
- **Booking** - 33% non-returnable deposit to secure the booking. Full payment due 10 weeks in advance.
- **Price per night** - Check website for latest prices. Two night minimum stay. Bank holidays 15% extra.
- **Public Transport** - Trains at Bangor and Porthmadog. Local buses stop nearby.
- **Directions** - Craflwyn Hall is approximately ¾ mile outside Beddgelert on the A498 towards Capel Curig.

CONTACT: Eirian Jones
The National Trust, Craflwyn, Beddgelert, Gwynedd, LL55 4NG
Tel: 01766 510120
eirian.jones@nationaltrust.org.uk www.craflwyn.org

SNOWDON LODGE
GROUP HOSTEL

Stay in the birthplace of Lawrence of Arabia! Snowdon Lodge hostel provides comfortable self-catering style group accommodation in a large grade 2 listed character building. The property is located in the picturesque village of Tremadog. Snowdon Lodge is perfect for a family reunion or simply as a base for a group of friends to explore this beautiful part of Snowdonia and the nearby Lleyn Peninsula. The hostel has 10 rooms of different sizes (twins, doubles and small dormitories). Bathroom and shower facilities are shared. There is a large fully equipped self-catering kitchen, a dining room seating 36, 2 lounge/TV rooms with real log fires in winter, a drying room and a private car park leading to extensive woodland walks. Snowdon Lodge is ideally positioned just 6 miles from Mount Snowdon, yet only 2 miles from beautiful beaches such as Black Rock Sands beach. The famous Italianate village Portmerion is also only 4 miles from the hostel. Within a mile are the Ffestiniog and Welsh Highland railways, the famous Tremadog rocks for climbers. Sorry, no stag or hen parties.

DETAILS

- **Open** - January – December , all day access
- **Number of beds** - 30 (sleeps a max. of 35 people): twins, doubles, small dorms
- **Booking** - Essential.
- **Price per night** - Sole use £450 per night. Minimum 2 nights, Bank Holidays minimum 3 nights.
- **Public Transport** - Half mile from Porthmadog train station and 250 yards from National Express coach stop.
- **Directions** - Half a mile from Porthmadog on Caernarfon road (A487).

CONTACT: Carl or Anja
Lawrence House, Tremadog, Nr Porthmadog, Snowdonia, LL49 9PS
Tel: 01766 515354
info@snowdonlodge.co.uk www.snowdonlodge.co.uk

CWM PENNANT
WALES **HOSTEL / TRAINING CENTRE**

Cwm Pennant Hostel is a 52 bed independent hostel offering relaxed accommodation for individuals, families and groups. It also offers residential adventure activities for groups provided by Outdoor UK Ltd. The hostel is set within stunning grounds in the Snowdonia National Park and has fantastic views of the Cwm Pennant valley and Moel Hebog. It is 6 miles from Porthmadog.

Cwm Pennant Hostel has a lounge, drying room, home cooked food and on-site parking. A self-catering kitchen may also be available. Currently guests have access to tea / coffee making facilities, a fridge and a microwave. A range of additional facilities are available including a power washer for mountain bikes and secure storage for bikes, kayaks and canoes. The area is ideal for hill walking, rock climbing and canoeing.

DETAILS

- **Open** - Open to advance bookings all year round, 7:30-12am; 5-10pm
- **Number of beds** - 52: 5 x 4, 1 x 8, 1 x 10, 1 x 14
- **Booking** - Advance booking is recommended and a deposit is required.
- **Price per night** - B&B £18 (adult) and £14.50 (under-18). Full-board £32.50 (adult) and £25.50 (under-18).
- **Public Transport** - Porthmadog train station is 6 miles away. Take the number 1 bus towards Caernarfon and get off at the Cwm Pennant turning on the A487. From here follow the brown hostel signs - 1 mile walk to the hostel.
- **Directions** - From Porthmadog take the A487 towards Caernarfon. Turn right after passing through Penmorfa village and follow the brown hostel signs.

CONTACT:
Golan, Garndolbenmaen, Gwynedd, LL51 9AQ
Tel: 01766 530888
info@cwmpennanthostel.com www.cwmpennanthostel.com

The Stone Barn and Studio are converted farm buildings at Tyddyn Morthwyl Farm and Caravan Park near Criccieth on the fringe of Snowdonia.

The farm provides a good centre for climbing and walking in Snowdonia and the Lleyn Peninsula. Tremadog Rocks (an all-year rock climbing venue) is only 7 miles away. Canoeing and wind surfing nearby.

The Barn has an alpine style sleeping platform. Hot showers and toilets are shared with the caravan park. There is a wood burning stove for heating and clothes drying (wood provided free) and a kitchen area with fridge and water. There is also The Studio, a small stone building with two single beds and wash basin, and a static caravan to let.

Several pubs in the locality serve good bar meals.

DETAILS

- **Open** - All year, flexible
- **Number of beds** - 12
- **Booking** - 48 hrs advanced booking required, with one night's fee as deposit.
- **Price per night** - £8 per person in the Stone Barn including wood (discount for groups). £9 per person in the Studio.
- **Public Transport** - Criccieth has a train station and National Express coach service. The hostel is 1.25 miles from Criccieth and a taxi service is available.
- **Directions** - 1.25 miles from Criccieth on B4411 Caernarfon road.

CONTACT: Mrs Trumper
Tyddyn Morthwyl, Criccieth, Gwynedd, LL52 0NF
Tel: 01766 522115
trumper@yrhenstabal.freeserve147.co.uk

SGUBOR UNNOS
BUNKHOUSE

Croeso Welcome. Sgubor Unnos provides luxury bunkhouse accommodation on a Welsh speaking, traditionally run, family farm in the village of Llangian, one mile from Abersoch, famous for it's watersports and surfing beaches, Hell's Mouth and Porth Ceiriad. Centrally located, it is the ideal centre for outdoor activities including walking the newly opened Llyn Coast Path, surfing, cycling, golf, fishing and sailing. Situated a few miles from Llangian, at the tip of the Peninsula lies Bardsey Island where 20,000 saints are buried!! Why not pay them a visit? Trips around the island for it's wildlife and heritage can be arranged. The modern bunkhouse offers 3 bedrooms ideal for individuals or groups. Fully equipped kitchen / lounge, disabled facilities, covered BBQ area, secure storage, private parking, traditional village shop, post office and phone 500m away. For details on area see www.abersoch-holiday.co.uk .
Photos taken by Tony Jones, www.llynlight.co.uk

DETAILS

- **Open** - All year, all day
- **Number of beds** - 14: 2 x 4 : 1 x 6
- **Booking** - Not essential but recommended.
- **Price per night** - £16 (adult), £8 (under 10 years), including a light breakfast. Discount for more than 2 nights.
- **Public Transport** - Nearest train station is Pwllheli (7 miles). Good local bus and taxi service to Llangian. Public transport details on web site.
- **Directions** - GR 296 288 On entering Abersoch from Pwllheli, take the right hand turning up the hill signed to Llangian (follow brown signs). On left on leaving village.

CONTACT: Phil or Meinir
Fferm Tanrallt Farm, Llangian, Abersoch, Gwynedd, LL53 7LN
Tel: 01758 713527
tanrallt@btconnect.com www.tanrallt.com

South Scotland

SKYE

396-398
395
393,394
392
391
405
406
Inverness 381
383 382
874
Aviemore
384,386
388 Newtonmore 371
387 370

389
Mallaig
EIGG 390
367
360 368
362,364
Fort William 356 359
365
366
354 353
Kinlochleven
352
338
329
TIREE
347
350
MULL 349
Oban
342-345
330 332,334
328
326 327
324
348
321
322
320 Stirling
346
COLONSAY
314-316
Tarbert
319
Glasgow

ARRAN
318
317
Ayr

307
Castle
Douglas
Stranraer
306

| 0 | miles | 50 |
| 0 | kilometres | 80 |

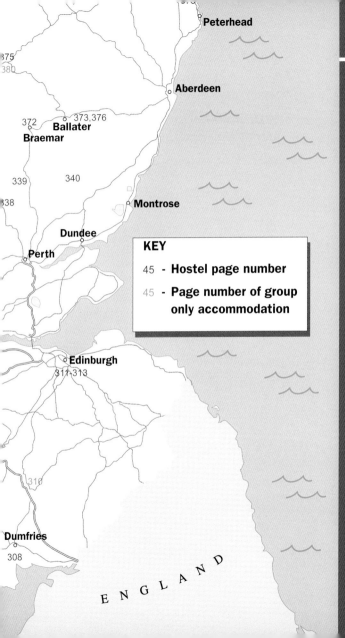

Peterhead

Aberdeen

375
380

372
Ballater
373,376
Braemar

339
340
338

Montrose

Dundee

Perth

KEY

45 - Hostel page number

45 - Page number of group only accommodation

Edinburgh
311-313

316

Dumfries
308

E N G L A N D

KEY

45 - **Hostel page number**

45 - **Page number of group only accommodation**

miles 0 ——— 50

kilometres 0 ——— 80

Durness 416

404

Stornoway 402,403

LEWIS

415

Ullapool
410

HARRIS 401

408
409

Gairloch

NORTH UIST

407

406

405

Portree

SKYE
396-398

383

382

395 393,394 391

384,386
388
387

392

Mallaig 389

SOUTH UIST

360 368
367 362,364
390 365
EIGG **Fort William** 356-359

BARRA
400

366 354 353

Kinlochleven
352

ORKNEY

429
428
427
426
425
423,424   Kirkwall
Stromness   422
420
419

Thurso   John O'Groats
418

413
Helmsdale
411

412 414
Inverness
381

374   375
Aviemore
380
370   371
Newtonmore
372   373,376
Braemar
339   340

Pitlochry 338
329,336

433
432   430
Lerwick
SHETLAND

Fraserburgh
378
Peterhead

Aberdeen

Ballater

Montrose

Castle Creavie Hayloft has recently been converted to a comfortable, family-friendly, camping barn. The ground floor has utility sinks, small area for kettle and microwave, shower room and toilet. Upstairs is the carpeted loft with 4 single beds and balcony doors opening to spectacular unspoiled views of the Galloway countryside. Bring your own sleeping bag or hire the bed-linen/duvets at £3.00 p.p.per stay. Breakfast available at the farmhouse if pre-booked. Guests are welcome to enjoy the farm footpaths and observe the daily life on this working sheep farm. Enjoy freshly baked bread and cakes, honey, and our own home reared lamb, pork and bacon.

Castle Creavie is named after the two Iron Age forts and is situated 4 miles from the popular harbour town of Kirkcudbright which has a good range of pubs, cafes and restaurants. Galloway is famed for its many castles, abbeys, first-class walking, long sandy beaches, and the Stanes.

DETAILS

- **Open** - All year, all day
- **Number of beds** - 4: 1x4
- **Booking** - Book by phone. Deposit required by post.
- **Price per night** - £12 pp. £3 to hire bedding.
- **Public Transport** - 4 miles from Kirkcudbright citylink services.
- **Directions** - From the A75 take the A711 to Kirkcudbright. In the town centre turn left at the Royal Hotel onto the B727 (Gelston), pass the cemetery and at the next road junction go straight on (Auchencairn / Dundrennan). Follow for approx 4 miles.

CONTACT: Charlie and Elaine Wannop
Castle Creavie, Kirkcudbright, Dumfries and Galloway, DG6 4QE
Tel: 01557 500238, Fax: 01557 500238
castle.creavie@btinternet.com www.castlecreavie.co.uk/

Whether you require a fully residential activity holiday or just a self catering base while you explore the Southern Upland Way or tackle the 7 Stanes, we offer accommodation to suit all requirements. Our Lodge has all the creature comforts you require after a hard day outdoors including fully self catered kitchen, hot shower rooms, dining area and TV sofa area for relaxing. There are launderette facilities on site and a drying room for wet kit.

We offer a range of activities from sailing, windsurfing, power boating, kayaking, canoeing, outdoor laser quest, archery, fishing, mountain biking and climbing, From instructor training to family fun days out. We have a new fleet of Trek 4300 disc mountain bikes for hire, fantastic trails from the doorstep and we are equi-distant between four of the 7 Stanes mountain venues. Our aim is to give you a memorable holiday experience in a safe friendly family atmosphere

DETAILS

- **Open** - All year, 9am-6pm (late arrivals catered for)
- **Number of beds** - 20: 5 x 4
- **Booking** - Preferable – the more notice the more likely we can take you. Last minute avaialabilty if space permits.
- **Price per night** - £15.00 pp or £13.50 for four or more people. Blankets or duvets provided at £5 pp for duration of stay.
- **Public Transport** - Just 1.5 hours from Glasgow and Carlisle and 1 hour from Prestwick and Dumfries. Buses (limited!) from Castle Douglas to the centre.
- **Directions** - Located on the A713 at the North East end of Loch Ken, in Dumfries and Galloway (SW Scotland).

CONTACT: Richard or Kieran
Parton, Loch Ken, Castle Douglas, Dumfries and Galloway DG7 3NQ
Tel: 01644 420626
gsc@lochken.co.uk www.lochken.co.uk

MARTHROWN
SCOTLAND OF MABIE BUNKHOUSE

Marthrown is set in the heart of Mabie Forest, about 6 miles south of Dumfries. It has a traditional sauna, a wood burning spring water hot tub, a large BBQ, garden areas and plenty of room for groups. The forest itself has newly developed mountain bike routes, ranging in length and difficulty. Bike hire is nearby as is the 7 Stanes mountain bike trails. Although we are a self-catering hostel meals are available to order.

Marthrown is suitable for all age groups. Facilities include secure dry store for bikes and equipment and a large dining area suitable for meetings. For something a little different why not try staying in the Roundhouse or Yurt. For more info see our web site below.

DETAILS

- **Open** - All year, 24 hours
- **Number of beds** - 26: 1x8:1x7:1x6:1x5 + Roundhouse, Yurt and Tipi
- **Booking** - Telephone a few days in advance.
- **Price per night** - £16-£17.50. Duvet £3.00.
- **Public Transport** - From Dumfries (White Sands) take the Stagecoach bus service 372 to Mabie Forest. It is best to arrive in daylight. 1.5 mile walk from road.
- **Directions** - From Dumfries take A710 (west) to Mabie Forest passing through the village of Islesteps. Turn right signposted Mabie Forest and Mabie House Hotel. Follow tarmac road over speed bumps to the end of the Hotel and Forest Rangers Office, through courtyard and onto forest track, Marthown is signposted and is exactly one mile into the forest.

CONTACT: Mike or Pam Hazlehurst
Mabie Forest, Dumfries, DG2 8HB
Tel: 01387 247900
mike@marthrown.com www.marthrown.com

WELL ROAD CENTRE
SCOTLAND GROUP ACCOMMODATION

The Well Road Centre is a large Victorian house set in its own grounds in the charming spa town of Moffat. The centre is ideal for youth groups, adult groups, conferences, residential workshops, sports events, multiple family gatherings and outdoor activity clubs. All rooms are fully carpeted and centrally heated. There are two spacious meeting rooms, a large bright self-catering kitchen fully equipped for 65, a games hall for indoor sports, a table tennis room and a snooker room. The are 13 bedrooms of various sizes, two of them with en-suite facilities. Two separate toilet/shower areas for mixed groups. Bring your own sleeping bags or duvets. Ample parking for cars, minibuses and equipment trailers and the nearby park can be used for football matches.

Moffat is in the Southern Uplands, an hour from Edinburgh and Glasgow. Ideal area for golfers, bird watchers, walkers and cyclists. All groups have sole use.

DETAILS

- **Open** - All year, all day
- **Number of beds** - 70: in 13 rooms (2 en-suite)
- **Booking** - Check availability and send £100 deposit to secure booking.
- **Price per night** - From £600 for two nights for up to 30 people. £20 per person for 31 people or more.
- **Public Transport** - Trains at Lockerbie(16m). Citylink bus to Glasgow/Edinburgh.
- **Directions** - From A74 take Moffat turning and enter the High Street (town square). Turning to the right around the shops on the south side of the square, follow Holm St to the T-junction. Turn left into Burnside, following up and right into Well Rd.

CONTACT: Ben Larmour
Huntly Lodge, Well Road, Moffat, DG10 9JT
Tel: 01683 221040
Ben8363@aol.com www.wellroadcentre.co.uk

CASTLE ROCK
HOSTEL
SCOTLAND

In a wonderful location, facing south with a sunny aspect and panoramic views over the city, Castle Rock Hostel is just steps away from the City Centre with the historic Royal Mile, the busy pubs and late-late nightlife of the Grassmarket and Cowgate, and of course the Castle. Most of the rooms have no traffic noise, there are loads of great facilities, 24 hour reception and no curfew.

With its beautiful and dramatic skyline Edinburgh is truly one of the world's great cities. The cobbled streets of the Old Town lead past mysterious gothic buildings up to the magnificent castle. Below the castle's rocky pinnacle lies the New Town's 200 year old Georgian splendour.

DETAILS

- **Open** - All year, 24 hours
- **Number of beds** - 235
- **Booking** - Booking not always essential. First nights payment needed to book
- **Price per night** - From £13 per person. ID required for check-in.
- **Public Transport** - 5/10 minute walk from Edinburgh Bus Stn and Waverley Train Stn. (taxis £3-£5). Airport bus goes to train station so it's easy to get to the hostel.
- **Directions** - 10 minutes walk from Waverley Train Station – turn left out of the station and continue to small roundabout. Cross over and continue up Cockburn Street to the top. Turn right onto the Royal Mile and follow uphill towards the Castle. Take the left fork at the Hub (church) and the hostel is situated 200 yards on the left side of Johnston Terrace next to two red telephone boxes. By Car – follow signs for City Centre towards the Castle turning onto Royal Mile uphill towards the castle then left fork at the Hub on to Johnston Terrace.

CONTACT: Receptionist
15 Johnston Terrace, Edinburgh, EH1 2PW
Tel: 0131 225 9666
castlerock@scotlandstophostels.com www.scotlandstophostels.com

HIGH STREET
HOSTEL

The High Street Hostel has become a hugely popular destination for world travellers since opening in 1985 and is one of Europe's best regarded and most atmospheric hostels.

Located just off the historic Royal Mile in a 400 year old building it is the perfect base for exploring all the city's attractions – and of course its wonderful nightlife!

Providing excellence in location, ambience and facilities, the hostel is highly recommended by more than ten of the world's top backpacker travel guides.

DETAILS

- **Open** - All year, 24 hours
- **Number of beds** - 152
- **Booking** - Booking in advance not always essential, 1 nights payment for booking.
- **Price per night** - From £13 pp
- **Public Transport** - Only a 5/10 minute walk from Edinburgh bus station or Waverley train station. Taxis cost between £3-£5 from each. The airport bus also stops outside the train station on the last stop so it is very easy to get to the hostel.
- **Directions** - From the bus station (St Andrews Square) turn left onto Princes Street then first right onto Northbridge. At top turn left onto the High Street on the Royal Mile and hostel is on Blackfriars St. on right. From railway station turn right then straight ahead up the Mound, at the junction go left, then at cross roads left again going down hill. After the traffic lights Blackfriars St is second on the left. From airport take bus 100 to last stop, Waverley Bridge (same instructions from Waverley Bridge).

CONTACT: Reception
8 Blackfriars Street, Edinburgh, EH1 1NE
Tel: 0131 557 3984
highstreet@scotlandstophostels.com www.scotlandstophostels.com

Royal Mile Backpackers is a small and lively hostel with its own special character. Its size means that you will quickly come to make friends with which to explore the town and swap travelling tales. Step outside and be on the doorstep of one of the most vibrant and exciting cities in Scotland! Enjoy the benefit of access to the lively bustling High Street with its wide range of facilities. Guests who stay with us can join our free walking tour of the Old Town which leaves from our sister hostel High Street Hostel on weekends. Only a few minutes walk from the castle and handy for just about everything!

DETAILS

- **Open** - All year, all day, Reception 7am – 3am (24hrs during August)
- **Number of beds** - 48
- **Booking** - Booking not always essential, first nights payment required for booking.
- **Price per night** - From £13 per person. ID required for check-in.
- **Public Transport** - Only a 5/10 minute walk from both Edinburgh bus station and Waverley train station. A taxi costs between £3-£5 from each. The airport bus also stops out side the train station on the last stop so it's very easy to get to the hostel.
- **Directions** - From main bus station turn left onto Princes Street then take first right onto Northbridge. At top turn left onto the High St. on the Royal Mile. From train station take the Princes Street exit (up Waverley Steps), at top go right then right again up Northbridge, then left at cross roads, hostel's on the left above the Oxfam Shop. From airport take bus no.100 to city centre, get off at Waverley Bridge. Walk away from Princes St. towards the roundabout, go over roundabout onto Cockburn Street. At the top of Cockburn Street turn left onto the High St. on the Royal Mile. Cross traffic lights at Northbridge and hostel is on left above the Oxfam Shop.

CONTACT: Receptionist
105 High Street, Edinburgh, EH1 1SG
Tel: 0131 557 6120
royalmile@scotlandstophostels.com www.scotlandstophostels.com

Cairncross House is in an excellent location within walking distance of the trendy West End and City Centre and is close to public transport. The West End is great for pubs and restaurants and has lots of good value places to eat. Nearby you will find some of Glasgow's top visitor attractions: Art Gallery and Museum, Transport Museum, University of Glasgow and its Visitor Centre, Hunterian Museum and Art Gallery.

The City Centre offers great shopping, clubs and pubs. The Hostel is part of the University of Glasgow's student residence and offers great value for money. Modern, well equipped with bed linen, wash basin in room, cooking facilities, showers, free laundry facilities and common room. Awarded the silver award for green tourism.

DETAILS

- **Open** - June to September, 8.00 am - 10.00 pm
- **Number of beds** - 242
- **Booking** - Advised but not essential, Booking address: Residential Services, University of Glasgow, 73 Great George Street, Glasgow, G12 8RR
- **Price per night** - £19.25 (inc. VAT) per person
- **Public Transport** - Buchanan Street Bus Station, Central Station and Queen Street Station are all 2 miles away. The nearest underground station is Kelvinhall (half mile) From George Square take buses 6 or 16, ask for Kelvinhaugh/Radnor St.
- **Directions** - From George St take St Vincent St, which becomes Argyle St after 1 mile. Through traffic lights take third left into Kelvinhaugh St, Cairncross House is on the right. From M8 J19 take A814 to Finnieston. Turn right into Finnieston St, continue to traffic lights and turn left into Argyle St. Kelvinhaugh St is third on the left.

CONTACT:
20 Kelvinhaugh Place, Glasgow, G3 8NH
Tel: 0141 330 4116/2318 or 0141 221 9334
vacationaccom@gla.ac.uk www.glasgow.ac.uk/cvso

EURO HOSTEL
GLASGOW

'Glasgow's Only City Centre Hostel' providing budget en-suite accommodation in Glasgow City Centre, only 2 minutes walk from Central Station. Ideally suited for international visitors to discover the city's cultural heritage and vibrant nightlife or convenient for guests to stay over after a concert or night out clubbing. We welcome groups of all sizes throughout the year and make an ideal choice for sports teams, concertgoers and school / college parties. Facilities include the 'Osmosis' bar, games room, chill-out lounges with Big-screen TV and SKY, 24hr reception, internet access, self-catering kitchen, guest laundry, luggage storage and free bike storage.

There are TVs in all the twin and double rooms and FREE WiFi.

DETAILS

- **Open** - All year, all day
- **Number of beds** - 364: Singles, 2, 4, 8 and 14 person all en-suite
- **Booking** - Individuals with credit card. Groups - 20% deposit required. Book on-line at www.euro-hostels.co.uk
- **Price per night** - From £12.95 B&B pp en-suite. Discount for mid-week bookings and long stays. Apply for group discounts.
- **Public Transport** - Central Railway Station 2 mins, Queen Street Railway Station 7 mins, Buchanan Bus Station 10 mins, Glasgow Airport 8 miles.
- **Directions** - From the bus station turn right into North Hanover St and right into West George St (past Queen St train station). Turn left into Buchanan St and right down Argyle Street (left if arriving from Central train station). Go down Jamaica St and the hostel is on the corner joining Clyde St.

CONTACT: Reception
318 Clyde Street, Glasgow, G1 4NR
Tel: 0141 222 2828, Fax: 0141 222 2829
glasgow@euro-hostels.co.uk www.euro-hostels.co.uk

This bunkhouse in a tranquil, rural setting is ideal for your group accommodation. The Isle of Arran is one of the most accessible Scottish islands; it's only a one hour ferry trip from the mainland. It offers the visitor hill-walking, mountaineering, golf, fishing, cycling, pony trekking and a bewildering choice of extreme sports. The bunkhouse is affordable, modern, comfortable and able to sleep up to 23. We supply all the bed linen, so no need to bring anything except your towels and of course, your food! We have a great, contemporary kitchen with all you'll need. Attached to the bunkhouse is the village hall which can provide extra rooms and an auditorium at extra cost. Ideal for educational groups, weddings, music workshop groups, clubs or any group needing extra facilities. We look forward to welcoming your family, club, group, school or any combination of these except stag parties!   Phone or email with your queries. Registered Scottish Charity SC028200.

DETAILS

- **Open** - All year, 24 hours
- **Number of beds** - 23: 2 x 8, 1 x 4 (en-suite) 1 x 3 (en-suite)
- **Booking** - Book ahead, 40% deposit. £100 security deposit on arrival.
- **Price per night** - £15 per person for groups of 15+. £20 per person for smaller groups.
- **Public Transport** - Buses stop on demand directly outside the Hall and Bunkhouse. These buses meet all the ferries that arrive and depart from the main ferry terminal at Brodick.
- **Directions** - Bunkhouse attached to Kilmory Public Hall located in village centre.

CONTACT:
Kilmory, Isle of Arran, KA27 8PQ
Tel: 01770 870345, Fax: 01770 870345
kilmory.hall@btinternet.com www.kilmoryhall.com

ALDERSYDE
BUNKHOUSE

Aldersyde Bunkhouse is a purpose built bunkhouse on the beautiful island of Arran (Scotland in miniature). Lamlash is a haven for golfers, there are 3x18 hole, 1x12 hole and 3x9 hole golf courses all very reasonably priced. Arran has lovely coastal and forestry walks and Goatfell at 874 metres. Both loch and sea fishing are available with boats for hire or organised trips. Bird life is plentiful and varied. We are a short sail from the Holy Island which has been bought by Same Ling as a retreat, visitors are welcomed. The 'Waverley', the only remaining sea-going paddle steamer in the world, calls at Arran twice weekly during the summer for trips on the Clyde. Arran offers a unique geology formation and is well used by universities. Brodick Castle and gardens are well worth a visit. There are standing stones at various sites, the most popular are at Machrie Moor. Crafts are part of island life and are varied, with visitor participation welcomed. A distillery and brewery are also very interesting. Food is available to suit all tastes, while the bunkhouse has self-catering with a new kitchen. Wheelchair friendly - electric wheelchair available.

DETAILS

- **Open** - All year, all day
- **Number of beds** - 21: 1 x 11, 1 x 7
- **Booking** - Advisable
- **Price per night** - From £12.50pp - group reduction and for length of stay
- **Public Transport** - Bus meets the ferry at Ardrossan.
- **Directions** - Due south from the ferry at Ardrossan. The Hostel is in Lamlash behind the Lamlash Bay Hotel (formally Aldersyde Hotel).

CONTACT:
Lamlash, Arran, KA27 8LS
Tel: 01770 600959
jpricelamlash@hotmail.com www.aldersydebunkhouse.co.uk

BUTE
BACKPACKERS
SCOTLAND

Bute Backpackers, your friendly independent hostel, has 40 beds with a mixture of single, twin, double & family rooms. Some rooms are ensuite and there are separate male and female shower facilities and also toilets on each level. There is also a separate self contained cottage dorm with its own fully equipped kitchen and bathroom and shower facilities. In the main house the self catering kitchen is equipped to the highest standard and there is a large seafront dining room with catering facilities. There is also a 40ft seafront lounge with woodburner and open fire, Sky TV, internet and wifi access. Also a drying room, laundry facilities, private car park for twelve cars and secure bike racks. There are regular live music sessions which includes open mike for any budding musos to join the fun. VisitScotland rated as 4 star.

DETAILS

- **Open** - All year, 24hr access, no curfew. Reception 10am - 10pm,
- **Number of beds** - 40: Main House 32 in 14 rooms; Cottage 8
- **Booking** - Deposit only required for group bookings.
- **Price per night** - From £15 to £25 per person.
- **Public Transport** - Take train to Wemyes Bay Station and Ferry Port (40 mins from Glasgow Central). Then ferry to Rothesay, Isle of Bute. Hostel 900m from ferry or take a taxi (taxi rank adjacent to port) which costs approximately £2.50.
- **Directions** - Turn right as you leave ferry and walk straight ahead for 200m past the discovery centre and putting green. Continue straight ahead for another 250m and Bute Backpackers is on your left. By car turn right on to main road. Continue for 300m to the mini roundabout . Head straight on for a further 300m and the hostel and access to the private car park is adjacent to the main road on your left .

CONTACT: Reception
The Pier View, 36 Argyle Street, Rothesay, Isle of Bute, PA20 0AX
Tel: 01700 501876
butebac@butebackpackers.co.uk www.butebackpackers.co.uk

Set on the Banks of Loch Lomond right on the West Highland Way Balmaha Bunkhouse offers 4 star quality assured accommodation at affordable prices. There is a self catering kitchen and breakfast and bedding are available for a little extra cost. Need more pampering? Then try Bed & Breakfast in the main house with ensuite rooms and breathtaking views over the loch. Boat trips are available on Loch Lomond, or for those with experience, Kayaks and Canadian Canoes can be hired from £20 per day. A catamaran and Topper are also available. Balmaha House is right on the shores of Loch Lomond and just some 5 mins paddling to the first of the islands (Inchcailloch), where you can hop and explore other islands with castles, deer, capercaille and even wallabies. There are ancient graveyards with the burial place of Rob Roy`s cousin and some of the most scenic landscapes in the world. Ideal for walkers, sailors, fishermen, and those who just want to get away from it all. We look forward to welcoming you to the romantic, adventurous and beautiful experience of Loch Lomond.

DETAILS

- **Open** - All year, all day
- **Number of beds** - 14: 1x6, 1x4 (family), 1x2 (double), 1x2 (twin)
- **Booking** - Please phone or email.
- **Price per night** - £15 per person. Sleeping bag hire £2. Breakfast £5 (full) or £3 (cont). B&B in house £35. No credit card facilities, nearest cash point 4 miles
- **Public Transport** - Bus stop is 100 metres from the hostel.
- **Directions** - The last house in the village on the right hand side opposite the bay and the telephone box.

CONTACT: Bob or Debbie Redley
Balmaha, Loch Lomond, Stirlingshire, G63 0JQ
Tel: 01360 870 218 Mob: 07711 904 902
Balmahabunkhouse@aol.com www.balmahahouse.co.uk

TROSSACHS
TRYST

SCOTLAND

Trossachs Tryst has been purpose-built on its own 8 acre site, set amidst beautiful scenery (on Sustrans route 7c) just outside the bustling tourist town of Callander. The hostel, which is the only one in the Trossachs area, opened in August 1997 and is finished to a very high standard, hence its nickname 'Poshtel' The rooms are all en-suite and are either 8, 4 or single bedded. The 4 bed family rooms have their own private kitchen / dining facilities and can be used as twin rooms on request. There is a spacious dining / common room, well equipped kitchen, a laundry and drying room. A large meeting / recreation room is also available and may be booked separately for conferences, parties, etc. We have an on-site Cycling Centre, which also sells basic provisions. Other activities available locally include hill walking, pony trekking, canoe hire / instruction, fishing and sailing.

DETAILS

■ **Open** - All year, Nov to Feb advanced bookings only, reception 8am - 11pm
■ **Number of beds** - 30
■ **Booking** - Booking advised at all times. Groups must book with deposit.
■ **Price per night** - £15 to £25 including linen & continental breakfast. Group and family discounts on request.
■ **Public Transport** - Nearest train station is at Stirling (15 miles). Nearest Citylink coach stop is at Callander (1.5 miles). Pick up from Callander can usually be arranged.
■ **Directions** - GR 606 072. The hostel is situated one mile up Invertrossachs Rd from its junction with the A81 (Glasgow Rd) in Callander.

CONTACT: Mark or Janet
Invertrossachs Road, Callander, Perthshire, FK17 8HW
Tel: 01877 331200, Fax: 01877 331200
mark@scottish-hostel.co.uk www.scottish-hostel.co.uk

LEDARD FARM
BOTHIES

Ledard Farm is a working hill farm and the centre for the Scottish Sheepdog School. It faces the Queen Elizabeth State Forest (25,000h), Ben Lomond and Loch Ard. Highland Adventure Outdoor Activity Centre is also sited on the farm and offers clay pigeon shooting, fishing, sailing, canoeing, mountain bikes, quad biking and hill walking. Ledard Farm has beautiful views across Loch Ard. The main path to the twin summits of Ben Venue passes through the farm and there are numerous forest paths for walking and cycling within easy reach.

Four Ledard Bothies each sleep 2 people. They are fully heated and also have fans. Guests can use their own sleeping bags or hire them for £5 (beds have quilt, sheet and pillow slip). The toilets and showers are in an adjacent building as are the self catering facilities. There is ample secure parking. Cars can be left safely when walking climbing or cycling in the area. For background information visit www.greattimescotland.com

DETAILS

- **Open** - Apr–Oct (inc), , all day. Arrive between 4pm and 8pm, depart before 11am
- **Number of beds** - 8: 4 x 2
- **Booking** - Booking essential – deposit for groups only.
- **Price per night** - First night £20pp, thereafter £15pp. Sleeping bag hire £5.
- **Public Transport** - Bus services to Aberfoyle from Stirling (adjacent to train station) or Glasgow (Buchanan Street Bus Station). We will pick you up from Aberfoyle or you can get a local taxi.
- **Directions** - Located in the middle of the Loch Lomond and The Trossachs National Park. From Aberfoyle take B829 in the direction of Kinlochard and Inversnaid for 5 miles (8kms). The farm is on the right 300m after Forest Hills Hotel.

CONTACT: Ferg or Fra
Ledard Farm, Kinlochard, Stirling, Stirlingshire, FK8 3TL
Tel: 01877 387219
ferg@ceilidh-band.demon.co.uk www.highland-adventure.co.uk

COMRIE
CROFT

Situated in a 200-year-old farmstead, Comrie Croft offers an attractive, great value escape amongst the Scottish hills. Just over one hour's drive from Edinburgh or Glasgow, the Croft is ideal for individuals, families or groups. There are endless things to see and do. Explore the mountains, have a go at adventure sports like quad-biking or white-water rafting, hold a team-building meeting or seminar, tour Scotland's oldest distillery, discover Loch Lomond National Park at Loch Earn, swim in our own mill pond, walk on the estate, hire a bike, find ruined castles, or simply read a book on the sofa.

Among the facilities are a choice of standard or en-suite private rooms, a cosy living room with books, games and movies and full self-catering facilities. We also have an eco campsite (tents only), shop, bike hire, indoor and outdoor games facilities, conference facilities, and our own 230 acre estate offering walks and mountain bike trails.

DETAILS

- **Open** - All year, all day
- **Number of beds** - 56 + 14 (2 units)
- **Booking** - Recommended
- **Price per night** - From £15 adults, £7.50 U16, U5 free.
- **Public Transport** - Train stations: Dunblane, Stirling, or Perth. Our own bus stop is served by no. 15 from Perth (approx. every hour). Summer only Citylink service to Oban and Fort William. Ask for Comrie Croft.
- **Directions** - Signposted from the A85 between Crieff (5 miles) and Comrie (2 miles).

CONTACT:
Comrie Croft, By Crieff/Comrie, Perthshire, PH7 4JZ
Tel: 01764 670140
info@comriecroft.com www.comriecroft.com

BY THE WAY
SCOTLAND HOSTEL AND CAMPSITE

By The Way Hostel and Campsite can be found in the Loch Lomond National Park halfway between Arrochar's peaks and the grandeur of Glencoe. The site, run by experienced hillwalkers, is aimed primarily at outdoor enthusiasts and with great walking (the West Highland Way passes by the hostel), climbing, white water paddling and gold-panning nearby, there is lots to be enthusiastic about (Munro-baggers can find 50 Munros within 20 miles). Accommodation options range from camping (with an indoor cooking/dining area and campers drying room), through basic trekker huts, to a purpose built four star hostel with twin and double rooms as well as dormitory accommodation, great self catering facilities and drying room. For more comfort still there's a three bedroom centrally-heated timber holiday chalet. By The Way is in Tyndrum with the village pub, shops, café and Tourist Information Centre nearby. The Glasgow to Fort William road is 250m from the site (far from the madding traffic noise) and both the Glasgow Oban and Glasgow Fort William trains stop in Tyndrum.

DETAILS

- **Open** - Hostel open all year. Camping from Easter to October, 24 hours
- **Number of beds** - 26 in hostel; 24 in huts; 50 camping.
- **Booking** - Always phone in advance. Deposit (Visa/Access) guarantees bed.
- **Price per night** - Hostel dorms from £16pp. Huts from £10pp. Camping £6pp
- **Public Transport** - Intercity coach and rail service pickup points in Tyndrum to Edinburgh, Glasgow, Fort William and Oban. Sleeper service to London.
- **Directions** - GR NN 327 302. Travelling on A82 follow sign in village for Tyndrum Lower Station. Hostel is immediately before station.

CONTACT: Manager
Lower Station Road, Tyndrum, FK20 8RY
Tel: 01838 400333
info@TyndrumByTheWay.com www.TyndrumByTheWay.com

STRATHFILLAN
WIGWAMS
SCOTLAND

On a working farm within the Loch Lomond and Trossachs National Park this is an ideal location for a single night, weekend or a week's let for families or groups. An ideal base for hill walking with monroes, the West Highland Way, canoeing, fishing, and skiing nearby. The Wigwams are comfortably equipped with mattresses, electric lights and heating etc (not metered). Large wigwam sleeps 4/5 on benches. Small wigwam sleeps 4 with mattresses on the floor. Each has own car park, picnic bench and campfire. Beaver is a deluxe wigwam sleeping 5 with kitchen, toilet, shower & TV. Also available: five self catering lodges, some with separate bedrooms, lounge, kitchen, shower and toilet; space for camping and caravans; Kirkton Farmhouse for groups up to 12; and a yurt sleeping 5. Logs,kindling and peat available in the shop, also our own sausages to cook on your camp fire. Site has toilet /shower block, hot and cold water and a fully equipped kitchen. Bedding & towels can be hired @£3/set.

DETAILS

- **Open** - All year, all day
- **Number of beds** -
- **Booking** - Book by phone or email.
- **Price per night** - Small wigwam £28 for 2. Large wigwam £33 for 2. Yurt £50 for 2. £10/extra adult, £8/extra child. From £175 per week with £20/extra person. Lodges from £190/week. Short breaks in lodges from £45/night.
- **Public Transport** -
- **Directions** - Situated on Scottish Agricultural College's research farm on the A82 three miles north of Crianlarich, thirty minutes south of Glencoe Ski-Centre.

CONTACT:
Auchtertyre, Tyndrum, Crianlarich, Perthshire FK20 8RU
Tel: 01838 400251
wigwam@sac.ac.uk www.sac.ac.uk/wigwams

BRAVEHEART
BACKPACKERS

Braveheart Backpackers is a cosy cottage with private, shared and ensuite bedrooms. A real 'home from home' hostel with open log fire, well equipped kitchen, cd player, TV, video, musical instruments, BBQ...

Situated in the scenic village of Killin ('one of Scotland's prettiest villages') by beautiful Loch Tay. Great hillwalking and 'munro bagging' location with Ben Lawers very nearby. Bikes, canoes and kayaks available to rent from the hostel and guided tours arranged too. This is a great place to chill out or to be active within the Loch Lomond and Trossachs National Park. There is much to do and see in the area with ancient castles, whisky distilleries, stone circles, early Celtic Christian & Druidic standing stones, crannogs (bronze age loch dwellings), ancient woodlands, Fortingall Yew Tree 'the world's oldest tree' and Glen Lyon 'Scotland's loveliest glen', all a short distance away. The area is steeped in history & mystery, so come & catch it whilst it is still a secret!

DETAILS

- **Open** - All year, all day
- **Number of beds** - 12
- **Booking** - Please book by phone or email.
- **Price per night** - Dorms £15.00 - £20.00 pp. Twin Room £20 pp. Special Rate: £12.50 pp for groups of 8 staying 1 week.
- **Public Transport** - 100m from nearest public transport. Buses to Callander and Stirling. Nearest train station Crianlarich (12 miles)
- **Directions** - Located next to Killin Hotel in a small courtyard behind the church.

CONTACT: Peter or Reception
Lochay Lodge & Cottage, Killin, Perthshire, FK21 8TP
Tel: 01567 829 089, Mob: 07796 886 899
peter@secretscotland.co.uk www.cyclescotland.co.uk

Situated 1,000 feet above sea level on a south facing mountain-side. The steading has been converted into two high standard units. They are perfect for relaxing after a busy day out on the local munroes / hills and lochs. Fantastic location for group gatherings, stag and hen parties, outdoor activity weekends or just a place to re-charge and take in the amazing views. There are 2 totally separate units which can be hired individually or as a whole. These units both have fully equipped kitchens and a dining area / seating area. There are extra tables / chairs and BBQs for outside eating and even a spit-roaster for that special occasion. Plenty of parking spaces and a large drying room. Bunks come with fitted sheets / pillow + case / duvet with cover. Activities in area include W/W/Rafting, Clay Shooting, Paintball, Quad Biking and many others.

DETAILS

- **Open** - All year, phone enquiries between 9am and 9pm
- **Number of beds** - 39: Original Unit 25:1x6, 1x8,1x4, 1x7. Newer Unit 14; 2x4,1x6
- **Booking** - Groups ONLY for Fri / Sat Weekends. Individuals / groups for Sun to Thur nights. Booking in advance essential and securing deposits required.
- **Price per night** - Whole place for a Fri + Sat weekend = £1,329 or Original Unit (25) = £881, or Newer Unit (14) = £494. Individuals/small groups are £17pppn from Sun to Thur nights. Check own website for Special Deals.
- **Public Transport** - Trains at Pitlochry (12 miles), bus at Aberfeldy (2.5 miles)
- **Directions** - See website to print directions. From the x-roads at The Black Watch in Aberfeldy, follow the B846 over River Tay at Wades Bridge. Turn right at the Aileen Craggan Hotel (signed Strathtay), approx 50mtrs after foot bridge on RH side over the Tay turn left (bunkhouse sign on RH side). Follow track for 1.5 miles.

CONTACT: Julian Rickard
Glassie Farm, Aberfeldy, Perthshire, PH15 2JN
Tel: Office: 01887 820265 or Mobile: 07849 689386
j_j_rickard@hotmail.com   www.thebunkhouse.co.uk

CULDEES
BUNKHOUSE

Culdees offers an independent hostel and bunkhouse accommodation in the heart of a caring community which aims to live at one with the natural environment. Whether you're a motorist, a cyclist or a Munro bagger, you'll find it a homely place for just a night or for all your holiday. The hostel and bunkhouse has a well equipped kitchen with dining area for 16 people, a living room with television area and a large music room with a baby grand piano and other instruments. Accommodation in the main house consists of two family rooms and one double room, each with digital lock, individual reading lights, duvets, fresh linen and an extra pillow. An 8 bed cottage is also available. There is a big open barn, ideal for barbecues and gatherings, great when it's raining! Drying room with washer and dryer. Toys, play area and plenty of space for outdoor games. Tourist Board 3 star recommended.
Gold Award for Green Tourism.

DETAILS

- **Open** - All year, 24 hours
- **Number of beds** - Bunkhouse 16: 4x4, main House 10: 2x4,1x2, cottage 8:2x4
- **Booking** - Book with credit card.
- **Price per night** - £17pp (bunkhouse), £22 main house, price on request for cottage.
- **Public Transport** - Train: Pitlochry 25 miles. Coach: Aberfeldy 9miles. Local bus four days a week and the school bus will drop at hostel track. Collection from Aberfeldy's bus stop if stuck.
- **Directions** - GR 716 447 From A827 Killin to Aberfeldy road turn left at the hotel in Fearnan. At top of hill turn left (Dalchiaran) signposted Culdees.

CONTACT: Maryse
Culdees, Boreland Farm, Fearnan, nr Aberfeldy, Perthshire, PH15 2PG
Tel: 01887 830519, Mobile 07904 954116, Fax: 01887 830664
contact@culdeesbunkhouse.co.uk www.culdeesbunkhouse.co.uk

Stunning rooms in Cottages & Bunkhouse at the foot of a south facing slope with beautiful walks and climbs in Sunny Weem Forest Park. Old barns have been converted to a 4star luxury bunkhouse and self catering eco-cottages with underfloor heating and log fired stoves. The sheltered sunny front garden and courtyard are midge free.

"Breakfast outside in the sunshine! What a great start to the day"

Home of the National Kayak School, ideal for whitewater kayaking, intro to advanced. Superb mountain biking also, on cycle route #7 and Rob Roy Way. .

Excellent riverside walk along the banks of the Tay.

Bar meals next door at Weem Hotel.

DETAILS
- **Open** - All year, flexible but generally all day
- **Number of beds** - Wade House 9 : 1x5, 1x4. Bunkhouse 25: 2x4/5, 1x2/3, 1x8/9, Two beautiful cottages 1x9, 1x4/5
- **Booking** - Advisable, book by phone or email
- **Price per night** - From £15 per person. Long stay rates available.
- **Public Transport** - Buses from Aberfeldy connect to trains at Pitlochry & Perth.
- **Directions** - North from traffic lights in Aberfeldy, over General Wade's bridge over the River Tay for 1km, the Adventurer's Escape is next to the Weem Hotel on the B846.

CONTACT: Stuart Wagstaff
Weem, Aberfeldy, PH15 2LD
Tel: 08456 436036
info@adventurers-escape.co.uk www.adventurers-escape.co.uk

DUNOLLY
SCOTLAND ADVENTURE OUTDOORS

Dunolly House comprises two units, the first is a 48-bed Victorian house, the other is a smaller 15-bed cottage. All rooms are fully carpeted and centrally heated with modern pine beds (linen and duvets provided). The complex can be taken together or as separate units for groups and individuals with catering to suit.

We have a fantastic range of activities on site which can be booked by groups and individuals. They include river rafting, duckying, kayaking, gorge ascent, archery, mountain biking, high ropes challenge and climbing wall. We have our own qualified instructors and we are licensed to run activities for children under the regulations of the Adventure Activities Licensing Authority.

Come and enjoy !!

DETAILS
- **Open** - All year, 24 hours
- **Number of beds** - 63
- **Booking** - Booking is normally necessary
- **Price per night** - From £13.50 per person
- **Public Transport** - Nearest train station is in Pitlochry (14 miles away). Citylink coaches stop at Ballinluig (11 miles away) and Pitlochry. Local buses to Aberfeldy.
- **Directions** - Turn off the A9 Road at Ballinluig. Travel for 5 miles. Turn right at the T junction. Travel 6 miles until Aberfeldy. Continue through the main street and we are the last house on the right as you exit Aberfeldy.

CONTACT: Booking Office
Taybridge Drive, Aberfeldy, Perthshire, PH15 2BP
Tel: 01887 820298
info@dunollyadventures.co.uk www.dunollyadventures.co.uk

THE GRANDTULLY

SCOTLAND

The Grandtully is perfectly situated about 40 metres from The River Tay, which makes it a brilliant base for canoeists / kayakers, with rapids and a slalom course on the doorstep. Munroe baggers / walkers have approximately 30 Munroes within sensible travelling distance, while there's plenty of other local walks for all abilities. Also ideally situated for mountain biking and golf with 20+ great golf courses nearby. The accommodation has 8 twin bedded rooms and 2 family rooms sleeping 4. The Grandtully has its own cafe bar 'The Tully'. We cater for larger groups, including stag / hen weekends and family gatherings etc. We can arrange for your own themed chocolate party or casino night There's an amazing selection of activities available for your whole group (w/w rafting, canyoning, quad biking, paintballing, etc). 10% discount for SCA members hiring the whole facility.

DETAILS

- **Open** - all year, phone enquiries between 9am and 9pm.
- **Number of beds** - 24
- **Booking** - Advanced booking is highly advised, deposit required.
- **Price per night** - A weeks exclusive use is £2796, or £998 for Fri & Sat nights. Weekday (Sun to Thur) £18 pp (inc.ensuites). 10% discount for SCA members hiring whole facility.
- **Public Transport** - Trains at Pitlochry (6 miles), bus stops outside the front door.
- **Directions** - See website for printable directions. The village of Grandtully is on the A827 5 miles from Aberfeldy and 4 miles from junction with the A9. The Grandtully is just on the main road with its car park around the back.

CONTACT: Wez
The Grandtully, Grandtully, By Aberfeldy, Perthshire, PH9 0PL
Tel: 07736 212617
info@thegrandtully.com   www.thegrandtully.com

PITLOCHRY
SCOTLAND BACKPACKERS HOTEL

Pitlochry Backpackers Hotel provides what is without doubt some of the most luxurious backpacker's accommodation in Scotland.

Set in the heart of beautiful rural Perthshire it makes a terrific first stop for any trip into the Highlands. Historic Dunkeld, Blair Castle and numerous whisky disilleries are just a few of the attractions within easy reach, and some of Scotland's finest walking and cycling trails are right on the doorstep of this very special hostel

It provides all the comforts of a hotel plus the ambience and facilities of a hostel. Twin, double and dorm rooms are available plus a wonderful sunny lounge overlooking the main street.

DETAILS

■ **Open** - March to October, 7.30am-12pm 4pm-11pm (please check at reception as times may vary)
■ **Number of beds** - 79
■ **Booking** - Booking in advance not always essential. First nights payment required.
■ **Price per night** - From £13 per night. ID required for check-in.
■ **Public Transport** - Buses will drop you off on Atholl Road and the hostel is only 1min walk. The train station exits onto Atholl Road also, only 5 mins walk.
■ **Directions** - If coming from the south, follow the A9 until you see signposts for Pitlochry. Once in the town you'll reach Atholl Road and the hostel is just on the right-hand side, with a customer car park behind the building – you can get to this by taking the immediate right after the hostel entrance. If coming from the north, once on Atholl Road hostel is on your left, with parking just before the entrance to the left.

CONTACT: Receptionist
134 Atholl Road, Pitlochry, PH16 5AB
Tel: 01796 470044
pitlochry@scotlandstophostels.com www.scotlandstophostels.com

Gulabin Lodge is beautifully situated in the heart of Glenshee at the foot of Beinn Gulabin offering the nearest accommodation to the Glenshee ski slopes. We offer nordic, alpine, telemark skiing and snowboarding and have a dry ski slope where lessons are available. Gulabin is an ideal base for climbing, walking or mountain biking, whether you are a beginner or an expert. Other activities available include rock climbing, gorge walking, abseiling, archery, rifle shooting, orienteering, canyoning, kayaking. Nine-hole golf course, 85m aerial runway and pony trekking nearby. Five minutes walk from the hostel are the Spittal of Glenshee Hotel and Dalmunzie Hotel both with friendly bars and excellent meals. The lodge offers comfortable accommodation for individuals, families and groups with two cosy lounges with log fires. Free hot showers. All rooms have wash basins and linen. Packages for groups. Ski, Snowboard & Nordic hire equipment, and Mountain bike hire with guided trips available.

DETAILS

■ **Open** - All year, 24 hours, arrive by 9pm
■ **Number of beds** - 37 :- 9 rooms available
■ **Booking** - Booking advisable with 20% deposit
■ **Price per night** - From £15pp (bed only). From £20pp B&B, Family rooms from £45. Full board available. Sole use available.
■ **Public Transport** - Train and bus stations at Pitlochry (22 miles), Blairgowrie (20 miles), Glasgow (100 miles), Edinburgh (70 miles). Post bus calls half a mile away.
■ **Directions** - Gulabin Lodge is on the A93 road at Spittal of Glenshee - 20 miles north of Blairgowrie and 19 miles south of Braemar. Transport can be arranged.

CONTACT: Darren and Tereza
Spittal of Glenshee, By Blairgowrie, PH10 7QE
Tel: 01250 885255 Mobile: 07799 847014
info@gulabinlodge.co.uk www.gulabinlodge.co.uk

PROSEN HOSTEL

SCOTLAND

Glenprosen is the most intimate of the Angus Glens on the southernmost edge of the Cairngorm National Park. Two Munros, the Mayar and Driesh, link Glenprosen to the Cairngorms plateau. The Minister's Path leads over to Glen Clova, whilst a new footbridge and path along the prettiest stretch of the river Prosen connects to Glenisla and the Cateran Trail in Perthshire. Prosen Hostel was recently converted from an old school to provide accommodation for those using the upgraded East Cairngorms footpath network. Converted to the latest and greenest specification, the living room has a wood burning stove, internet connection, and raised area for admiring the view (& red squirrels) through the school's huge windows. A drying room and laundry facilities complete the cosy welcome. It sleeps a total of 18 in 4 bunkrooms, sleeping 4, 4 & 6 and a family room sleeping 4. The nearby village hall is available to rent for ceilidhs, music sessions, parties and celebrations. STB 4 star.

DETAILS

- **Open** - All year, all day
- **Number of beds** - 18:1x6, 3x4
- **Booking** - Book by phone or email
- **Price per night** - £16 - £20 per person. Minimum periods apply for Christmas and New year.
- **Public Transport** - Trains Dundee; buses Kirriemuir (regular to Dundee & Forfar)
- **Directions** - From Kirriemuir follow B955 signed to Prosen, Clova and Cairngorms National Park. At Dykehead fork left. Carry on for 7 miles until public road ends at telephone kiosk. Turn acute right and follow tarmac 200m uphill to hostel.

CONTACT: Hector or Robert
Prosen Hostel, Balnaboth, Kirriemuir, Angus, DD8 4SA
Tel: 01575 540238/302
sih@prosenhostel.co.uk www.prosenhostel.co.uk

JEREMY INGLIS
HOSTEL

Jeremy Inglis Hostel is only 150 yards from the station and the bus terminus in Oban.

Prices include a continental breakfast with muesli, toast and home made jams, marmalade and Vegemite. Tea and coffee are available at any time.

The rooms are mostly double and family size so you have some privacy. All linen is included in the price.

Kitchen facilities are provided and the hostel is heated by meter.

WIFI available.

DETAILS

■ **Open** - Closed for periods outside of the summer season, no curfew, access with key.
■ **Number of beds** - 37
■ **Booking** - Booking preferred. Deposit in certain circumstances.
■ **Price per night** - From £15 per person (in a shared room). Including continental breakfast. Single rooms (when available) £22.
■ **Public Transport** - Nearest train and Citylink drop off 150 metres from hostel. Ferries to Islands 350 metres. For ferry enquiries phone 01631 566688.
■ **Directions** - The hostel is in Airds Crescent, one of the streets off Argyll Square. The hostel is on the second floor, pink door.

CONTACT: Jeremy Inglis, Katrin or Michael
21 Airds Crescent, Oban, Argyll, PA34 5SJ
Tel: 01631 565065, Fax: 01631 565933
jeremyinglis@mctavishs.freeserve.co.uk

CORRAN
HOUSE

Corran House is part of a Victorian terrace with magnificent sea-scapes across the bay to the Isle of Kerrera and the hills of Mull. There is a warm welcome for visitors and reasonably priced accommodation for singles, couples, families and groups. The house has a large self-catering kitchen, spacious TV lounge, comfortable, commodious, well appointed guest rooms and 4 bed dormitories with generous size beds - most rooms have en-suite facilities. Corran House is well situated for exploring Argyll and visiting the inner Hebrides. It is only a short walk along the sea front to the bus, train and ferry terminals. Downstairs is Markie Dans bar with patio and spectacular views. The pub offers great highland hospitality, tasty meals, live entertainment, wide screen TV, pool table and a late licence all year round to enable the discerning drinker to sample the best range of malt whiskies on the west coast.
Pony trekking trips now available - prior booking advisable.

DETAILS

- **Open** - All year, reception 10am-9pm. Check in after 3pm.
- **Number of beds** - 36 : 7x4 : 1x2 : 1x6. plus Guest rooms : 11.
- **Booking** - Advisable. Credit card secures bed. Early / late arrival with notice.
- **Price per night** - Bunk room from £14pp. Guest rooms from £25pp.
- **Public Transport** - Oban train, bus and ferry terminals are 900m from the house.
- **Directions** - Corran House overlooks Oban Bay to the west of the town centre. From the Tourist Information and all the Oban transport terminals, with the sea on your left, walk along George Street past the Columba Hotel into Corran Esplanade. Follow the seafront for 300m. Corran House is on your right above Markie Dans Bar.

CONTACT:
1 Victoria Crescent, Corran Esplanade, Oban, Argyll, PA34 5PN
Tel: 01631 566040, Fax: 01631 566854
enquiries@corranhouseoban.co.uk www.corranhouseoban.co.uk

OBAN
BACKPACKERS

Oban Backpackers has become many people's favorite hostel thanks to its friendly atmosphere, excellent facilities and beautiful seaside town setting. There's an enormous self catering kitchen, a pool table and lots of information about things to do in Oban and Argyll. Oban is a picturesque town possessing spectacular views across to the islands - the view at dusk from McCaig's Tower provides a sunset you are unlikely to forget. The bustle of fishing boats, ferries, yachts and seabirds make the waterfront a lovely place to be. Boat trips leave Oban to the many beautiful Scottish Isles and more remote areas of Scotland. Ancient standing stones, medieval castles and whisky distilleries all in the area, with seal colonies, hairy coos and the best fish and chips in Scotland all within walking distance. Minibus available for transfers and custom made tours.

DETAILS

■ **Open** - All year, reception open 5pm-10.30pm and 7am-10.30am
■ **Number of beds** - 48: 3 x 6, 1 x 8, 1 x 10, 1 x 12 plus double and twin rooms
■ **Booking** - Booking is strongly recommended but not essential – deposit equivalent to first night's accommodation to be paid in full to confirm the booking.
■ **Price per night** - From £13.50 pp,, private rooms from £16.50pp
■ **Public Transport** - Close to Oban train station and Citylink buses.
■ **Directions** - From A85 turn left onto Deanery Brae as you are coming into Oban. Follow the road onto Breadalbane Street. A pub with green lights is on the right, we are a little further on the left. Parking is usually available out the front. If arriving by bus or train, walk along the waterfront through town, keeping the ocean on your left. Continue straight on up George Street, past a cinema on the right, then the Taj Mahal Indian restaurant. We are a few doors further, a white building on the same side.

CONTACT: Receptionist
Breadalbane Street, Oban, Argyll PA34 5NZ
Tel: 01631 562107
oban@scotlandstophostels.com www.obanbackpackers.com

COLONSAY
SCOTLAND BACKPACKERS LODGE

The Lodge is located on a peaceful and idyllic Inner Hebridean island to the south of Mull which boasts magnificent sandy beaches, ancient forests and beautiful lochs. The place is teeming with wildlife which includes dolphins, seals, otters and many rare species of bird. There are ancient standing stones and a 14th-century priory with exceptional carved Celtic tombstones. The famous Colonsay House gardens and café are open to visitors to enjoy twice a week. We offer for hire mountain bikes and tennis racquets to use on the free court. The pub, café, shop and village hall, where there are regular Ceilidhs, are all within three miles. Fresh lobster, crab and langoustines can be bought from fishing boats in the harbour and don't forget the best oysters in the world are grown on Colonsay. The lodge is a refurbished former gamekeeper's house with bothies. It is centrally heated and has 3 large twin, 3 small twin and 1 family room. It has a large dining / cooking / sitting area and a separate sitting room with a log fire. Bed linen provided.

DETAILS

- **Open** - All year, 24 hours
- **Number of beds** - 16   6 x 2 : 1 x 4.
- **Booking** - Required 24 hours in advance.
- **Price per night** - £18pp twin, £14pp bothy, £16pp 4 bed dorm.
- **Public Transport** - Train and coach in Oban. Ferry to Colonsay takes 2.5 hours.
- **Directions** - Ferry departs Oban 5 times a week April to October, Sun, Mon, Wed, Thurs, Fri (rest of year Mon, Wed, Fri). From Kennacraig and Port Askaig, Islay on Weds. Transport from the harbour can be arranged if required.

CONTACT: The Manager
Colonsay Estate Cottages, Isle of Colonsay, Argyll, PA61 7YP
Tel: 01951 200312
colonsaycottages@dial.pipex.com www.colonsayestate.co.uk

Tiree is an idyllic Hebridean Island, perfect for outdoor pursuits, wildlife enthusiasts, and those yet to experience the total tranquility of stunning white beaches and crystal clear seas.

A warm welcome and excellent facilities await you at Millhouse. Bikes are for hire to explore the island, visit the thatched cottage and lighthouse museums, find the standing stones, wonder at the machair flowers or watch the seals. Watersports take place on adjacent Loch Bhasapol, and the secluded Cornaig beach is a ten minute walk away. There is a resident RSPB warden on the island and a bird hide near the hostel.

For walkers, Millhouse is on the Tiree Pilgrimage route linking the ancient chapels and monuments around the island. STB 4star Hostel

DETAILS

- **Open** - Mar-Oct, open in winter by arrangement, open all day (quiet after 11.30pm, check out 10am)
- **Number of beds** - 16/18 : 2 x 2/3 : 2 x 6 plus 3 family rooms : 12 beds: 3 x 4
- **Booking** - Advisable, please check vacancies before boarding the ferry
- **Price per night** - Twin £17.50pp, Dorms £14.50pp, Family £44 - £58 per room
- **Public Transport** - Caledonian MacBrayne ferry from Oban to Tiree or Flybe flight from Glasgow. Local Ring and Ride bus 01879 220419.
- **Directions** - From ferry turn right at T junction, then left at next fork. Continue for 4 miles to Millhouse Hostel

CONTACT: Judith Boyd
Cornaigmore, Isle of Tiree, Argyll, PA77 6XA
Tel: 01879 220435
tireemillhouse@yahoo.co.uk www.tireemillhouse.co.uk

IONA
HOSTEL

Tucked into the rocky outcrops at the north end of the island, Iona Hostel has spectacular views to Staffa and the Treshnish Isles, and beyond Rhum to the Black Cuillins of Skye. The hostel is situated on the working croft of Lagandorain (the hollow of the otter). This land has been worked for countless generations, creating the familiar Hebridean patchwork of wildflower meadow, crops and grazing land, home to an amazing variety of plants and birds. We offer quiet sanctuary for those that seek it, within easy reach of island activities.

Iona Hostel is new, well-reviewed and recommended. Whether travelling on your own, with friends, or as part of one of our many visiting groups, Iona Hostel offers you a warm welcome - with the best views and duck eggs this side of heaven. 4 star STB. Green Tourism Gold Award.
We regret no dogs are allowed.

DETAILS

- **Open** - All year , closed 11am-1pm for cleaning - no curfew
- **Number of beds** - 21: 1 x 2 : 2 x 4 : 1 x 5 : 1 x 6.
- **Booking** - Is strongly advised, 50% deposit.
- **Price per night** - £18.50 adult £15.50under 10s (bedding included).
- **Public Transport** - Caledonian Macbrayne ferry service from Oban or Mull 08705 650000. For buses on Mull 01546 604695. Taxi service on Iona 0781 0325990.
- **Directions** - You cannot bring your car onto Iona, but there is free parking in Fionnphort on Mull at the Columba Centre. Iona Hostel is the last building at the north end of the island, 2 km from the pier and up beyond the abbey.

CONTACT:
Iona Hostel, Iona, Argyll, PA76 6SW
Tel: 01681 700781
info@ionahostel.co.uk www.ionahostel.co.uk

We're right on the sea, with views to Ben Nevis. There are regular sightings of seals and otters, and sometimes of porpoises, dolphins and eagles. Stroll to the ferry, pub, shops, swimming pool and miniature steam railway. Walk to Torosay and Duart Castles. Catch the bus for Tobermory; for Iona (where Columba brought Christianity to Scotland) and for Staffa (home of puffins, and inspiration for Mendelssohn's overture 'Fingal's Cave').

Your accommodation is in Shielings, unique carpeted cottage tents, made by us on Mull, which are clean, bright and spacious, and have real beds for 2, 4, or 6. There are super showers, and communal Shielings with woodburner, TV, payphone and launderette. Our campsite is rated '5 stars, exceptional, World Class' by the Scottish Tourist Board.

DETAILS

- **Open** - April to October, 24 hours (Reception 8am - 10pm)
- **Number of beds** - 18: 6 x 2 : 1 x 6.
- **Booking** - Please email a booking enquiry from our website www.shielingholidays.co.uk
- **Price per night** - £12.50 pp, Under 15's £9 pp, bedding £3pp
- **Public Transport** - From Glasgow, rail (08457 484950) or bus (08705 505050) at 12.00, ferry (01680 812343) at 16.00 from Oban, arrive Mull 16.46; back by 10.55 ferry, arrive Glasgow 15.45. Please check times before travel.
- **Directions** - GR 724 369 From ferry, left on the A849 to Iona. After 400 metres, left opposite church past old pier to reception - 800 metres in all.

CONTACT: David Gracie
Craignure, Isle of Mull, Argyll, PA65 6AY
Tel: 01680 812496
info@shielingholidays.co.uk www.shielingholidays.co.uk

GLENAROS
LODGE

A warm welcome awaits you at this unique house on the magical Isle of Mull. There are wonderful views over the sea and to the ruins of ancient Aros Castle. It is an ideal central location for hikers, cyclists and motorists wishing to see the whole island, view its wildlife and special geology whilst also being near Tobermory. Red deer can be glimpsed in the early morning grazing in front of the Lodge. Bird watchers can spot heron, mallard, puffins and sea eagles amongst many other birds. Seals are common off the shore and dolphins, whales and the occasional otter may also be seen in the bay right outside the house. Glenaros Lodge is a traditional, homely, cosy house with much information on the island's history and wildlife. For those visitors who just want a holiday away from it all then here is that special, peaceful oasis with extensive grounds & woodlands. There are five private, family and shared rooms, three of which have magnificent sea views. Also two yurts and camping in the grounds. Meals are available on request. There is a self-catering kitchen, guest lounge & log fire. Bikes and canoes for hire. Tours of Mull and Iona can be arranged too.

DETAILS

- **Open** - All year, all day
- **Number of beds** - 18
- **Booking** - Book by phone or email.
- **Price per night** - Dorm £15pp, twin room £25pp.
- **Public Transport** - Ferry from Oban to Craignure is generally met by a Bowman's Bus which goes to Glenaros (not on Sundays). Ask for Glenaros Lodge.
- **Directions** - Approximately 1 mile north of Salen on A848. Hostel is on the left.

CONTACT: Peter
Glenaros Lodge, Aros, Salen, Isle of Mull, PA72 6JP
Tel: 01680 300301 Mob: 07796 886899
peter@hostel-mull.co.uk www.glenaroslodge.net

GLENCOE
SCOTLAND INDEPENDENT HOSTEL

Glencoe Independent Hostel (signed Glencoe Bunkhouse), is centred around an historic west highland croft in the heart of beautiful Glencoe, offering great value accommodation for groups, families and individuals. It is set in secluded and peaceful woodland midway between Glencoe village and the Clachaig Inn with immediate access to world class cycling, walking, climbing and kayaking and 20 mins from Glencoe Ski Centre, 40 minutes from Nevis Range. Relax and enjoy the beautiful surroundings. The hostel has 3x6, 1x8 bed rooms, a lounge with open fire, cooking and dining facilities. The Alpine bunkhouse sleeps 16 in 2 rooms of 4 beds and 1 of 8 beds. Ideal for outdoor activity and school groups. Caravans for 4 to 6 people and log cabin for 2-3 people. Top class drying room, small shop, bike storage, and mountains all around.

DETAILS

- **Open** - All year (phone in Nov and Dec) , 9am - 9 pm
- **Number of beds** - Hostel: 26, bunkhouse: 16, 4 caravans of 4/6, Log cabin: 2/3
- **Booking** - Booking advised in summer. 30% non refundable deposit (min. £10).
- **Price per night** - From £10.50 to £20 per person.
- **Public Transport** - 1.5miles from bus stop in Glencoe Village (crossroads). Citylink buses 914, 915 and 916 from Skye, Fort William, Glasgow. Bus 44 from Fort William and Kinlochleven. For West Highland Way take White Corries near Kingshouse Hotel to Glencoe Crossroads (20 mins) then 1.5 miles walk.
- **Directions** - Sign-posted Glencoe Bunkhouse. From A82 south, take right turn for Clachaig Inn, 1 miles after pub on left. From north, take left turn for Kinlochleven, then immediate right to Glencoe Village. 1 mile out of village on right .

CONTACT: Keith or Davina
Glencoe Independent Hostel, Glencoe, Argyll, PH49 4HX
Tel: 01855 811906
info@glencoehostel.co.uk www.glencoehostel.co.uk

BLACKWATER
HOSTEL & CAMPSITE SCOTLAND

Blackwater Hostel is in the centre of the scenic village of Kinlochleven surrounded by the Mamore mountains midway between Glencoe and Ben Nevis. An ideal stopover for families, cyclists, walkers, climbers and those who are walking the West Highland Way. There are high and low-level, half-hour to full-day walks, all with great views, or if you prefer there is a regular bus service from the village to Glencoe, Ballachulish and Fort William. Water sports are available nearby. Ice Factor, Europe's first indoor 14 metre ice/climbing wall is only 200 metres away. This is comfortable, high-quality STB 4 star bunkhouse accommodation. All rooms have en-suite facilities, TV and central heating. Facilities include self-catering kitchens, lounge, dining conference area and drying room. There are supermarkets, pubs & restaurants within two minutes walking distance. Campsite has drying room, showers & covered area.

DETAILS

- **Open** - All year, 24 hours
- **Number of beds** - 39 - 2,3,4,8 bedded rooms
- **Booking** - Essential (between 8am-8pm)
- **Price per night** - From £14pp including bed linen. £32 for twin.
- **Public Transport** - The nearest train station is Fort William and National Express travels from Glasgow to Glencoe and Fort William. Regular bus service to Kinlochleven all day from Glencoe, Ballachulish and Fort William.
- **Directions** - GR 188 618. OS sheet 41. From A82 Glasgow to Fort William road at Glencoe turn right to Kinlochleven. The hostel is situated near the centre of Kinlochleven. Just past the Co-op a large sign with an arrow will point you to Hostel.

CONTACT: Caroline
Lab Road, Kinlochleven, Argyll, PH50 4SG
Tel: 01855 831253 or 0791 9366116
black.water@virgin.net www.blackwaterhostel.co.uk

CORRAN
BUNKHOUSE

Corran Bunkhouse 4 star accommodation is situated in a stunning loch side location surrounded by mountains in the magnificent Highlands of Scotland, 8 miles south of Fort William and 7 miles north of Glencoe. The Corran Bunkhouse is made up of two fully equipped self catering bunkhouses which between them can offer comfortable accommodation for up to 32 people. One bunkhouse sleeps 12 and the other sleeps 20 making Corran Bunkhouse an ideal base for small and large groups. Individual travellers are welcome and the room sizes make the bunkhouse ideal for family groups. All bedrooms have a TV and ensuite facilities. There are fully equipped kitchen / dining areas, drying room, central heating, laundry facilities, private parking and a steam room situated in the smaller bunkhouse. Children and pets welcome. Group discounts. Come and enjoy the many outdoor activities available in the area such as climbing, walking, canoeing, kayaking, cycling and mountain biking.

DETAILS

- **Open** - All year, all day (reception 9am -10pm)
- **Number of beds** - 32: 8x2 1x3 2x4 1x5
- **Booking** - Advisable but not necessary - major credit cards accepted.
- **Price per night** - £16 per person, £14 per person for block bookings of 12 or more. £24 for single occupancy. Prices included bedding and power
- **Public Transport** - Trains at Fort William (8 mile bus or taxi ride to hostel). Regular busses toward Fort William from the south and from Inverness stop 100m from hostel (ask for Onich). Check the Citylink web site for bus details.
- **Directions** - Corran Bunkhouse lies on the Onich side of the Corran/Ardgour Ferry 8 miles south of Fort William on the A82 trunk road from Glasgow to Inverness .

CONTACT:
Onich, Fort William, PH33 6SE
Tel: 01855 821000
corranbunkhouse@btconnect.com www.corranbunkhouse.co.uk

CALLUNA

Situated within fifteen minutes walk of Fort William High Street, Calluna is ideal for short or long stays. The modern accommodation consists of one flat, an alpine loft and two apartments. Bedding is supplied, along with a spacious kitchen, comfortable lounge and efficient drying rooms. On the spot advice from Alan Kimber (Mountain Guide) and an on-site indoor bouldering wall, with over 60 problems set by David Macleod (Britain's best rock and ice climber), make this an ideal all weather climbing venue. Waterproofs, boots, axes, crampons and mountaineering courses are also available (see website for details). Calluna is well known for peace, quiet and fine views over Loch Linnhe to the hills of Ardgour. A popular base for climbing and canoeing groups, families and individual globe trotters. Plenty of parking for mini-buses and trailers.
Lecture room available for groups

DETAILS

- **Open** - All year, 24 hours (keys supplied)
- **Number of beds** - 26: 5 x 2 (twin beds), 4 x 4
- **Booking** - Phone up beforehand
- **Price per night** - Dorm beds £15 a night and Twin beds £17pp a night.
- **Public Transport** -   Fort William train and coach/bus stations are 20 mins walk away. Alan & Sue offer a free lift from the stations when available - just phone.
- **Directions** - By vehicle: from roundabout (West End Hotel) go uphill on Lundavra Rd and take third on left (Connochie Rd) between four-storey flats. Follow Connochie Rd (do not take right turns) and arrive at our back door! On foot: ask for directions to the West End Hotel and follow the route above (15/20 mins on foot).

CONTACT: Alan or Sue
Heathercroft, Fort William, Inverness-shire, PH33 6RE
Tel: 01397 700451, Fax: 01397 700489
info@fortwilliamholiday.co.uk www.fortwilliamholiday.co.uk

FORT WILLIAM
BACKPACKERS

Deep in the Highlands, surrounded by spectacular mountain scenery lies Fort William, a mecca for those with a spirit of adventure. You can start (or end) the 'West Highland Way' in Fort William, hike or bike along mountain trails, go for a boat trip on the sea loch or just take it easy amidst the wonderful scenery. Even in winter Fort William stays busy with skiing, snow-boarding, mountaineering and ice-climbing. Nestling on a hillside above the town, with wonderful views, our characterful and comfy hostel provides everything you'll need after a day in the hills. In the evening put your feet up in our elegant lounge in front of a real fire or stroll down to the choice of local pubs. Ben Nevis, Britain's highest mountain, is just around the corner and below it is Glen Nevis, perhaps Scotland's prettiest glen, with wonderful waterfalls and ancient pine forest. Dramatic and eerie, Glencoe awaits a few miles away for an excellent day trip.

DETAILS

- **Open** - All year, all day. Reception 7am-12pm and 5pm-10.30pm (times may vary)
- **Number of beds** - 38
- **Booking** - Booking not always essential, first nights payment required for booking.
- **Price per night** - From £13 per person. ID required for check-in.
- **Public Transport** - Train and bus stations are only 5/10 minute walk from hostel.
- **Directions** - From north on the A82 go right at roundabout towards town centre. Turn left onto Victoria Road, then left at fork onto Alma Road, From south on the A82 go straight over first roundabout, At second roundabout go right onto Belford Road following Inverness signs, then turn right up Victoria Road then into Alma Road at left fork. From stations walk past supermarket, turn left before the underpass, heading onto the Belford Road. The hostel is just a bit further up, on Alma Road on the right.

CONTACT: Receptionist
Alma Road, Fort William, PH33 6HB
Tel: 01397 700 711
fortwilly@scotlandstophostels.com www.scotlandstophostels.com

BANK STREET
LODGE
SCOTLAND

Bank Street Lodge is situated 100 metres from Fort William High Street which has numerous shops, pubs, restaurants, banks etc.

There is a fully equipped kitchen with cooker, fridge, microwave, cutlery and crockery provided. The common room lounge has a TV, it also provides tables and chairs for eating self prepared meals, and a snack vending machine. All bedding is provided. Some rooms are en-suite (twins, doubles and family).

The Stables Restaurant, at the front of the building, serves fine food for lunches and dinners - treat yourself.

Fort William is an ideal base from which to enjoy walking, climbing, cycling or mountain biking. The world-renowned Nevis Range Mountain Bike Trails and Ski Centre are only a short distance from the town centre. Three star STB rating

DETAILS

- **Open** - All year, 24 hour reception
- **Number of beds** - 42: 6 x 4 : 3 x 3 : 1 x 7 : 1 x 2
- **Booking** - Booking advised. Deposit required for long stays or groups.
- **Price per night** - £14, £15 or £17.50 per person. Group rates available.
- **Public Transport** - Train and bus stations at Fort William, 500 metres from Lodge.
- **Directions** - Head for Town Centre via the underpass, turn left after Tesco supermarket on Bank Street, then head up the hill for 150 metres. Hostel is above the Stables Restaurant. Car parking is available.

CONTACT: Kenny / Reception
Bank Street, Fort William, PH33 6AY
Tel: 01397 700070
bankstreetlodge@btconnect.com www.bankstreetlodge.co.uk

CHASE THE
WILD GOOSE HOSTEL

Chase The Wild Goose Backpackers Hostel is located on the Great Glen Way and cycle route in the village of Banavie, near Fort William and at the end of the West Highland Way. You can be sure of a warm welcome, a comfortable bed and the company of like-minded travellers in a pleasant out-of-town environment.

Chase The Wild Goose is ideal accommodation, whether you are on a relaxing holiday break with family or friends, enjoying the adventure of a lifetime, travelling the world or living life in the extreme.
Take time out in the Scottish Highlands. The scenery is breath-taking! The hospitality is second to none!

DETAILS

- **Open** - All year, 7am - 10pm (late keys)
- **Number of beds** - 48 : 2x8, 3x6, 2x5, 1x4
- **Booking** - Pre-booking is advised. Credit or debit card secures booking.
- **Price per night** - From £9.95 to £20.45 per person. Reductions for under 16s and groups. Exclusive use is available to groups at excellent rates.
- **Public Transport** - The hostel is located just 100m from Banavie train station. The Fort William-Mallaig-Isle of Skye bus stop is nearby on the A830.
- **Directions** - Travel north from Fort William on the A82, signed Inverness. After 1.5 miles, turn left on the A830 'Road to the Isles' for Mallaig. After 1 mile, cross the canal and take a right turn, then 2nd left. Expect to see a large building with flags on the roof. If walking, take a short-cut to Banavie along the Great Glen Way.

CONTACT: Fergus
Great Glen Way, Lochiel Crescent, Banavie, Fort William, Inverness-shire, PH33 7LY
Tel: 07979 407980 or 01397 772531
enquiries@great-glen-hostel.com www.great-glen-hostel.com

SMIDDY
BUNKHOUSE

A friendly welcome at our comfortable, family run, mountain hostels in a loch-side location overlooking the Caledonian Canal. The pine clad interior gives a cosy, friendly atmosphere. Stunning mountains and water at the doorstep with the meeting of the West Highland Way and Great Glen Way. Hot showers. Fully equipped kitchens available at all times (food available from local shop until 10pm daily). Use of 2 efficient drying / laundry rooms. Bedding provided. Fully heated for all year round use. Outdoor information / daily snow and avalanche reports.

Advice/instruction available from resident mountain and water based instructors and guides for: winter and summer walking/climbing; river,loch and sea kayaking; dinghy sailing. Hire for sea and river of kayaks/open canoes, dinghy and other equipment. AALA licensed outdoor centre. Group and family accommodation. Meeting / lecture room facilities available by arrangement.

DETAILS

- **Open** - All year, all day (with key). Key deposit required.
- **Number of beds** - 26 : 3x4, 1x6, 1x8
- **Booking** - Telephone to pre-book.
- **Price per night** - £11.50 - £14.00 (seasonal) pp (incl. bedding).
- **Public Transport** - Two minutes walk from Corpach Railway Station on the Mallaig Line. Three miles from Fort William (trains from Glasgow and London).
- **Directions** - Take A82 north out of Fort William towards Inverness. After one mile take A830 north towards Mallaig and follow for 2 miles to village of Corpach. Turn left before shops, signposted 'Snowgoose Mountain Centre'. The hostel is 30yds on left.

CONTACT: John or Tina
Snowgoose Mountain Centre, Station Road, Corpach, Fort William, PH33 7JH
Tel: 01397 772467, Fax: 01397 772467
ihg@highland-mountain-guides.co.uk www.highland-mountain-guides.co.uk

FARR COTTAGE LODGE

Farr Cottage is a 4 star hostel situated in Corpach just 4 miles from Fort William town centre, with a breath-taking view of Ben Nevis and across Loch Linnhe, in the outdoor pursuits capital of Scotland. There is a full range of in-house facilities including cable television in the lounge, licensed bar, self-catering facilities, drying room and laundry service. Newly installed central heating and hot showers.

We also organise outdoor pursuits which comprise white water rafting, canyoning, climbing, abseiling, skiing, snowboarding, fishing, golf and many many more! We can provide evening meals, breakfast, picnic lunches and we will ensure you have the break or holiday of a lifetime with us. Our professional team are geared to meet your needs and requirements.

DETAILS

■ **Open** - All year, 24 hours
■ **Number of beds** - Cottage 30: 2 x double, 2 x 8,1 x 10. Lodge 18: 1 x 2, 1 x 4, 2 x 6. Both buildings fully self-contained.
■ **Booking** - Advance booking advised
■ **Price per night** - £15pp, From £17pp in double room. Group rates available.
■ **Public Transport** - Corpach train station is 200m from the hostel. The nearest Citylink service is three miles away at Fort William. Taxi fare from Fort William centre is approximately £7.50.
■ **Directions** - Follow the A82 north from Fort William centre towards Inverness for 1.5 miles. Turn left at the A830 to Mallaig. Follow this road for 1.5 miles into Corpach. We are on the right.

CONTACT: Cliff or Dee
Corpach, Fort William, PH33 7LR
Tel: 01397 772315
mail@farrcottage.com www.farrcottage.com

BEN NEVIS INN
BUNKHOUSE
SCOTLAND

The Ben Nevis Inn is located in one of the most beautiful and famous areas of Scotland, at the very foot of Ben Nevis, Britain's highest mountain. The Inn sits in Braveheart country at the start of the Ben Nevis path and a mile from the end of the West Highland Way. The bunkhouse offers everything that walkers and mountaineers will need, with self catering facilities including a large kitchen, comfortable bunks, and a separate drying area. All bunks have a duvet and all bed linen (no sleeping bags allowed). The bunkroom sleeps 24 divided into three sections and has some great views onto Glen Nevis.

The Inn offers an extensive menu with plenty of local produce and something to suit all tastes. There is frequent live music, check out events on the Inn's website . The bunkhouse is 20 minutes walk from the centre of Fort William which has cafes, provisions shops, outdoor-ware shop, pubs, and a well-equipped and recently refurbished leisure centre with swimming pool.

DETAILS

- **Open** - All year, all day
- **Number of beds** - 24: 3x8
- **Booking** - Strongly recommended. Book online with full payment.
- **Price per night** - £14 to £15 per person per night.
- **Public Transport** - Train station and bus stop in town centre, 2 miles (30 mins walk) from bunkhouse. There is a taxi rank outside the station.
- **Directions** - From A82 in Fort William take road to Inverness. Just before lights turn right onto Achintee Rd towards Claggan. At Spar shop turn right and follow road.

CONTACT:
The Ben Nevis Inn, Claggan, Achintee, Fort William, Inverness-shire, PH33 6TE
Tel: 01397 701227
info@ben-nevis-inn.co.uk www.ben-nevis-inn.co.uk

ARIUNDLE
BUNKHOUSE

The Ariundle Centre is located at the beginning of the Ariundle Oakwoods, close to glorious walks, bird song, climbing, cycling, canoeing and fishing. It is a friendly family run business with a licensed restaurant, tea room, craft shop and bunkhouse. The 4 star Bunkhouse was completed in February 2006 and sleeps 26 people. The rooms are large and airy and there is a drying area and self catering facilities. Linen is supplied, towels can be hired for 50p. The Bunkhouse is ideal for walkers and climbers. Groups, individuals and families are all welcome and family rooms are available. Cooked breakfasts, morning coffee, light lunches and scrumptious home baking are available in the restaurant and the sandwiches and baking make ideal packed lunches. Candlelit suppers are served using local products, sometimes with a local musician to entertain. The Centre can cater for parties or weddings with guests sleeping in the bunkhouse. The village of Strontian has a petrol station and a well stocked shop.

DETAILS

- **Open** - All year,
- **Number of beds** - 26: 2x8, 2x4,1x2
- **Booking** - Advance bookings accepted all year
- **Price per night** - From £15 pp. Cont. b/fst £3. Grp discount for advance payment.
- **Public Transport** - 1 mile from the nearest public transport.
- **Directions** - If travelling from north, east or south the quickest way to arrive at the Centre is to take the A82 to the Corran Ferry and then follow the road to Strontian. (Turn left when you come off the ferry).

CONTACT: Kate Campbell
Ariundle Centre, Strontian, PH36 4JA
Tel: 01967 402279
ariundle@aol.com www.ariundle.co.uk

Glenfinnan sleeping car provides unique, comfortable accommodation in an historic railway carriage adjacent to Glenfinnan Station.

It is an ideal location for the mountains of Lochaber, Rough Bounds, Moidart and Ardgour. It makes a good starting point for bothy expeditions and is a useful stopping off point on the route to Skye.
Why not use it also for extended stays using road or rail for trips to fishing, golf, ferries, cruises, and beach locations.
There is a fully equipped kitchen, showers, a drying room and total hydro electric heating. The adjacent dining coach provides excellent meals to give you a break from self catering.

Your overnight stay includes free admission to the railway museum housed in the railway buildings

DETAILS

- **Open** - All year , 24 hours
- **Number of beds** - 10
- **Booking** - Booking preferred and advisable to avoid disappointment.
- **Price per night** - £14 pp, £120 for exclusive use of whole coach.
- **Public Transport** - Bunkhouse is adjacent to Glenfinnan Railway Station on the West Highland Line (Glasgow-Fort William-Mallaig) and is 100m from a bus stop.
- **Directions** - On the A830, 15 miles from Fort William and 30 miles from Mallaig with ferry connections to the Small Isles and Skye.

CONTACT: John or Hege
Glenfinnan Station, Glenfinnan, nr Fort William, PH37 4LT
Tel: 01397 722295, Fax: 01397 722495
susanjohnson75@tiscali.co.uk   www.glenfinnanstationmuseum.co.uk

Àite Cruinnichidh, 15 miles northeast of Fort William, occupies a unique sheltered spot adjacent to the Monessie Gorge; explore remote glens, mountain passes and lochs. Numerous easy walks within minutes of the hostel and seven magnificent canoeing rivers within 20 miles. The location is also ideal for climbing (rock & ice), mountain biking, skiing or just relaxing. A warm, peaceful, friendly, country hostel in a converted barn. Àite Cruinnichidh has been renovated to high standards and sleeps 32 in five rooms of four, one of six, one twin and one double/family room en-suite. All bedding supplied. A fully equipped kitchen/dining room, sitting room, excellent showers. Additional facilities:- sauna suite, garden, seminar room, dark room, use of maps, advice on walking/cycling routes. Groups and individuals welcome. We do not have wheelchair access but we are glad to accommodate people with all forms of disability whenever we can, and know some sign language.

DETAILS

■ **Open** - All year
■ **Number of beds** - 32: 1x6, 5x4, 1x twin, 1x family / double en-suite
■ **Booking** - Booking advised, 50% deposit.
■ **Price per night** - £12 per person.
■ **Public Transport** - Roy Bridge train station and bus stop (2 miles) has several trains and buses to and from Fort William daily. Pick up available from Roy Bridge.
■ **Directions** - From Fort William follow A82 for 10 miles to Spean Bridge, turn right onto A86 for 3 miles to Roy Bridge. Pass though village and continue for 2 miles. The hostel is on right 100m after Glenspean Lodge Hotel on left.

CONTACT: Gavin or Nicola
1 Achluachrach, By Roy Bridge, Near Fort William, PH31 4AW
Tel: 01397 712315
gavin@highland-hostel.co.uk www.highland-hostel.co.uk

NEWTONMORE
HOSTEL

Newtonmore, a traditional village in the Cairngorms National Park, is a great base for outdoor activities, relaxing or touring. The village has shops, a petrol station and several hotels which serve good value food and drink. See where Monarch of the Glen was filmed, visit the Highland Folk Museum, the MacPherson Museum and Waltzing Waters! Walk, climb, ski, canoe, windsurf, cycle, fish, golf, birdwatch or sail.

Our purpose built hostel has showers, a brilliant drying room, a well equipped kitchen, central heating and a lounge/dining area with wood burning stove. No meters.

Inverness 46 miles, Fort William 50 miles, Glasgow/Edinburgh 110 miles

Come and stay in our hostel, the area is unique.

DETAILS

- **Open** - All year, all day, no curfew
- **Number of beds** - 10: 1 x 2, 2 x 4
- **Booking** - Phone to check availability (20% deposit) or book online.
- **Price per night** - From £14 (adult), reductions for children. Private rooms £36(twin), £51(triple), £68(quad).
- **Public Transport** - Newtonmore train station + bus stops nearby.
- **Directions** - GR 713 990. The hostel is behind Craigellachie House in the centre of the village at the junction of the A86 and B9150. Look for blue signs.

CONTACT: Kathryn or Peter
Craigellachie House, Main Street, Newtonmore, Inverness-shire, PH20 1DA
Tel: 01540 673360
pete@HighlandHostel.co.uk www.HighlandHostel.co.uk

INSH HALL
LODGE
SCOTLAND

Situated between Loch Insh and the foothills of Glenfeshie, Insh Hall Lodge provides comfortable double, twin and family rooms on a room-only, B&B or full board basis. Rooms are equipped with bed linen and TVs.

Facilities include self catering kitchens, large meeting room, laundry/drying room, sauna and mini gym, outdoor volleyball and basketball, as well as private car parking.

FREE WATERSPORTS OFFERED TO GUESTS STAYING TWO OR MORE NIGHTS (SET TIMES.)

Meals are available in the Boathouse Restaurant situated by the shore, 120 yds from the lodge. Loch Insh is the starting point for many local walks, lochside trails and cycle routes (located on Sustrans Cycle Way, Route 7).

DETAILS

- **Open** - All year, All day
- **Number of beds** - 28: double, twin and family rooms
- **Booking** - Booking is recommended but not always required. Deposit taken.
- **Price per night** - From £16 - £35 per person.
- **Public Transport** - Trains at Aviemore and Kingussie (7 miles from Loch Insh). Nearest airport is Inverness, approximately one hour north of Loch Insh.
- **Directions** - Situated near Kincraig, 7 miles south of Aviemore, 7 miles north of Kingussie on the B9152, follow signs for Loch Insh Watersports. Local bus routes from Aviemore to Kincraig, approx 1 mile from the Lodge.

CONTACT: Receptionist
Insh Hall, Kincraig, Inverness-shire, PH21 1NU
Tel: 01540 651272
office@lochinsh.com www.lochinsh.com

BRAEMAR LODGE
BUNKHOUSE

Surrounded by the beauty of Deeside, Braemar Lodge is in a quiet setting only a two minute walk from the village itself. Braemar Lodge Hotel was formerly a Victorian shooting lodge and is set in extensive grounds two minutes from the centre of Braemar in the heart of Royal Deeside.

Our great value Bunkhouse provides comfortable accommodation for up to 12 people within the hotel grounds. The bunkhouse is equipped with two shower rooms, one of which is suitable for wheelchair access. The bunkhouse also has excellent drying and laundry facilities, excellent for damp clothes and ski boots. A generous fully equipped kitchen is also available for all your self catering needs. Guests are also welcome to use the hotel's excellent dining facilities if a rest from self catering is required. All bed linen and towels are supplied for the duration of your stay.

DETAILS

- **Open** - All year, all day
- **Number of beds** - 12: 3x4
- **Booking** - Book by phone or email
- **Price per night** - From £13 per person
- **Public Transport** - Aberdeen airport 59 miles. Railway stations at Perth (50 miles) and Aberdeen. Buses to Braemar from Aberdeen where the bus and rail station are side by side. Two minute walk to hotel from Braemar village bus stop.
- **Directions** - The hotel is situated on the A93 on the left if you are arriving form the south. Two minutes walk from the village centre.

CONTACT: Reception
6 Glenshee Rd, Braemar, Aberdeenshire, AB35 5YQ
Tel: 013397 41627
mail@braemarlodge.co.uk www.braemarlodge.co.uk

Exceptional accommodation in the Scottish highlands for families, friends, couples and groups. Guests from all over the world have been delighted by this refreshingly stylish base in Royal Deeside, in the dramatic surroundings of the Cairngorm Park. The owners Alan and Cathy Low are committed to meeting the highest standards. Cathy is a professional storyteller and both speak French and German and teach English. For details of English programmes, please visit www.schoolhouse-english.eu. There's a large lounge with giant sofas and open fire, a bright dining room and a choice of family, double or twin rooms. The beds are superkingsize and all rooms have excellent ensuite showers. There's a large garden with BBQ hire, outdoor eating facilities and car park. Schoolhouse can provide excellent accommodation for groups of up to 24 in 3 ensuite dorms with up to 8 bunks in each. Bed linen and towels are supplied and breakfast is included. In-house catering can be provided, delicious meals and lunches being freshly prepared often using ingredients straight from the garden.

DETAILS

- **Open** - All year, all day
- **Number of beds** - 22
- **Booking** - Booking essential for groups
- **Price per night** - From £18 per person, includes breakfast.
- **Public Transport** - From Aberdeen bus station (bus enquiries 01224 212266).
- **Directions** - From Aberdeen follow the A93 to Ballater (43 miles). From Inverness follow Grantown-on-Spey then A939 to Ballater (70 miles). From Perth follow A93 to Blairgowrie then continue to Ballater (65 miles).

CONTACT: Alan or Cathy Low
Anderson Road, Ballater, Aberdeenshire, AB35 5QW
Tel: 013397 56333
info@school-house.eu   www.school-house.eu

SLOCHD MHOR
LODGE

Slochd Mhor Lodge is perfectly situated in the spectacular Strathspey in the Cairngorm National Park and halfway between the villages of Carrbridge and Tomatin. The Lodge is on an 'off road' section of the No 7 Sustrans cycle route and surrounded by hills and forests. This is also perfect walking country and in winter there are nordic ski trails from the doorstep. All other outdoor pursuits are within easy reach. Slochd Mhor Lodge offers a genuine welcome in warm cosy surroundings. Fully equipped kitchen with wood burning stove and a spacious dining area together with large lounge / lecture room with woodburner, tv, books and games. Other facilities include a drying room and laundry facilities, some en-suite rooms, a shower and toilet room suitable for wheel-chair users, an on-site cycle shop / workshop, MT bike hire, and in winter nordic ski hire. Free range eggs when available. Coffee and tea. There is an outside seating and BBQ area. Ample parking. Visit Scotland 4 star graded. Silver Green Business Award. Cyclists Welcome and Walkers Welcome members.

DETAILS

- **Open** - All year, 24 hours
- **Number of beds** - 28: 1x10 : 1x6 : 2x5 : 1x2
- **Booking** - Booking recommended
- **Price per night** - From £15pp. Sole use rates available.
- **Public Transport** - Nearest bus and train station Carrbridge (4miles). City Link London/Edinburgh and Glasgow/Inverness stop at Carrbridge.
- **Directions** - From south on A9, after mileage board 'Inverness 23' travel 1.5 miles north, take first opening on left marked 'Slochd'. Then first opening on right (¼ mile)

CONTACT: Liz or Ian
Slochd, Carrbridge, Inverness-shire, PH23 3AY
Tel: 01479 841666
Slochd666@aol.com www.slochd.co.uk

ARDENBEG
BUNKHOUSE
SCOTLAND

Ideal accommodation for groups and families visiting the stunning Cairngorms National Park, near Aviemore, in the Highlands of Scotland!

Four family / group rooms with private / en-suite shower rooms. Two fully equipped kitchen / dining rooms with televisions, stereos. Large, enclosed garden, BBQ, campfire area, play equipment. Outside covered seating area for use from Spring to October. Ample off road parking, discount card and free wireless broadband. A superb location for year round activities! Summer / winter mountaineering, skiing / snowboarding. rock climbing & abseiling, kayaking & canoeing, mountain biking, gorge swimming, orienteering, sailing, windsurfing, golf. Many other local attractions, ideal for families / rest days.

VisitScotland 3star Hostel, Hospitality Assured.

DETAILS

- **Open** - All year, all day
- **Number of beds** - 24 : 1x4 : 2x6 : 1x8
- **Booking** - In advance to avoid disappointment.
- **Price per night** - £16.50 pp for 2 or more nights, £18 for a single night. Private rooms from £46.50
- **Public Transport** - Nearest train station Aviemore. Nearest airport Inverness. Good bus services from both to Grantown Square. Ardenbeg is 2 minutes walk.
- **Directions** - From the A9 approach Grantown on the A95 passing Dulnain Bridge. At first roundabout turn left into Grantown.Just before traffic lights turn left into Chapel Road. Turn right at the end of road into Grant Rd. Ardenbeg is 2nd house on left.

CONTACT: Rebecca
Grant Road, Grantown-on-Spey, Moray, PH26 3LD
Tel: 01479 872824
enquiries@ardenbeg.co.uk www.ardenbeg.co.uk

HABITAT
@ BALLATER

Set in the village of Ballater, with a range of shops, pubs and restaurants, this is a stunning, purpose built hostel, ideal for families, groups and independent travellers. Within the Cairngorms National Park it is a great position for enjoying a variety of outdoor activities.

All rooms are ensuite, ranging from 8 bed dorms to 4 bed rooms suitable for families. Bedding is included.

There's a large kitchen /dining / lounge area with wood burning stove and under-floor heating throughout. There is an excellent drying and laundry room and secure storage for bikes.

Ballater is an ideal location for exploring the Eastern Cairngorms, Royal Deeside and Aberdeenshire.

Habitat@Ballater is a VisitScotland five star hostel.

DETAILS

- **Open** - All year, all day
- **Number of beds** - 37: 2x8, 1x7, 3x4, 1x2. All ensuite.
- **Booking** - Book by phone or email.
- **Price per night** - From £15 per person.
- **Public Transport** - From Aberdeen bus station (phone 01224 212266)
- **Directions** - On A93 just west of bridge over river in centre of Ballater.

CONTACT: Harry and Claudia Leith
Bridge Square, Ballater, Aberdeenshire, AB35 5QJ
Tel: 013397 53752
info@habitat-at-ballater.com www.habitat-at-ballater.com

RATTRAY HEAD
ECO-HOSTEL

Rattray Head Eco-Hostel is a former lighthouse shore station among huge dunes on an isolated 11 mile sandy beach. Come and relax in this gorgeous most easterly part of mainland Scotland, and enjoy one of its driest, sunniest, midge-free areas.

The 1892 granite building has been renovated to form a modern, non-smoking, dog-friendly coastal retreat. The hostel has self-catering kitchens, bunkrooms, and double and family bedrooms.
It is part of the SIH network and has a Visit Scotland 3-Star grading.

The North Sea Cycle Route (Sustrans 1) is 17 miles inland and passes through historic Aberdeenshire with stone circles, castle ruins and golf courses.

DETAILS

- **Open** - All year, phone in winter, , Check-in 4–8pm, check-out 11am. No curfew.
- **Number of beds** - 22: 1x2, 5x4
- **Booking** - Booking is available with first night as deposit.
- **Price per night** - Bunk £14pp, triple £16pp, double/twin £21pp. Includes bedding and drinks.
- **Public Transport** - Airport, coach and train stations at Aberdeen (43 miles). Buses 260, 263 run frequently between Aberdeen and Peterhead. Bus 269 runs hourly between Peterhead and Fraserburgh. Taxi from Peterhead about £17.
- **Directions** - NK103577 Rattray is signed from the A90 Peterhead to Fraserburgh road. The hostel is at the end of the lane near the lighthouse, about 3 miles from the A90.

CONTACT: Rob and Val
Lighthouse Cottages, Rattray Head, Peterhead, Aberdeenshire, AB42 3HA
Tel: 01346 532236
hostel@rattrayhead.net www.rattrayhead.net/hostel

NETHY STATION

SCOTLAND ABERNETHY BUNKHOUSES

Sharing a car park with the Speyside Way and just yards from the river, the converted Nethy Station offers all that a group could expect from a bunkhouse. It is well-equipped, fully central heated and has two public areas. Most rooms have triple bunks. We have 2 bunk rooms with unusual access: we call it Narnia, as you can reach them through a wardrobe! There is also 'The Shed'!

Whether you self-cater or we cook for you as a group you will have access to the kitchen at all times. We never ask people to share the building so you may sleep, walk, ski, board, hike, ride, fish etc…. at your own convenience!

The station is only 200 yards from the centre of Nethy Bridge with its shop, butcher, pub and interpretive centre and half way between two wintersports areas. Dogs are welcome but please do not let them sleep on the beds!

DETAILS

- **Open** - All year, anytime
- **Number of beds** - 24: 2 x 9 :3 x 2.
- **Booking** - Essential (with deposit)
- **Price per night** - £11.75pp May-Sep. £12.75pp Oct–Apr. Minimum of 7 people.
- **Public Transport** -   Take train or Citylink coach to Aviemore. Local buses are available from Aviemore to Nethy Bridge Post Office, phone 01479 811566.
- **Directions** - GR 002 207.   Hostel is adjacent to the Speyside Way. From the B970, with Post Office on your right, go over the bridge and turn left immediately. Past the butcher turn second right.

CONTACT: Patricia or Richard
Croftbank, Nethy Bridge, PH25 3DS
Tel: 01479 821370
info@nethy.org www.nethy.org

INVERNESS
STUDENT HOTEL
SCOTLAND

Inverness, capital of the Highlands, is set amongst some of Scotland's most fascinating attractions. The bustling town centre soon gives way to lochs, hills, forests and glens. Close to Inverness Castle, the intimate and lively Student Hostel enjoys wonderful panoramic views of the town and the mountains beyond. After a hard day's Nessie hunting, our hostel provides a friendly cosy place to unwind, just yards from the city's varied nightlife and a few minutes walk from the bus and train stations. Visit the beautiful ancient pine forest of Glen Affric, tranquil but deeply historic Culloden Battlefield, the 4,000-year-old standing stones at Clava Cairns or stroll down the river bank to the waterfront to try to glimpse the wild dolphins in the nearby Moray Firth. Famous Loch Ness lies just a few miles upstream and of course has its own special wild animal.

DETAILS

- **Open** - All year, all day, reception 7am-11pm (times may vary)
- **Number of beds** - 57
- **Booking** - Booking not always essential. First nights payment needed to book.
- **Price per night** - From £13 per person, ID required for check-in.
- **Public Transport** - Inverness train station and bus station are a mere 10 minute walk from the hostel. Alternatively jump in a taxi for around £5.
- **Directions** - Head to the city centre and the castle. Hostel is up from Castle Terrace past the castle. Where road forks take the left onto Culduthel Road. Hostel is second building on right. From train / bus station turn left onto Academy St. When you see the Marks and Spencers ahead of you, cross at the traffic lights and go down Inglis St. At the end turn right along the High Street, and then left at the bottom going up Castle St past the castle. Continue up Culduthel Road and hostel is on right.

CONTACT: Receptionist
8 Culduthel Road, Inverness, IV2 4AB
Tel: 01463 236556
inverness@scotlandstophostels.com www.scotlandstophostels.com

LOCHNESS
SCOTLAND BACKPACKERS LODGE

Loch Ness Backpackers is a warm and friendly little hostel with a relaxed atmosphere, good music and no curfew. It has grown from an 18th-century farm cottage and barn and provides a warm open fire to greet you on cold nights. The house forms the main area of the hostel with reception, lounges, dining room, kitchen and toilets / showers on the ground floor, and two dormitories and one double room in the upstairs area. A converted barn (the bunkhouse) contains four more dormitories, toilets / showers and a kitchen / dining area. There is also a great BBQ area, garden & car park.

Loch Ness Backpackers is within easy walking distance of Loch Ness, Urquhart Castle, three pubs, restaurants, a supermarket, a fish & chip shop, post office, bank, gift shops and bus stops. A perfect location for activity or relaxation amongst spectacular scenery. Horse riding, fishing on the loch and mountain biking can all be arranged locally (great bikes available for hire).

DETAILS
- **Open** - All year, all day
- **Number of beds** - House 16: Bunkhouse 24: (1x2, 2 x family room, 6 x dorms).
- **Booking** - Check availability on website or by phone.
- **Price per night** - From £15 per person.
- **Public Transport** - Nearest trains at Inverness. Rapsons, Megabus and Citylink buses all pass close to the hostel.
- **Directions** - Near the A82 Inverness to Fort William road. Turn off is next to the stone bridge in Lewiston near the Smiddy pub.

CONTACT: Wendy and Neil MacIntosh
Coiltie Farm House, East Lewiston, Drumnadrochit, Inverness, IV63 6UJ
Tel: 01456 450807
info@lochness-backpackers.com www.lochness-backpackers.com/

BCC LOCHNESS
HOSTEL
SCOTLAND

BCC Lochness Hostel is a top quality purpose built-hostel (graded 5 star by VisitScotland) with superb facilities. All rooms are en-suite and offer the very latest in facilities for the discerning traveller. It lies in the heart of one of Scotland's most stunning glens, enabling you to escape from modern life.

This is an excellent base from which you may explore the world famous Loch Ness, Urquhart Castle, Glen Affric (National Nature Reserve) and Glen Strathfarrar which are renowned for their stunning beauty and variety of wildlife. From the hostel there are 6 golf courses all within 30 minutes drive. It is also ideally placed for hill walking, Munro bagging, mountain biking, cycling, fishing and horse riding. A good stop off point for those travelling to Skye and the Outer Hebrides and yet only twenty minutes drive from the historic city of Inverness. The hostel is situated near the main bus route and is within easy walking distance of the nearby pub / restaurant.

DETAILS

- **Open** - All year, all day
- **Number of beds** - 30: 5 x 6/4
- **Booking** - Book by phone or email.
- **Price per night** - From £12 per person. From £30 for twin room.
- **Public Transport** -   Buses from Inverness, Drumnadrochit and Fort William stop nearby.
- **Directions** - We are midway between Drumnadrochit and Cannich on the A381 which leads to Glen Affric National Nature Reserve.

CONTACT: Donald MacLean
Bearnock, Glen Urquhart, Drumnadrochit, Inverness-shire, IV63 6TN
Tel: 01456 476296 Mob: 07780 603045, Fax: 0778060945
info@bcclochness.co.uk www.bcclochnesshostel.co.uk

MORAG'S
LODGE

Morag's Lodge is an award winning hostel overlooking Fort Augustus and is the perfect base to explore the Loch Ness area. We offer great budget accommodation for backpackers, independent travellers and groups and we're a perfect stop off if you're on The Great Glen Way.

We have a range of dorms, twins, doubles and private family rooms and most are en-suite. Fantastic facilities include a fully licensed bar, TV lounge, drying room, wi-fi and internet access, self-catering kitchen and dining room.

We can also provide breakfast and evening meal with packed lunches on request. Ample car parking is available in the hostel grounds and bike hire is available.

VisitScotland Grading 4 Stars. Green Tourism Silver Award.

DETAILS

- **Open** - All year, all day. Check-in from 5pm (earlier by arrangement)
- **Number of beds** - 81: 5x6, 3x5, 6x4, 4x3
- **Booking** - Booking recommended.
- **Price per night** - From £17 pp bunk.
- **Public Transport** - Bus stop for Fort William and Inverness only 200m away.
- **Directions** - From Inverness, arrive at Fort Augustus, turn first right up Bunoich Brae. From Fort William, go through village past petrol station and car park. Take next left up Bunoich Brae.

CONTACT: Liz
Bunoich Brae, Fort Augustus, Inverness-shire, PH32 4DG
Tel: 01320 366289
info@moragslodge.com www.moragslodge.com

BIKE HIRE

STRAVAIGERS
LODGE

Stravaigers Lodge is an independent, purpose-built, family-run hostel with 30 private rooms sleeping 60 people (no dorms). It offers comfortable, low priced accommodation for individuals, families and groups.

Situated in Fort Augustus on the shores of Loch Ness, our hostel is only five minutes walk from the Caledonian Canal, Loch Ness and the Great Glen Way. Pubs, restaurants and shops are also within 5 minutes walk.

The lodge provides a warm welcome, friendly service and an excellent place to stay. situated in the beautiful village of Fort Augustus at the southern end of Loch Ness.

DETAILS
- **Open** - April to New year, 10am onwards
- **Number of beds** - 60: 30 x 2
- **Booking** - Notice required for bookings in off peak season.
- **Price per night** - £15 to £20 per person.
- **Public Transport** - Regular air links from London to Inverness and daily bus service from airport via Inverness and Loch Ness to Fort Augustus.
- **Directions** - From the white canal bridge head towards B862 (Whitebridge) and follow for 100metres, hostel is on your right

CONTACT:
Glendoe road, Fort Augustus, Inverness-Shire, PH32 4BZ
Tel: 01320 366257
stravaigerslodge@aol.com

Nestled between mountains and lochs in the heart of the "Outdoor Capital of the UK", 20 miles north of Fort William and 10 miles south of Loch Ness, the Great Glen Hostel is an ideal location whether you're touring the Highlands, bagging Munros or paddling rivers and lochs, and we are only a few minutes' walk from the Great Glen Way.

We provide comfortable accommodation in twin, family and dormitory rooms. Hostel facilities include a self-catering kitchen, drying room, laundry, bike and canoe storage, free internet access, hot showers and a hostel store.

The whole hostel is available for exclusive rental for groups throughout the year.

DETAILS

■ **Open** - Open all year, all day. Please call first Nov-March.
■ **Number of beds** - 50: 3 x 2, 1 x 4, 4 x 5, 2 x 6, 1 x 8
■ **Booking** - Booking recommended. Please telephone in advance or book online
■ **Price per night** - Dorm beds £14.50-15.50. Twin rooms from £34. Whole hostel available for exclusive hire from £350 per night.
■ **Public Transport** - Citylink bus services between Glasgow and the Isle of Skye, and between Fort William and Inverness will stop nearby. Nearest railway station: Spean Bridge. Nearest airport: Inverness.
■ **Directions** - We are located 11 miles north of Spean Bridge and 3 miles south of Invergarry on the A82 in a small settlement called South Laggan. Citylink buses stop 100m north of the hostel on the A82. If you are walking the Great Glen Way, stay on the Way until you see signs directing you to the hostel.

CONTACT: Clem or Kirsty
South Laggan, Spean Bridge, Inverness-shire, PH34 4EA
Tel: 01809 501430
bookings@greatglenhostel.com www.greatglenhostel.com

INVERGARRY
LODGE

Invergarry Lodge is a 4-star self-catering hostel located in the Great Glen, surrounded by mountains, glens, rivers and lochs. Ideally situated for most outdoor pursuits, it also provides a great base for exploring the Highlands. We are a short drive from Loch Ness and are ideally placed for day trips to Fort William, Fort Augustus, Inverness and the Isle of Skye.
The lodge is spacious and comfortable, accommodating up to 24 in 5 dormitory-style bedrooms. Facilities include a large kitchen, spacious lounge and dining areas and free wireless internet access and broadband. The hostel also has provision for bike and kayak storage and has a large drying room if required.
The hostel is open all year round to individuals, families and groups.

DETAILS
■ **Open** - All year (phone first November to March), all day
■ **Number of beds** - 24:- 2x6 : 1x4 : 2 x family (double + 3 single). Subject to availability rooms can be booked as doubles/twins
■ **Booking** - Recommended. Same and next day bookings, card number secures. Advance bookings 25% deposit please.
■ **Price per night** - From £15 per person
■ **Public Transport** - Citylink buses 915, 916 (Glasgow-Fort William-Skye) and 919 (Fort William-Inverness) serve Invergarry.
■ **Directions** - Take the A82 to Invergarry. From the south, Mandally Road is on the left, before the village, just past St Finnans Church. From the north, take the first turning on the right after the A87. From the village, the hostel is a 10min walk. Go south on the A82 towards Fort William. After the bridge, take the first road on the right.

CONTACT: Matt or Jenny
Mandally Road, Invergarry, PH35 4HP
Tel: 01809 501412
mail@invergarrylodge.co.uk www.invergarrylodge.co.uk

SHEENAS
BACKPACKERS LODGE SCOTLAND

The Backpackers Lodge in Mallaig offers a homely base from which you can explore the Inner Hebrides, the famous white sands of Morar and the remote peninsula of Knoydart. Mallaig is a working fishing village with all the excitement of the boats coming in. You can see the seals playing in the harbour waiting for the boats and whale watching trips are available from the harbour.

The hostel provides excellent budget accommodation with two rooms each with six beds, a drying room, full central heating and fully equipped kitchen/common room. It has three star plus grading with the Scottish Tourist Board.

On site is the Tea Garden Cafe open 9am-6pm serving quality meals, snacks, speciality coffee and home baking. In the evening The Garden Restaurant (open from 6pm to 9pm) serves home cooked bistro style seafood. Meals available from April to October. See website for pictures of our food and the beautiful countryside around.

DETAILS

- **Open** - All year 24 hours
- **Number of beds** - 12: 2 x 6
- **Booking** - Telephone ahead for availability and bookings.
- **Price per night** - £15 per person.
- **Public Transport** - Mallaig has a train station and services by Citylink coaches. For information on local buses phone 01967 431272.
- **Directions** - From railway station turn right, hostel is two buildings along.

CONTACT:
Harbour View, Mallaig, Inverness-shire, PH41 4PU
Tel: 01687 462764
backpackers@btinternet.com www.mallaigbackpackers.co.uk

A new conversion of a 19th-century building, the Glebe Barn has charm and character whilst providing comfortable accommodation with magnificent views. You can enjoy breathtaking scenery along numerous walks; study fascinating geological formations, or explore varied natural habitats with incredible varieties of plant and animal species. Relax on beautiful sandy beaches, listen to the famous singing sands and watch the eagles soar above the spectacular Sgurr of Eigg. Just a mile away there is a well-stocked shop and café / restaurant with regular traditional music sessions. Facilities at the Barn include a well-equipped kitchen, spacious lounge/dining room (polished maple floor, log fire), a combination of twin, triple, family and dormitory rooms, each with wash hand basins (linen provided), central heating, hot showers plus laundry facilities.

DETAILS

- **Open** - Individuals April to October, Groups all year, all day
- **Number of beds** - 22: 1 x 2 : 2 x 3 : 1 x 6 : 1 x 8.
- **Booking** - Booking essential prior to boarding ferry. Deposit required.
- **Price per night** - £16 (1/2 nights), £14 (3+ nights). Twin room £36 (1/2 nights), £32 (3+ nights). Sole use (min 14 persons) £15pp (1/2 nights), £12.50pp (3+ nights).
- **Public Transport** - Fort William is the nearest National Express coach stop. The early train from Fort William to Arisaig and Mallaig meets the ferry. Daily summer sailings from Arisaig or Mallaig.
- **Directions** - We generally meet visitors at the pier. Follow tarmac road around the shore and up hill until you cross a small stone bridge over a burn. Continue up hill and take first track on right. Taxi / minibus service available on request.

CONTACT: Karen or Simon
Isle of Eigg, PH42 4RL
Tel: 01687 482417
simon@glebebarn.co.uk www.glebebarn.co.uk

KINTAIL LODGE
BUNKHOUSES
SCOTLAND

Kintail Lodge stands at the foot of the Five Sisters of Kintail, right on the shores of Loch Duich. It is an ideal base for touring Skye and the Western Highlands or for bagging some of the 30 Munroes in the area. In the grounds of the hotel there are two budget accommodation units which are especially popular with walkers, climbers and fishermen. The Wee Bunk House has a cosy room with bunks to sleep 6 people and a snack kitchen containing fridge, hot rings, kettle, microwave and basic cooking utensils. There is a shower room with a toilet and the building is wheelchair friendly. The Trekkers' Lodge sleeps 6 people in two twin rooms and two single rooms, each with their own washbasin. There are 2 shower rooms with toilets and a snack kitchen equipped as in the Wee Bunkhouse. After a long day in the hills you can unwind in the relaxed atmosphere of the traditional Kintail Bar, where good food is served and beer is plentiful, or enjoy the lochside garden and patio.
Packed lunches are available if ordered the night before.

DETAILS

- **Open** - All year, all day (restricted winter hours)
- **Number of beds** - Trekkers Lodge 6: 2 x 2,2 x 1, Wee Bunkhouse 6:1 x 6
- **Booking** - Book by phone or email.
- **Price per night** - £14pp, 3+ nights £13pp, Sole use of Trekkers Lodge £80 per night. Sole use of Wee Bunkhouse £65 per night.
- **Public Transport** - See Citylink website
- **Directions** - Kintail Lodge is situated on the A87 between Invergarry and the Skye Bridge.

CONTACT: Reception
Kintail Lodge Hotel, Glenshiel, Kyle of Lochalsh, Ross-shire, IV40 8HL
Tel: 01599 511275
kintaillodgehotel@btinternet.com www.kintaillodgehotel.co.uk

FLORA MACDONALD
HOSTEL
SCOTLAND

Flora Macdonald Hostel offers clean, comfortable accommodation in the magnificent surroundings of the Sleat Peninsular in the south of the isle. In this region, also known as the Garden of Skye, visitors may see golden eagles, sea eagles, red and roe deer, otters and lots of other wildlife. It is also of enormous interest to geology students.

The owner Peter Macdonald, a direct descendent of the Lords of the Isles, the Macdonald Chiefs and Robert the Bruce, is a local historian happy to share his knowledge of the area, and breeds rare Eriskay ponies on the family croft.

The hostel has solid pine bunks and is fully centrally heated. It has a modern well equipped kitchen, a drying room with washer and tumble dryer, and a conservatory to sit in and enjoy the views.

DETAILS

- **Open** - All year, 9am to 9pm.
- **Number of beds** - 24: 1x10, 3x4, 1x2
- **Booking** - Booking is not essential but strongly advised. Deposits required with all bookings, at least 1 week in advance.
- **Price per night** - £14 dorm beds, private rooms £30 to £60. 20% reduction for block bookings and individual stays in excess of 7 nights.
- **Public Transport** - Regular bus service between Broadford and Armadale (bus stop at end of hostel road by the church).
- **Directions** - 3 miles from Armadale opposite Kilmore church, 22 miles from Skye bridge on the A851.

CONTACT: Peter Macdonald
Kilmore Sleat, By Armadale, Isle of Skye, IV44 8RG
Tel: 01471 844272/440
peter.macdonald@cillemhor.freeserve.co.uk

DUN CAAN
HOSTEL

SCOTLAND

This warm and friendly hostel, set on the harbour front in the romantic fishing village of Kyleakin, is the ideal base for your Isle of Skye visit. Overlooking the ancient ruins of Castle Moil (once home of a Viking princess known as Saucy Mary) you'll be enjoying beautiful sea and mountain views from every room.

We provide you with a well-equipped self-catering kitchen, free teas and coffees, hot showers, a cosy common room with TV, freshly laundered bed linen, a drying room for wet outdoor clothing, lots of books to read, games to play and advice on what to see and do on this truly magnificent island. Also available at the hostel: laundry services and bike hire. Please note that this is a non smoking hostel. Local facilities include a coffee shop, bars, restaurants and a general store and post office. Let's Go recommended and STB 4-star.

DETAILS

- **Open** - 1st March to 1 Oct, all day
- **Number of beds** - 15: 1x6, 1x5, 1x4
- **Booking** - Booking advisable in June, July and August. All major credit cards accepted. Secure on-line booking.
- **Price per night** - From £15 inc. bedlinen, teas and coffees. No hidden costs.
- **Public Transport** - Kyle of Lochalsh train station arrivals connect with Skye Bridge bus to Kyleakin (last stop Dun Caan Hostel). City Link coaches stop near to Hostel. Ferries Armadale, Kylerhea (summer only).
- **Directions** - After crossing the Skye Bridge turn left at the roundabout for Kyleakin. Through village towards harbour and old ferry pier.

CONTACT: Terry or Laila
The Pier Rd, Kyleakin, Isle of Skye, IV41 8PL
Tel: 01599 534087
info@skyerover.co.uk www.skyerover.co.uk

SKYE
BACKPACKERS

Skye Backpackers sits in the picturesque fishing village of Kyleakin, skirted by mountains and sea. A real 'home away from home', the hostel is a sanctuary for any weary traveller. Curl up by the open fire with a good book, or in the summer enjoy the hostel's large garden. Whatever you're looking for - hillwalking, sightseeing or the legendary faeries, this island will not disappoint. Our lovely hostel staff can also help arrange bus tours and hiking treks!

Kyleakin is on the main bus route and is also easily accessible by boat or from the train station at Kyle on the mainland. The village offers a shop, café, choice of pubs and spectacular scenic views. One of Europe's most dramatic and haunting lands, words can do little justice in describing the awesome beauty of the Isle of Skye. The majestic Cuillin Mountains dominate the rugged landscape, which is peppered with lochs, glens and tiny fishing villages.

DETAILS

- **Open** - All year, all day. Reception 7am-12pm and 5pm-10.30pm (times may vary)
- **Number of beds** - 39
- **Booking** - Booking in advance not always essential, first nights payment required for booking.
- **Price per night** - From £13 per person. ID required for check-in.
- **Public Transport** -   Kyle of Lochalsh train station is the closest train station and is only a short bus ride (approx 5/10mins) from the hostel. The bus drops you just opposite the hostel.
- **Directions** - From Kyle of Lochalsh go over the Skye Bridge then take first exit at roundabout, which takes you into Kyleakin. The hostel is on the right hand side after the Kings Arms Hotel. Park in the car park opposite hostel or on the hostel grounds.

CONTACT: Receptionist
Benmhor, Kyleakin, Isle of Skye, IV41 8PH
Tel: 01599 534510
skye@scotlandstophostels.com www.scotlandstophostels.com

Sligachan Bunkhouse overlooks the 'Black Cuillins' and is an ideal base for exploring the magnificent mountains of Skye. Several routes up the peaks pass the Bunkhouse and the path to 'Loch Coruisk' can be seen from the verandah.

The Bunkhouse is surrounded by peaceful mountain scenery on a track easily accessible by car. It is only a 5 minute walk from the bus stop at Sligachan, which sees a regular bus service from the mainland and Portree. The Sligachan Hotel can be seen from the Bunkhouse, about a 5 minute walk, and will provide a hot meal from breakfast through to dinner. The bar is a great place to relax after a long day's trekking and has a great display of malt whiskies and we make our own real ale at the Cuillin Brewery. The Bunkhouse has 4 bedrooms, full kitchen facilities and a lounge with open fire.

DETAILS

■ **Open** - March 1st to October 31st, all day
■ **Number of beds** - 20
■ **Booking** - Booking essential for large groups. Deposit required.
■ **Price per night** - £16pp. Linen Hire £3. Block bookings £300 per night. Discounts for longer stays.
■ **Public Transport** - Train - 1) Fort William to Mallaig, crossing by ferry to Armadale, buses to Sligachan (30m). 2) Inverness to Kyle of Lochalsh, catch bus over Skye Bridge to Kyleakin, connect with bus to Sligachan.
■ **Directions** - Inverness: A82 Invermoriston take A887 then A87 to Kyle of Lochalsh, cross Skye Bridge, continue on A87. Fort William: A830 to Mallaig, cross to Skye on ferry, take A851 to Broadford, then A87

CONTACT: Sligachan Hotel
Sligachan, Isle of Skye, IV47 8SW
Tel: 01478 650204
reservations@sligachan.co.uk www.sligachan.co.uk

WATERFRONT
BUNKHOUSE

Waterfront Bunkhouse has been purpose-built to provide a high degree of style and comfort. Twenty feet from the edge of Loch Harport, the accommodations command breathtaking views of the Cuillins. The bunkhouse is an ideal base for hill walkers or sightseeing tourists, with spectacular scenery and abundant wildlife in the surrounding hills and glens. The hostel sleeps 24 and consists of dormitory type rooms with 6 or 4 beds and one en-suite room. Upstairs there is the kitchen and common room with a balcony overlooking the loch. Full laundry facilities and showers are available (also open to visiting yachtsmen). The Waterfront Bunkhouse is about 40 mins from Broadford, 25 mins from Portree and next to The Old Inn, a traditional highland pub providing breakfast, lunch and dinner if required. Live traditional music every weekend and a welcoming open fire.

DETAILS

- **Open** - All year (please ring for availability), 24 hours
- **Number of beds** - 24: 2 x 6 bed & 3 x 4 bed
- **Booking** - In peak season booking 4 weeks or more in advance is advised (deposit required).
- **Price per night** - £14 per person, £16pp for en-suite room. Sole use £270.
- **Public Transport** - The nearest railway station is Kyle of Lochalsh. Citylink coaches (from the mainland and north Skye) drop off at Sligachan. Two local buses run each weekday from Portree via Sligachan to Fiskavaig
- **Directions** - From Sligachan take the A863 for 4 miles then left onto B8009 for 4 miles to Carbost The Waterfront Bunkhouse is in the centre of the village next to the Old Inn public house and opposite the school

CONTACT: Angus or Spencer
The Old Inn, Carbost, Isle of Skye, IV47 8SR
Tel: 01478 640205, Fax: 01478 640325
waterfront@oldinn.f9.co.uk   www.carbost.f9.co.uk

Come and visit the award winning, family run Skyewalker Hostel, rated 4 star by VisitScotland, and experience a warm welcome and true Scottish hospitality. Skyewalker Hostel is ideally situated as a base for exploring the island and offers a very high standard of clean, cosy accommodation at a budget price. We have a range of rooms from 2 bedded private rooms to larger dormitories (fresh bed linen provided free of charge), a comfortable lounge and a fully equipped self catering kitchen. We also have a large garden with BBQ area, giant chess, fantastic glass chill-out dome and off street free parking. Free Wifi is available and the local hotel / pub is a five minute walk from the hostel. Skyewalker hosts regular Scottish folk music sessions and it is also possible to book the whole place for special occasions such as birthdays, family get-togethers, Munro completion parties, etc.

DETAILS

- **Open** - 1st April - 31st October (or all year for group bookings), check in between 3pm and 10pm.
- **Number of beds** - 40:
- **Booking** - Book early to save disappointment. On-line booking available.
- **Price per night** - From £14.50 per person.
- **Public Transport** - Two local buses run each weekday from Portree via Sligachan to Portnalong and back. Citylink coaches from the mainland and north Skye drop off at Sligachan. Please note there is no bus to / from the hostel on Sundays.
- **Directions** - From Sligachan (in the centre of Skye), take A863 for 5 miles to the turn off for Carbost which takes you onto the B8009. Proceed through Carbost to Portnalong. Alternatively, follow the green signs from Sligachan! GR 348 348

CONTACT: Brian or Lisa
Old School, Portnalong, Isle of Skye, IV47 8SL
Tel: 01478 640250, Fax: 01478 640420
enquiries@skyewalkerhostel.com www.skyewalkerhostel.com

CROFT BUNKHOUSE
SCOTLAND BOTHIES AND WIGWAMS

We offer a variety of accomodation, including a fully equipped bunkhouse, self-contained family units, twin rooms and heated wooden wigwams.

Situated on a 12 acre croft in Portnalong beside Loch Harport, we are ideally situated for all outdoor activities. The Cuillins are easily accessible via nearby Sligachan and Glenbrittle, there is a pier and slipway for launching boats 500m down the road, and the pub is 500m up the road.

It is possible to block book all of our accommodation for large groups, and it is also possible for smaller parties to exclusively book our self-contained units (bothies), each of which have their own kitchens, toilets & showers.
Visit Scotland Quality Assurance Grading –
4 Star Hostel. "The best value hostel on Skye"

DETAILS

- **Open** - All year, 24 hours
- **Number of beds** - 40 + camping.
- **Booking** - Deposit or credit / debit card details required to confirm bookings.
- **Price per night** - Dorm £10. Twin £12.50. For Bothies & Wigwams see website.
- **Public Transport** - Cross Island Citylink coaches from mainland pass through Sligachan. Two buses daily (excl. Sun) from Portree via Sligachan to Portnalong.
- **Directions** - GR 348 353. From Sligachan take the A863 for 4 miles then left onto B8009 for 6 miles through Carbost and Fernilea to Portnalong. Follow signs for Croft Bunkhouse & Loch Harport Gallery, it is 500yds past the pub.

CONTACT: Dave
Portnalong, Isle of Skye, IV47 8SL
Tel: 01478 640254. Mobile 07841 206 157, Fax: 01478 640254
skyehostel@lineone.net   www.skyehostels.com

DUNARD
HOSTEL

Dunard is a warm, friendly, family-run hostel on the beautiful island of Barra in Scotland's Outer Hebrides.   The hostel has a cosy living room with a lovely fire, hot showers and spacious kitchen. There are bunk, twin and family bedrooms.
Situated in Castlebay the hostel has views over the castle to beaches and islands beyond.   We are close to the ferry terminal, a handful of shops, and bars which often fill with live music. During the summer the island is alive for 'Feis Bharraidh' a gaelic festival of music, song and dance. Take time and explore this truly beautiful island with stunning white beaches, quiet bays where otters hunt and seals bask on rocks, dunes and meadows carpeted in flowers, and wild windswept hills home to golden eagles. Join one of our friendly guided sea kayaking trips and paddle amongst sheltered islands for really close-up wildlife encounters (no experience needed). www.clearwaterpaddling.com

DETAILS

■ **Open** - All year, except Christmas and New Year , all day
■ **Number of beds** - 16: 3 x 4 : 2 x 2.
■ **Booking** - Booking advised, especially during the summer. Booking essential for groups.
■ **Price per night** - £14 per person. £18 pp twin room. £50 per family room (sleeps 4). £180 - £235 sole use.
■ **Public Transport** - The hostel is a 3 minute walk from the Ferry Terminal in Castlebay. If using a local bus ask to be dropped at the hostel.
■ **Directions** - From Ferry terminal in Castlebay head up hill, turn left and we are the third house past the old school. (200m from Terminal)

CONTACT: Katie or Chris
Dunard, Castlebay, Isle of Barra, Western Isles, HS9 5XD
Tel: 01871 810443
info@dunardhostel.co.uk www.dunardhostel.co.uk

DRINISHADER
HOSTEL

SCOTLAND

Drinishader Hostel is a traditional crofter's cottage situated 5 miles from Tarbert, 8 miles from the white sandy beaches. It is located on the Golden Road, above Drinishader Harbour, overlooking the beautiful East Loch Tarbert. A cottage with character and warm atmosphere, it has a cosy lounge with open fire, a well-equipped kitchen and comfortable orthopaedic bunks. Hot showers and laundry facilities are available. Pick-up services from Tarbert can be arranged if there are no bus services. There is a shop / post office nearby & you can pre-order fresh, delicious home-made bread and cakes to be delivered to your breakfast table. Among the activities guests enjoy are coastal / hill walking, cycling, sightseeing, bird / wild life watching or simply chilling out.

If you're not fresh when you arrive, you will be when you leave! We hope it will be a home from home for you. So come and discover the magic of Drinishader!

DETAILS

- **Open** - All year, 8am till 11pm
- **Number of beds** - 12
- **Booking** - Advisable to confirm beds, may require deposit.
- **Price per night** - From £12 per person.
- **Public Transport** - Caledonian MacBrayne ferries (01876 500337) from Ullapool to Stornoway or from Uig (Skye) to Tarbert. Drinishader is a 10 min bus journey from Tarbert (01851-705050). Bus stop at hostel. There are 5 buses each day.
- **Directions** - From Tarbert follow the A859 south. After 3.5km turn left along the Golden Road. The hostel is located just above the harbour in Drinishader.

CONTACT: Roddy or Warden
Drinishader, Isle Of Harris, HS3 3DX
Tel: 01859 511255
drinishaderhostel@yahoo.co.uk

HEB
HOSTEL

The Heb Hostel is a family-run backpackers hostel in the heart of Stornoway on the enchanting Isle of Lewis. It is an ideal stop / stay for travellers visiting the Hebrides. Surfers, cyclists, walkers, families and groups are all welcome,

Clean, comfortable, friendly and relaxed - Heb Hostel aims to provide you with a quality stay at budget prices.

There are many facilities, including a common room with TV, peat fire, local guides & information.

DETAILS

- **Open** - All year, all day. New arrivals phone to get access code.
- **Number of beds** - 26: 1x8, 2x7,1x4
- **Booking** - Booking is not essential but may be advisable at busier times. Deposits are only required for groups. Payment is due on arrival by cash or cheque.
- **Price per night** - £15 per person per night. 10% discount on booking the whole hostel for more than one night
- **Public Transport** - By plane: From Glasgow, Edinburgh or Inverness (British Airways), Aberdeen (Eastern Airways), Inverness & Benbecula (Highland Airways). By Ferry (Caledonian McBrayne) Ullapool to Stornoway (Lewis), Uig(Skye) to Tarbert (Harris) or Berneray (Uists) to Leverburgh (Harris)
- **Directions** - From bus station : exit front door, cross South Beach St & walk up Kenneth St. Pass 1st intersection & we are 2nd on the right. From ferry terminal come out main exit, turn left, follow pedestrian walk-way to the bus station. From Airport take bus to Stornoway bus station.

CONTACT: Christine Macintosh
25 Kenneth St, Stornoway, Isle of Lewis, HS1 2DR
Tel: 01851 709889
christine@hebhostel.com www.hebhostel.com

Laxdale Bunkhouse is contained within Laxdale Holiday Park which is a small family-run park set in peaceful tree-lined surroundings. Located 1.5 miles away from the town of Stornoway this is an ideal centre from which to tour the islands of Lewis and Harris. Built in 1998, the bunkhouse consists of four bedrooms with four bunks in each room and caters for backpackers, families or larger groups looking for convenient, low cost accommodation. There is a spacious fully equipped dining kitchen which provides two cookers, fridge and microwave, and a comfortable TV lounge in which to relax. There is also a drying room. Toilets and showers are located within the building and are suitable for the disabled. Outside there is a covered veranda, picnic table and BBQ area.

DETAILS

- **Open** - All year, 8am - 10pm
- **Number of beds** - 16: 4 x 4
- **Booking** - July and August booking advisable one week in advance.
- **Price per night** - £15pp (high season), £14pp (low season). £210 sole use (high season), £195 sole use (low season).
- **Public Transport** - Buses every 30 mins stop close to hostel. Taxi fare from town centre approximately £2.50.
- **Directions** - From Stornoway Ferry Terminal take the A857. Take the second turning on the left past the hospital. Follow camping signs for one mile out of town. The Bunkhouse is located inside the holiday park. From Tarbert or Leverburgh take A859 for 40 miles to Stornoway. Turn left at the roundabout and 2nd left after hospital then as above.

CONTACT:
Laxdale Holiday Park, 6 Laxdale Lane, Stornoway, Isle of Lewis, HS2 0DR
Tel: 01851 706966 / 01851 703234
info@laxdaleholidaypark.com www.laxdaleholidaypark.com

GALSON FARM
HOSTEL

Our comfortable, cosy, fully equipped hostel provides the perfect haven from which to explore the crofting townships of Ness and the west side of Lewis, with sandy beaches, wildlife, historic sites and culture on the doorstep. Situated within a cobbled stone courtyard enjoying stunning views of the Atlantic Coast towards the Butt of Lewis Lighthouse.

A short walk through our croft, with its network of footpaths, takes you to the shore and river, with otters regular visitors.

Comprising of one dormitory with up to 8 beds, two shower / toilets and a kitchen / dining room. Bedding can be supplied if required as can meals by order. Bus service to Stornoway, shop within 2 miles. Visit Scotland 4star hostel. Stay a while, for memories of a lifetime.

DETAILS

- **Open** - All year, 24 hours
- **Number of beds** - 8
- **Booking** - Always phone in advance. Deposit (Visa/Access) guarantees bed.
- **Price per night** - £15pp. Sole use : 2 people £48, up to 8 people £75.
- **Public Transport** - The nearest ferry runs from Ullapool on the mainland to Stornoway which is 20 miles from the hostel. Local buses run from Mondays to Saturdays. Enquire at Stornoway Bus Station.
- **Directions** - GR 437 592. Follow A857 Stornoway to Ness (Nis) road for 20 miles. At Galson (Gabhsann) turn left at phone box. Bunkhouse is ¼ mile.

CONTACT: David and Hazel Roberts
Galson Farm House, South Galson, Isle of Lewis, HS2 0SH
Tel: 01851 850492, Fax: 01851 850492
GalsonFarm@yahoo.com www.galsonfarm.co.uk

GERRYS
HOSTEL

405

SCOTLAND

Gerrys Hostel is situated in an excellent mountaineering and wilderness area on the most scenic railway in Britain.

The photo shows the hostel, looking North West. The hostel has a comfortable common room with log fire and library.

Come and go as you please. No smoking inside or out.

Accommodation for non-smokers.

PLEASE CONTACT THIS HOSTEL BY PHONE OR POST

DETAILS

- **Open** - All year (check by phone), book in 5pm to 8.30pm. Later by arrangement only.
- **Number of beds** - 20: 1 x 10 : 2 x 5. Double and twin also.
- **Booking** - Prepay to secure bed, or phone.
- **Price per night** - From £13 pp, discount for long stay large groups.
- **Public Transport** - Achnashellach station is 4km west of the hostel. Nearest Citylink coaches drop off at Inverness. Local bus between Inverness and Lochcarron: Wednesday and Saturday 3pm.
- **Directions** - GR 037 493. 95 miles north of Fort William, 50 miles west of Inverness on A890.

CONTACT: Gerry Howkins
Craig, Achnashellach, Strathcarron, Wester-Ross, Scotland, IV54 8YU
Tel: 01520 766232
www.gerryshostel-achnashellach.co.uk

LEDGOWAN HOTEL
AND BUNKHOUSE
SCOTLAND

Ledgowan Lodge is a traditional country house hotel with cosy log fires, original features and friendly bar open to residents and non-residents. The bunkhouse is adjacent to the hotel and bunkhouse guests have full use of the hotel's facilities. Ledgowan Lodge is perfectly situated for the hill walker, climber or anyone wanting low cost basic overnight accommodation. It is within easy driving distance of the Torridon and Fannich Mountain ranges and Fionn Bheinn Mountain is on the doorstep. The lodge sleeps twelve adults in six separate rooms, each with a set of bunk beds, wash hand basin, chest of drawers and thermostatically controlled heating. There is a one off charge for providing towels and linen. The two bathrooms contain large baths with shower facilities and a toilet. There are basic cooking facilities and a refrigerator for self catering, but it is recommended that guests socialise within the hotel where the welcome provides a restaurant, bar meals, real fires and lively conversation. There is ample car parking in the grounds and an excellent drying room within the hotel. Camping available.

DETAILS

- **Open** - All year, all day
- **Number of beds** - 12: 6 x 2
- **Booking** - Book by phone or email
- **Price per night** - £12pp. £24 for sole use of 2 bed bunkroom. Linen £5 (one off charge). Camper vans and tents (with use of bunkhouse) £5pp.
- **Public Transport** - Achnasheen Station is one mile from the bunkhouse.
- **Directions** - On the A890, 1 mile south of Achnasheen

CONTACT: Reception
Legowan Lodge Hotel, Achnasheen, Ross-shire, Scottish Highlands, IV22 2EJ
Tel: 01445 720252
info@ledgowanlodge.co.uk www.ledgowanlodge.co.uk

Walkers, climbers and mountain bikers enjoying the Torridon Mountains and wilderness areas will be delighted to find the Kinlochewe Hotel with its warm welcoming bar and bunkhouse accommodation. There are over 20 Munros within 20 miles of Kinlochewe and the hotel provides a great base from which to explore them. The Hotel Bar is open all the year round, and serves excellent home-made food at affordable prices. It also has a selection of real ales and 50 malt whiskies. The bunkhouse is ideal for outdoor enthusiasts with a drying room and hot showers. It has one dormitory with 12 bunks (this makes it unsuitable for children). Each bunk has an individual locker and is provided with a pillow and pillow case (bring your own sleeping bags, towels and padlock for the locker). The bunkhouse has its own showers, toilets, drying room and a self catering kitchen.

DETAILS

- **Open** - All year, 8am - midnight
- **Number of beds** - 12
- **Booking** - Essential for groups, deposit required. Advisable for individuals.
- **Price per night** - £12.50 per person.
- **Public Transport** - Nearest train station is in Achnasheen (10 miles away). In summer trains run four times a day (twice a day on Sundays) from Inverness and the lunchtime train can be met by the local Dial-a-Bus which comes to Kinlochewe. Phone 01520 722205 for further details. On Tuesdays, Thursdays and Fridays the 5pm Westerbus from Inverness to Gairloch stops outside the Bunkhouse at 6.45pm.
- **Directions** - Kinlochewe is situated at the junction of the A832 Garve to Gairloch road and the A896 north from Torridon.

CONTACT: Andrew and Gail Staddon
Kinlochewe by Achnasheen, Wester Ross, IV22 2PA
Tel: 01445 760253
bookings@kinlochewehotel.co.uk www.kinlochewehotel.co.uk

RUA REIDH
LIGHTHOUSE

Perched on the cliff tops 12 miles north of Gairloch, Rua Reidh Lighthouse must have one of the most dramatic settings of all the Scottish hostels. The lighthouse still beams out its light over the Minch to the Outer Isles and Skye, but since its automation the adjoining house, no longer needed for keepers, has been converted into a comfortable independent hostel. The centrally heated house has two sitting rooms with log fires, a self-catering kitchen, a drying room, three private rooms and four dorms (each sleeping four), some rooms with en-suite shower. Meals are available from the main dining room and guided walking is also offered. The area of the lighthouse is unspoiled and makes a perfect place to watch for whales, dolphins etc.

For an away from it all experience travel to the 'edge of the world' and Rua Reidh Lighthouse.

DETAILS

- **Open** - All year (except last 3 weeks in Jan), 9am - 11pm
- **Number of beds** - 26: 3 x 4; 2 x 3; 4 x 2
- **Booking** - Pre-booking advisable.
- **Price per night** - From £10.50pp (dorm) to £22pp (private with en-suite facilities)
- **Public Transport** - Nearest train station Achnasheen (40 miles). Nearest Citylink coaches Inverness (80 miles). Westerbus 01445 712255 and Scotbus run a daily connection between Inverness/Gairloch (12 miles from hostel).
- **Directions** - From Gairloch take the road signed Big Sands and Melvaig, follow this road for 12 miles to the lighthouse. The last 3 miles is a private road with 20mph limit.

CONTACT:
Melvaig, Gairloch, IV21 2EA
Tel: 01445 771263
info@ruareidh.co.uk www.ruareidh.co.uk

Sail Mhor Croft is a small rural hostel which is situated at Dundonnell on the shores of Little Loch Broom. The mountain range of An Teallach, which has the reputation of being one of the finest ridge walks in Great Britain, is right on our doorstep and the area is a haven for walkers of all experience as well as for photographers.

Whether you wish to climb the summits, walk along the loch side, visit a beautiful sandy beach or just soak up the tranquillity of the area, you know the scenery cannot be beaten anywhere in the country. The hostel offers accommodation for up to 16 persons in three dorms which are fitted with anti-midge screens. Guests have a choice of using our self-catering facilities or we can provide a full breakfast. It is advisable to ring in advance in order to book yourself a bed, the next self-catering hostel is many miles away.

DETAILS

- **Open** - All year except Xmas, New Year and January, flexible
- **Number of beds** - 16:- 2 x 4 : 1 x 8
- **Booking** - Always phone in advance. Groups should book as soon as possible.
- **Price per night** - £13.50 per person, self-catering. £175 sole use.
- **Public Transport** - Nearest train station is Inverness (60 miles). Nearest City Link bus drop off is Braemore Junction (15 miles). Wester bus passes the hostel 3 times a week; Mon, Wed and Sat. It also provides a service between Gairloch and Ullapool on Thursday afternoon.
- **Directions** - GR 064 893 (sheet 19) 1.5 miles west of Dundonnell Hotel on A832.

CONTACT: Dave or Lynda
Camusnagaul, Dundonnell, Ross-shire, IV23 2QT
Tel: 01854 633224
dave.lynda@sailmhor.co.uk www.sailmhor.co.uk

BADRALLACH
BOTHY AND CAMPSITE
SCOTLAND

On the tranquil shores of Little Loch Broom overlooking An Teallach, one of Scotland's finest mountain ranges, Badrallach Bothy and Camp Site with its welcoming traditional buildings offers a fine base for walking and climbing in the hills of Wester Ross, Caithness and Sutherland. You can fish in the rivers, hill lochs and sea, or simply watch the flora and fauna including many orchids, golden eagles, otters, porpoises, pine martens, deer and wild goats. Guests often sit around the peat stove in the gas light (there is now electric here too) and discuss life over a dram or two. Hot showers, spotless sanitary accommodation (STB graded 4 star excellent), an unbelievable price (thanks to S.N.H), and the total peace makes our Bothy and camp site (12 tents only) one that visitors return to year after year. We also have a caravan, 4 star cottage and dinner, B&B. Hire canoes, kites, bikes, boats and blokarts.

DETAILS

- **Open** - All year, all times
- **Number of beds** - 12 plus bedspaces (Alpine style platforms). We have had 20 at a squeeze, mats & sleeping bags required.
- **Booking** - Recommended
- **Price per night** - £6 pp £1.50 per vehicle. £70 sole use (£100 Xmas & New year).
- **Public Transport** -   Westerbus (01445 712255) operate Mon/Wed/Sat between Inverness/Gairloch and drop at road end Dundonnell, 7 miles from hostel. Pick-up can be arranged.
- **Directions** - GR 065 915   Located on the shore of Little Loch Broom 7 miles along a single track road off the A832, one mile east of the Dundonnell Hotel.

CONTACT: Mr / Mrs Stott,
Croft No 9, Badrallach, Dundonnell, Ross-shire, IV23 2QP
Tel: 01854 633281
mail@badrallach.com www.badrallach.com

SLEEPERZZZ.COM

Stay on a first class train in Rogart in the heart of the Highlands halfway between Inverness and John O'Groats. The three railway carriages have been tastefully converted, with many original features. Two sleep 8, one is subdivided to sleep 4 and 2. There are two beds per room, and a kitchen, dining room, sitting room, showers and toilets. They are heated and non-smoking. All bedding is included. We also have a cosy showman's wagon which sleeps two. Four trains per day in each direction serve this small crofting community which has a shop, post office and pub with restaurant. Glenmorangie and Clynelish distilleries, Dunrobin Castle and Helmsdale's Heritage Centre are easy to reach by train or car. See the silver salmon leap at Lairg and the seabirds and seals in Loch Fleet. Or just enjoy the peace of Rogart.

The climate is good and the midges are less prevalent than in the west! Families welcome. Free use of bikes for guests.

DETAILS

- **Open** - March to November inclusive , 24 hours
- **Number of beds** - 26:   8 x 2 : 1 x 4 : 3x 2.
- **Booking** - Booking is not essential.
- **Price per night** - £14 per person, 12yrs and under £9 per person. (10% discount if you arrive by bike or train).
- **Public Transport** - Wick to Inverness trains stop at the door.
- **Directions** - We are at the railway station, 4 miles from the A9 trunk road, 54 miles north of Inverness.

CONTACT: Kate or Frank
Rogart Station, Pittentrail, Sutherland, Highlands, IV28 3XA
Tel: 01408 641343   Mobile/Text 07833 641226
kate@sleeperzzz.com www.sleeperzzz.com

BLACK ROCK
BUNKHOUSE

Situated in beautiful Glenglass and sheltered by Ben Wyvis, this comfortable bunkhouse is named after the breathtaking Black Rock Gorge. It is an ideal base for touring the highlands and seeing wildlife, including seals in the Cromarty Firth and dolphins at Cromarty. Highland Games are held throughout the area. It is sited at the eastern end of a hikers' route across Scotland and on the Lands End to John O'Groats route for walkers and cyclists. The village has a general shop, Post Office, bus service and an inn (serving good bar meals and breakfasts) 250m away.

Available to groups or individuals, accommodation is in four rooms of four and one room for 1. Blankets are available and sheet sleeping bags can be hired. There is a self-catering kitchen and dining area with TV, showers and launderette facilities. There is also a camping ground. All areas of the bunkhouse are easily accessible by wheelchair and suitable for the disabled.

DETAILS

- **Open** - April 1st to October 31st, 24hr access. New arrivals 9am - 9pm
- **Number of beds** - 17 : 4 x 4, 1 x 1
- **Booking** - Not always essential. Deposit of 1 night's fee to secure booking.
- **Price per night** - £12- £14 per person. 10% off for groups of 8+.
- **Public Transport** - Nearest train station Dingwall (6 miles) Nearest Citylink drop off Inverness (15 miles). There are local buses hourly.
- **Directions** - Follow A9 north from Inverness, 2 miles north of Cromarty Firth bridge take left turn for Evanton. Follow camping signs.

CONTACT: Lillian
Evanton, Dingwall, Ross-shire, IV16 9UN
Tel: 01349 830917
enquires@blackrockscotland.co.uk www.blackrockscotland.co.uk

HELMSDALE
HOSTEL
SCOTLAND

Set in the scenic coastal village of Helmsdale, halfway between Inverness and John O´Groats, Helmsdale Hostel is an ideal stop when travelling to and from Orkney. On the main Land´s End to John O´Groats route, and surrounded by nearby Marlyn hills, the hostel is popular with cyclists and walkers.

The surrounding area also offers beach walks, bird watching and gold panning opportunties.

The hostel has excellent facilities and all rooms are en-suite. Groups, families and individuals all welcome.

DETAILS

- **Open** - Easter to Sept; other dates by request (all year group booking available). Open during the day.
- **Number of beds** - 24: 2x8, 2x4
- **Booking** - Advance booking not essential - book on line, by email or phone
- **Price per night** - Dorm £15pp, family room for 4 £60.
- **Public Transport** - Helmsdale is served by the City Link bus service and is on the railway line from Inverness to Thurso.
- **Directions** - The hostel is situated on the corner of the A9 and Old Caithness Road (park in Rockview Place). Arriving by bus: walk up the slope for 100 metres. The Hostel is after the old church on your left. (200 metres). Arriving by train: cross over the old bridge, turn right along Dunrobin Street, then left up Stafford Street. Hostel is at the top of the slope on the left (half a mile).

CONTACT: Irene
Helmsdale Hostel, Stafford Street, Helmsdale, Sutherland, KW8 6JR
Tel: 01431 821636, Mob: 07971 516287
irene.drummond@btinternet.com   www.helmsdalehostel.co.uk

BALINTRAID HOUSE
SCOTLAND HIGHLAND RETREAT

Balintraid House is a rambling house in a beautiful location looking directly out onto historic Cromarty Firth. It offers a comfortable alternative to staying in Inverness when driving north or west, or an ideal location to base your Highland holiday. Locally you can see dolphins, seals, swans and migrating birds in the firth. Take a short drive to Shin Falls or Rogie Falls and see salmon leaping up the waterfalls. Explore the Pictish Trail, sample whisky at nearby Glenmorangie or Dalmore Distilleries and enjoy walks to the Fyrish monument, Ben Wyvis and numerous others. Discover original Caledonian forests at Glen Affric. Visit a castle or two. Relax to traditional feis or other music at local venues and hotels.
Facilities include a well-equipped kitchen, central heating, warm duvets and comfy beds, internet access, table tennis, musical instruments and small library.
Free range eggs available, and tea/coffee. Please note: we have cats.

DETAILS

- **Open** - All year, please phone for access times.
- **Number of beds** - 9: flexible, single/double/family/group dorm.
- **Booking** - Recommended, please advise if arrival time changes.
- **Price per night** - From £18
- **Public Transport** -   Stagecoach stop at house. Trains from Inverness (Thurso / Wick) will stop at Invergordon. Phone for pick up, 3 miles away (charge).
- **Directions** - 26 miles north of Inverness. Turn off A9 for Invergordon and follow coastal road (B817) northwards for 2 miles, passing through small village of Saltburn. After the last house there are two big fields then a clump of trees with two drives on left leading to house.

CONTACT: Anita
Balintraid House, Balintraid, by Invergordon, Ross-shire, IV18 OLY
Tel: 01349 854446 Mob: 07917710279
balintraid.house@virgin.net www.balintraidhouse.co.uk

INCHNADAMPH
LODGE
SCOTLAND

Situated at the heart of the dramatic Assynt mountains, Inchnadamph Lodge has been tastefully converted to provide luxury hostel accommodation at a budget price. Twin, family and dormitory (4-8 people) rooms are available and a continental-style breakfast is included. We have a large self-catering kitchen, a lounge and a dining room (both with real fires), and a games room. Packed lunches are available on request and bar meals are served at the Inchnadamph Hotel. At the foot of Ben More Assynt, and overlooking Loch Assynt, you are free to explore one of the wildest areas in the Highlands. Mountains can be climbed from our door! The Inchnadamph Nature Reserve is right by us - home to a wide diversity of birds, plants, animals and full of exciting geological features. Nearby lochs are popular for trout fly fishing.
Details and photos on our website.

DETAILS

- **Open** - All year - phone November - March inclusive, 24 hours
- **Number of beds** - 38: 8x2 : 7x2 : 4x2 (dormitory) 12 (twin/double)
- **Booking** - Advised, required Nov-March.
- **Price per night** - £16.00-£17.50 (dormitory), £22-£26 (twin room) inc. continental breakfast and linen. Group discounts.
- **Public Transport** - Transport is available to our door from Inverness 6 days a week, either by train to Lairg and then postbus, or by coach to Ullapool and minibus to Inchnadamph. Times vary - please call us for details.
- **Directions** - Inchnadamph is 25 miles north of Ullapool on the Lochinver/Durness road. The lodge is the big white building across the river from the hotel.

CONTACT: Chris
Inchnadamph, Assynt, Nr Lochinver, Sutherland, IV27 4HL
Tel: 01571 822218, Fax: 01571 822232
info@inch-lodge.co.uk www.inch-lodge.co.uk

LAZY CROFTER
BUNKHOUSE

The Lazy Crofter is a small hostel, traditional yet modern with a cosy and informal atmosphere. It offers self-catering accommodation to groups, families and individuals at unbeatable prices. Set between magnificent mountains and stunning seascapes it enjoys wonderful views over the North Atlantic Ocean. It is owned and managed by Robbie and Fiona Mackay, who pride themselves on the warm atmosphere and genuine highland hospitality and invite you come, relax and enjoy a slower pace of life.

The Bunkhouse sleeps 20 in a mix of dorms and two-man bunkrooms. The bedrooms are warm, bright and airy; linen is provided and all rooms are fully made-up for your arrival. There's a modern, fully equipped self-catering kitchen, a drying room with American-style washing machine, powerful hot showers, ample parking, bike storage, and secure lockers.

A well stocked village store and Post Office are 100 metres away and it's only a short walk to pubs / restaurants / tourist information and amazing golden beaches.

DETAILS

- **Open** - All year, check in after 12 noon
- **Number of beds** - 20: 2x8, 2x2
- **Booking** - Booking is preferred. Deposits required for group bookings.
- **Price per night** - £15 per person
- **Public Transport** - Nearest trains at Lairg, just over an hours drive away. A daily bus service (May- September) leaves Inverness in the morning, driving via Ullapool.
- **Directions** - Grid reference NC 406 679 OS sheet 9.

CONTACT: Fiona
Durine, Durness, Sutherland, Scotland, IV27 4PN
Tel: 01971 511202
fiona@durnesshostel.com   www.durnesshostel.com

CORNMILL
BUNKHOUSE

Cornmill Bunkhouse is situated on a traditional croft which has been in the family for many generations. The croft runs ewes, spring-calving cows, and grows winter feed and woodland. The mill was built in the early 1800s and was active until around 1926. It has been converted into 4 star affordable and comfortable accommodation for individuals or groups. The Bunkhouse can sleep up to 14 people. It has a large self catering kitchen and open-plan sitting room on the first floor, in which the old grinding wheel now serves as a coffee table. There is level access to the first floor at the rear of the building, with an easy going stair down to the ground floor, which has two bunk rooms, a disabled access toilet/wetroom and a toilet with a shower. The first bunk room sleeps 8. The second sleeps 6 and has a patio door looking onto the workings of the old mill with its large wooden cog driving wheels. Activities can be organised for groups including Laser Tagging, Shooting and Clippage. Hen and Stag parties welcome. Come and enjoy this historic setting. 4 star tourist board graded.

DETAILS

- **Open** - All year, advanced notice required 1st Oct - 1st April, all day
- **Number of beds** - 14: 1x8,1x6
- **Booking** - Please enquire for availability by phone or email.
- **Price per night** - £14 per person. Discounts available for group bookings.
- **Public Transport** - Forsinard railway station is only 10 miles away. The line runs from Inverness - Wick, stopping at Forsinard three times a day.
- **Directions** - The Cornmill Bunkhouse is located on the A897, 6 miles from Melvich, 20 miles to Thurso, 42 miles to John O'Groats and 34 miles to Helmsdale.

CONTACT:
Cornmill Bunkhouse, Achumore, Strathhalladale, Sutherland, KW13 6YT
Tel: 01641 571219   Mob: 07808 197350
sandy.murray2@btinternet.com   www.achumore.co.uk

St. Margarets Hope Backpackers is a traditional stone building. It has two family rooms, one single room, one four bedded room and one dorm with eight beds. It also has a fully equipped kitchen, laundry room and shower room.

St. Margarets Hope Backpackers is situated in one of the prettiest villages in Orkney. There are three well stocked shops, a Post Office, three pubs serving good beer & food, an award-winning restaurant and a craft shop.

During the summer the passenger-only ferry Pentland Venture sails three times a day and docks seven miles from the village. Pentland Ferries docks in the village, she sails all year three trips a day and takes vehicles.

The bus stop is just across the road from the hostel for the bus which goes to Kirkwall four times a day.

DETAILS

■ **Open** - All year, arrival up until 9pm (unless otherwise arranged) and checkout by 10am
■ **Number of beds** - 17: 1x8, 1x4, 2x2, 1x1
■ **Booking** - Not essential, payment on arrival.
■ **Price per night** - £13 per person
■ **Public Transport** - The hostel is a 10 min walk from Pentland Ferries and just 50 yards from the bus stop for Kirkwall. (Buses go 4 times a day except Sundays).
■ **Directions** - Situated in the centre of St Margaret's Hope village in South Ronaldsay, the most southerly of the Orkney Isles.

CONTACT:
Back Road, St Margaret's Hope, Orkney, KW17 2SP
Tel: 01856 831225
orkneybackpackers@hotmail.co.uk orkneybackpackers.com

Surrounded by magnificent scenery the Hoy Centre is ideally situated for a peaceful and relaxing holiday. The centre was completely refurbished in 2005 and offers high quality, four star accommodation. All rooms are en-suite (with shower) and each room has twin beds and a bunk bed, seats, lockers and all bedding. One room is equipped for wheelchair access. There is a well equipped kitchen, comfortable lounge area with TV and a separate spacious dining hall. Underfloor heating ensures a comfortable temperature. Washing and drying facilities are also available. Much of North Hoy is owned and managed by the RSPB. The reserve comprises 3,500 ha of upland heath and cliffs with a large variety of birds. Off the west coast is The Old Man of Hoy, a 137m sea stack, perhaps Orkney's most famous landmark and a great place to see puffins. The dramatic hills of North Hoy and stunning sea cliffs offer excellent walking. The shop at Lyness has closed so the nearest shop is 20 miles away. Walkers and groups welcome scheme awarded.

DETAILS

- **Open** - All year, all day
- **Number of beds** - 32: 8x4
- **Booking** - Preferred. Groups send 25% deposit, balance 28 days prior to arrival
- **Price per night** - Adult 13.30, £10.25 (child), £3.35 (under3). Family room (4 beds) £32.20. Private rooms:- 2 adults £36.60, 3 ad £43.25, 4 ad £53.25. Sole use £277.
- **Public Transport** - Short walk from Moaness Pier (pedestrian ferry from Stromness) www.orkneyferries.co.uk (01856 872044). Taxis/minibuses are available.
- **Directions** - Car ferry arrives from Houton to Lyness, which is 16km from centre.

CONTACT: Recreation Department
Hoy Centre, Hoy, Orkney, KW16 3NJ
Tel: 01856 873535 ext 2417
recreation@orkney.gov.uk   www.hostelsorkney.co.uk

PEEDIE
HOSTEL

The Peedie Hostel (Peedie is an Orcadian word meaning "small") is a quaint hostel overlooking the harbour in the town of Kirkwall, and lies within easy strolling distance of the Main Street and many local attractions. Kirkwall is the heart of the Orkney Archipelago and the hub of nearly all transport within the isles. The Peedie Hostel is within 300m of the island's main bus station and 200m of the inner and outer North Isles ferry terminals, making it the ideal base for your Orkney adventure. It is close to many local amenities, including pubs, restaurants shops and supermarkets.

The Peedie Hostel has one single room, three double rooms and a 4 bed dorm room (or family room). Shared facilities include two kitchens and two shower/bathrooms. All rooms have TVs and most enjoy views over the bay. All rooms are heated. Each room has its own key and the hostel and its facilities are open 24/7 giving guests complete freedom during their stay. We also understand that travel to and from Orkney sometimes involves checking in or out at odd times and this can be accommodated.

DETAILS

- **Open** - All year, all day
- **Number of beds** - 11: 1x1, 3x2,1x4
- **Booking** - Bookings can be made by phone, email or letter.
- **Price per night** - £15 pp.
- **Public Transport** - 200m to North Isle & Shapinsay ferries. 300m to bus station.
- **Directions** - Situated on the sea front on Ayre Road.

CONTACT:
1 Ayre Houses, Ayre Road, Kirkwall, Orkney, KW15 1QX
Tel: 01856 875477
kirkwallpeediehostel@talk21.com www.davidwild.co.uk/peediehostel/

On the Stromness waterfront, a short distance from the ferry terminal, Hamnavoe Hostel makes an ideal base for your visit to Orkney. It has single, twin and family rooms with one recently upgraded to en-suite. The rooms have easy access to the shower, bathroom and toilet on each floor. They are fitted with wash hand basins, pine bunk beds and have stunning views out across Hamnavoe. The light and airy kitchen has two cookers, microwave, double fridge, freezer, toasters, kettle and sandwich toaster. The large dining table has fantastic views over the harbour and marina. The lounge has comfortable seating, freeview TV, video, stereo and a stock of books, cards and games. There is a small laundry room with coin operated washing machine, tumble drier and iron. There's is a pay phone and wi-fi internet connection. Entry is by a coded door lock and individual rooms have keys. Free long stay car park. Come and visit the nearby islands of Graemsay and Hoy, check out the World Heritage Sites or just relax in the tranquillity of island life.

DETAILS

- **Open** - All year, all day, no curfew, check in from 2pm and check out by 10am., Reconfirm your booking by 7pm on the scheduled date of arrival.
- **Number of beds** - 13: 1x4, 1x1, 4x2
- **Booking** - Book with deposit of first night, re-confirm by 7pm on the arrival day.
- **Price per night** - From £16pp. Private rooms £16. Family room £45.
- **Public Transport** - Orkney Ferries run to Stromness Ferry terminal. There is a regular bus service to and from the town of Stronmness from the terminal.
- **Directions** - On the waterfront a short walk from Stromness ferry terminal.

CONTACT: Mr George Argo
10a North End Road, Stromness, Orkney, KW16 3AG
Tel: 01856 851202
info@hamnavoehostel.co.uk www.hamnavoehostel.co.uk

BROWNS
HOSTEL AND HOUSE

Stromness - a small friendly town where both the hostel and house are centrally situated in Victoria Street, near shops, pubs, restaurants, Post Office, bank. museum and the Pier Art Centre. An ideal base for the tourist as it is also within walking / cycling distance of the wildlife, high cliffs, beaches, beautiful sunsets, the historical sites of Skara Brae, Standing Stones, the Palace and Brough of Birsay etc., and for fishing, golfing, bowling, surfing, to dive on the many wrecks in Scapa Flow, or (for the beginner) to book a Scuba-dive course. Free internet access available. Hostel - very popular with all ages, is praised for its cosy well equipped kitchen, seating all guests at one sitting. In the evenings the big table is a great gathering place and many enjoyable times have been had. Sleeps 14. House - self-catering, has kitchen, sitting room, en-suite bedrooms and laundry room. Let as a whole or per room. Sleeps 12-14

DETAILS

- **Open** - All year, all day. No curfew, keys provided.
- **Number of beds** - Hostel 14: 3 x 1 :2 x 2 : 1 x 3: 1 x 4. House 12-14:
- **Booking** - Booking advisable during March to October. Pre-paid bookings secure (send sae for receipt). Telephone bookings kept only for limited time.
- **Price per night** - From £13.50 (inc linen), special rate for groups.
- **Public Transport** - Train or bus to Thurso, bus 2 miles to Scrabster then boat to Stromness. Alternatively from Gills Bay to St Margarets Hope by boat or John O'Groats by boat to Burwick then bus to Stromness via Kirkwall.
- **Directions** - Browns accommodation is near to the harbour in Stromness, just two minutes along street. Next door to Royal Hotel.

CONTACT: Sylvia Brown
Stromness, Orkney, KW16 3BS
Tel: 01856 850661
info@brownshostel.co.uk www.brownsselfcatering.co.uk

BIRSAY
OUTDOOR CENTRE SCOTLAND

The Birsay Outdoor Centre is situated in the northwest corner of the Orkney mainland, in close proximity to spectacular and varied coastline scenery and beaches. Nearby at the Brough of Birsay you can see the remains of early Christian and Norse settlements on a tidal island. You can also visit Orkney's 5,500 year old Neolithic Heartland which has World Heritage Status and includes the Ring of Brodgar. Close by are the Standing Stones of Stenness, the tomb of Maeshowe and, in Sandwick, the well-preserved village of Skara Brae. The Centre offers comfortable accommodation, with all new furniture, beds and appliances. It sleeps up to 30 in 5 bedrooms; family rooms are available and all linen is provided. It has a well equipped kitchen, dining area, lounge, drying room and disabled access. Camping available (20 pitches).

DETAILS

- **Open** - All year (excl. Christmas and New Year), 6-7pm
- **Number of beds** - 28: 2x4, 1x2, 1x6, 1x12 plus camping.
- **Booking** - Bookings preferred. If it's a group booking 25% deposit required with balance payable 28 days prior to arrival
- **Price per night** - Adults £12.20, £9.25 (juniors), £3.35 (under 3s). Family room (4 beds) £29.95. Private rooms:- 2 adults £34, 3 adults £41, 4 adults £47. Sole use of Centre (28 beds) £222 per night
- **Public Transport** - For buses from Kirkwall and Stromness contact Orkney Coaches (01856 870555). Ferries from Scrabster, (Northlink Ferries 01856 872044), from Gills Bay, (Pentland Ferries 01856 831226). Foot passenger ferries from John O'Groats, summer only (John O'Groats Ferry 01955 611353)
- **Directions** - OS sheet 7 GR 253267

CONTACT: Recreation Department
Birsay, Orkney, KW17 2LY
Tel: 01856 873535 ext. 2417
recreation@orkney.gov.uk www.hostelsorkney.co.uk

ROUSAY
HOSTEL

Rousay Hostel is situated on a working organic farm within easy walking distance of shops, restaurant, pub, bike hire and the pier. Modern, purpose built and well equipped, the hostel has two dormitories and one single room, showers, kitchen and laundry facilities. There's a camp site adjacent to the hostel and campers have use of the hostel facilities. Organic produce may be available to buy from the farm and bike hire is available at the hostel.

The island of Rousay is a walker's and birdwatcher's paradise with many footpaths and a nearby bird reserve. Often called "the Egypt of the North" Rousay contains some of the best preserved archaeological sites in the north of Scotland, set in spectacular scenery rich in wildlife, plants and flowers. The small, friendly community creates a unique welcome for the visitor to this beautiful island.

DETAILS

- **Open** - All year, all day
- **Number of beds** - 11
- **Booking** - Book by phone or email.
- **Price per night** - £10.00 (£12 with linen), £5 camping,
- **Public Transport** - Travel to Orkney via a choice of four ferry routes from John O'Groats (summer only), from Scrabster, from Aberdeen or from Gills Bay. Once on mainland Orkney travel from Kirkwall to Tingwall Pier to cross by frequent ferry to Rousay. Easy walk from the pier to the hostel.
- **Directions** - Ask directions from the pier.

CONTACT: Carol or Eric
Trumland Organic Farm, Rousay, Orkney, KW17 2PU
Tel: 01856 821252, Fax: 01856 821252
trumland@btopenworld.com

AYRES ROCK
HOSTEL
SCOTLAND

Sanday is the perfect place to take time out. You'll find long stretches of unspoilt sandy beaches, an abundance of birds, seals and other wildlife, glittering seas, clear air and spectacular skies. Those of us lucky enough to live here enjoy a rare quality of life in a small, friendly and safe community. Ayre's Rock Hostel has accreditation by Visit Scotland and is rated at four stars. There are two twin rooms and one family ensuite room. Our brand new lounge area with expansive views over the Holms of Ire offers a comfortable place to relax after a day's exploration of our beautiful island. A further visitors' sitting area is provided in the conservatory of the main house. A kitchen is available for self-catering, or guests can have B&B. Evening meals can be provided by arrangement. Takeaways are also available from the Ayre's Rock Chip Shop when open.

DETAILS

- **Open** - All year, 8am to 10pm
- **Number of beds** - 8 : 2x2 1x4
- **Booking** - Book by phone or email.
- **Price per night** - From £13.50 in shared room. Single occupancy of twin room £18. Group booking from £50. Breakfast £5. Evening meals from £8pp
- **Public Transport** - The direct ferry from Kirkwall Pier to the Loth terminal in Sanday takes an hour and twenty minutes. Passenger fares are about £13 return (Orkney Ferries 01856 872044 www.orkneyferries.co.uk). Flying direct from Kirkwall airport to Sanday takes 11 minutes and a return flight costs about £65. There are usually two flights per day and they are well used by the islanders (LoganAir - 01856 872494 - www.loganair.co.uk). For local buse and taxi phone 01857 600410.
- **Directions** - 6 miles from Loth ferry terminal and 3 miles from Sanday air field.

CONTACT: Julie or Paul
Ayre, Coo Road, Sanday, Orkney KW17 2AY
Tel: 01857 600410
paul_allan1967@hotmail.co.uk www.ayres-rock-sanday-orkney.co.uk

THE BARN
CHALMERSQUOY

The Barn offers four-star quality hostel accommodation and camping facilities, all year round, in Westray (The Queen O' The Isles), Orkney.

The Barn has excellent kitchen and lounge facilities and offers twin and family rooms, all with a sea view. It is in a great location to explore the many cliffs, beaches, seabirds and walks that our island has to offer. You can also explore the Heritage Centre, craft businesses and well stocked local shops. If you don't want to cook in, the Pierowall Hotel is 3 minutes walk from the Barn and offers excellent food and bar facilities.

DETAILS

- **Open** - All year, if we're in, we're open.
- **Number of beds** - 13: 1x4, 1x3, 3x2
- **Booking** - Booking advisable. No deposit required.
- **Price per night** - £16 pp or £160 per night for exclusive use . Special winter rates available for exclusive use if two nights booked.
- **Public Transport** - There is a bus service available from Rapness Ferry Terminal to The Barn from mid May to mid September. This bus service is available on request during the winter season. The number to phone to request the bus is 01857 677758 (Kenneth Harcus).
- **Directions** - Westray is one of the north isles of Orkney. Travel to Westray with Orkney Ferries (Tel: 01856 872044 to book car) or Loganair (Tel: 01856 872494). From Rapness Ferry turn right and drive north for 7 miles. You will then see Pierowall Village. The Barn is on the outskirts of Pierowall Village. It is well signposted and central to all facilities.

CONTACT: The Harcus family
Chalmersquoy, Westray, Orkney, KW17 2BZ
Tel: 01857 677214
johnharcus@btinternet.com www.thebarnwestray.co.uk/

The North Ronaldsay Bird Observatory is situated at the south west corner of the island with outstanding views and an adjacent shell sand beach. Seals and the unique seaweed-eating sheep are abundant along the coast which skirts the 34 acres of croft managed by the observatory. The observatory sees spectacular bird migration through the island in Spring and Autumn. It offers a special attraction for those interested in wildlife, but welcomes all visitors. The Observatory Hostel consists of three dormitories and a self-catering kitchen in a converted barn and byre of the croft. The Byre sleeps four in two bunks and has en-suite washing, shower and toilet facilities. It is particularly suitable for family use. The Barn also sleeps four and shares facilities with the Bøl which has a single bunk sleeping two. Adjacent is the Observatory Guest House (3 star) which has a lounge bar and meals which are available to hostellers.

DETAILS

- **Open** - All year, 24 hours, open all day, no curfews.
- **Number of beds** - 10: 2x4, 1x2 ; house: 8: 2x4 and private rooms
- **Booking** - Advance booking essential
- **Price per night** - Hostel £13-£14. Half board in hostel from £28. Guest House private rooms £43-£55 half board
- **Public Transport** - Loganair flights from Kirkwall (Orkney) leave daily. Ferry from Kirkwall on Fridays and between May-Sept also on Tuesdays (subject to tides and weather). Small boats may be chartered. Orkney can be reached by vehicle ferries from Aberdeen, Thurso (Scrabster) and Gill's Bay, and a passenger summer service from John O'Groats.
- **Directions** - Situated at the south west corner of the island

CONTACT: Duty Warden
NRBO, North Ronaldsay, Orkney Islands, KW17 2BE
Tel: 01857 633200, Fax: 01857 633207
bookings@nrbo.prestel.co.uk www.nrbo.co.uk

The Shetland camping böd network offers low cost accommodation in nine historic buildings with fantastic scenery - giving the opportunity to tour these beautiful islands, staying in böds en route. Due to the böd's historic nature, no two buildings are the same and facilities vary. The smallest böd sleeps four and the largest sixteen. Electricity, hot water and showers are available in six of the nine buildings and solid fuel stoves and mains water in all. Each böd has a story to tell, for example Voe Sail Loft was once a knitwear workshop, where the jumpers for Sir Edmund Hillary's expedition to reach the peak of Mount Everest in 1953 were produced. 7 out of 9 have local meals available within 2 miles and 7 out of 9 have (variable) facilities for less able people. Under 16s must be accompanied by an adult. No pets allowed. Explore Shetland, bed down in a böd. For further info log onto: www.camping-bods.co.uk.

DETAILS

- **Open** - 1st March – 31st October, The böds are unmanned but a custodian is contactable until 9pm, please call to arrange entry
- **Number of beds** - 4 to 16 (depending on böd).
- **Booking** - Booking is not essential however, as böds are unmanned it is best to book in advance to ensure the custodian is available before arrival.
- **Price per night** - £6 to £8 pppn. Group discounts are also available.
- **Public Transport** - Information on public transport within Shetland: www.shetland.gov.uk/transport/ Information on cycle and car hire: www.visitshetland.com/getting-around/
- **Directions** - Ferry from Aberdeen to Shetland (NorthLink). Flights to Shetland from Orkney, Inverness, Aberdeen, Edinburgh and Glasgow (Flybe).

CONTACT: Reception
For info: Shetland Amenity Trust, Garthspool, Lerwick, Shetland, ZE1 0NY
Tel: 01595 694688
info@shetlandamenity.org www.camping-bods.co.uk

HURDIBACK
SCOTLAND BACKPACKERS HOSTEL

Papa Stour is a beautiful unspoilt island, with spectacular cliffs and caves, ideal for walkers, bird watchers and photographers, or just to enjoy the fresh air and peace. Spot the seals, otters and the occasional dolphin, or visit sights of historical interest. There are long hours of daylight in the summer and in the autumn and winter you can spy the northern lights. Glimpse the untamed wildness of this remote corner of the world.

Hurdiback is a comfortable bunk house on a working croft, overlooking a picturesque bay. There are two bedrooms and a kitchen/sitting room. Equipment includes electric cooker, microwave, toaster, kettle and fridge. Heating, bed-linen, quilts and towels are included in the price and cots are available. We can order in your groceries with a couple of weeks notice and there is complimentary tea and coffee at the hostel

DETAILS

- **Open** - All year, all day
- **Number of beds** - 8: 2 x 4
- **Booking** - Advisable, groups require deposit.
- **Price per night** - Adults £20pp, 5-16 yrs and OAPS £10pp, under 5's free.
- **Public Transport** - Ferry (booking required 01957 722 259) West Burrafirth to Papa Stour return. Bus (booking required 01595 860 266) Margaret public/private bus. By air use Direct Flight Ltd (01595) 840246.
- **Directions** - Hurdiback is a short walk / drive from the ferry pier, or airport pick -up on request.

CONTACT: Peter or Esther
Hurdiback, Papa Stour, Shetland, ZE2 9PW
Tel: 01595 873227 or 0808 1920 006 (freephone), Fax: 01595 873229
enquiries@hurdibackhostel.co.uk www.hurdibackhostel.co.uk

Gardiesfauld Hostel is on Unst, the most northerly of the Shetland Isles. The island has spectacular cliffs, sculpted by the Atlantic Ocean on the west and secluded, golden, sandy beaches on the east with rocky outcrops where seals and otters appear. The Gulf Stream provides a moderate climate and the clean peaceful setting offers an invigorating chance to relax in a community where crime is unknown. During the summer enjoy long hours of daylight and the twilight of the "simmer dim" while in winter the long nights provide the backdrop for a vibrant cultural life. Situated on the picturesque shore at Uyeasound, this refurbished hostel combines superb facilities with a relaxed atmosphere. There is a kitchen, dining room, lounge, conservatory, coin operated laundry, showers (coin operated) and rooms with ensuite facilities. Caravans and tents welcome, caravan hook up facility planned for 2010.

DETAILS

- **Open** - April to September, Open in winter for prebooked groups, all day
- **Number of beds** - 35: 1 x 11, 2 x 6, 2 x 5, 1x 2
- **Booking** - Book by phone or email
- **Price per night** - Adults £12pp, children (under 16) £8pp. Camping from £6 a tent.
- **Public Transport** - Ferry from Aberdeen to Shetland (Northlink Ferries). The bus meets the ferry and continues to Unst. Ask for Uyeasound. Flights to Lerwick (BA). From Fetlar catch 7:55am ferry from Oddsta (Bus meets ferry)
- **Directions** - Take the A970 north from Lerwick to Voe then the A968 north to Toft . Take the ferry from Toft to Ulsta in Yell. Take the A968 north to Gutcher. Take the ferry from Gutcher to Belmont. Follow the A968 north and head into Uyeasound (B9084). Follow the road to the pier and look out for the hostel sign board.

CONTACT: Warden
Uyeasound, Unst, Shetland, ZE2 9DW
Tel: 01957 755279
enquiries@gardiesfauld.shetland.co.uk www.gardiesfauld.shetland.co.uk

KEY

435 - **Hostel page number**

0   miles

0   kilometres

435
Coleraine

Londonderry

Strabane   Ballymena
                                               Larne

                    Cookstown
Omagh   Belfast

Enniskillen   Armagh   Craigavon

                                               Downpatrick

                                    Newry   Newcastle

Belturbet
Cavan

For details of accommodation in the
Republic of Ireland, mainland Europe
and worldwide, see the map and table
on pages 436-441

Dublin
Dun Laoghaira

Kildare

RICKS
CAUSEWAY COAST HOSTEL N IRELAND

Rick's hostel is situated in the town of Portstewart, only 50 metres from the ocean. It has a mix of accommodation including small dormitories, private rooms for two and family rooms. Some of the rooms are en-suite. All have central heating with duvets and all bed linen provided. There is a self-catering kitchen and it is planned soon to provide meals for those who require them. The spacious common room has an open fire, contains books, games, music, a video-recorder and is overflowing with plants. Portstewart itself is a relaxed seaside town with a 3.5 kilometre long sandy beach. It contains lively pubs and great value restaurants. There are excellent public transport connections to Belfast, Derry and Dublin. It is an ideal base from which to explore the north coast including the Giant's Causeway, Bushmills whiskey distillery, Carrick-a-rede Rope Bridge and Dunluce Castle or for trips to the glens of Antrim or Derry.

DETAILS

- **Open** - All year, all day
- **Number of beds** - 34
- **Booking** - Recommended by phone or email
- **Price per night** - £12 pp dorm. £14.50 pp double/twin. £15pp 3/4 bed ensuite, £18 pp double/twin en-suite,
- **Public Transport** - Nearest train station Coleraine with frequent buses to Portstewart. Direct bus links from Belfast, Derry, Dublin, The Giant's Causeway and Coleraine, all stop at Atlantic Circle Bus Stop 100 metres from Hostel.
- **Directions** - By car from the A2 take road signposted Portstewart Point/The Herring Pond, the hostel is 100 metres from this turn.

CONTACT:
4 Victoria Terrace, Portstewart, BT55 7BA
Tel: UK (028) 708 33789, IR (048) 708 33789
rick@causewaycoasthostel.fsnet.co.uk

IRELAND

1 Belfast
8
12 Donegal
7 6,13
Galway
9
Dublin
4
2,3,10,15
Waterford
5
14 Cork
11 16

IRELAND
see inset

SWEDEN

NORWAY

DENMARK

UK

NETH.
20
29
22,28,31
24-26 Berlin POLAND
BELGIUM
52
19
GERMANY
32
27
Paris
21
49,50,51
53,54
23
CZECH
SLOV-
REP.
AKIA
30
FRANCE
SWITZ.
AUSTRIA
see inset
SLO,
HUN.
CRO.
BOS.
PORTUGAL
SPAIN
ITALY
17
48
Rome
18
47 46
ALB.
34 Zurich
SWITZERLAND
42 Bern
39
Interlaken
38,35
33,41,43,44
Geneva
45
37
36,40

KEY

45 - **Hostel number in table on pages 438-441**

FINLAND

EST.

LAT.

LITH.

56

BELARUS

KAZAKHSTAN

U K R A I N E

MOLDOVA

ROMANIA

55

FED REP YUG.

BULGARIA

MAC.

GEORGIA

AZER.

ARMENIA

IRAN

GREECE

57

T U R K E Y

SYRIA

IRAQ

CYPRUS

LEBANON

JORDAN

R U S S I A

○ Moscow

| 0 | miles | 500 |
| 0 | kilometres | 800 |

Europe

EUROPE AND

IRELAND

1	RICKS HOSTEL CAUSEWAY	Portstewart (see pg 435)	UK (028) 708 33789,	rick@causewaycoast hostel.fsnet.co.uk
2	ISAACS HOSTEL	Dublin	+353 (0) 1 8556215	www.isaacshostel.com
3	JACOBS INN	Dublin	+353 (0) 1 8555660	www.jacobsinn.com
4	JAMAICA INN	Sixmile bridge	+ 353 (0)61 369220	www.jamaicainn.ie
5	FÁILTF HOSTEL	Kenmare	1 088 84 0042333,	www.kenmare.eu/failte-hostel
6	OLD MILL HOLIDAY HOSTEL	Westport	+353 (0) 98 27045	www.oldmillhostel.com
7	INISHBOFIN ISLAND HOSTEL	Inishbofin	+353 (0) 95 45855	www.inishbofin-hostel.ie
8	THE RITZ ACCOM.	Killybegs	+353 (0)74 9731309	www.theritz-killybegs.com
9	WOODQUAY HOSTEL	Galway	+ 353 (0) 91 562618	www.woodquayhostel.ie
10	LITTON LANE HOSTEL	Dublin	+353 (0) 1 872 8389	www.irish-hostel.com
11	GARRANES HOSTEL	Beara	353 (0)27 73147	www.dzogchenbeara.org
12	HARBOUR HOUSE HOSTEL	Sligo	+353 (0) 71 171547	www.harbourhousehostel.com
13	ABBEYWOOD HOUSE	Westport	+353 (0) 98 25496.	www.abbeywoodhouse.com
14	SHIPLAKE MOUNTAIN HOSTEL	Dunmanway	+ 353 (0) 23 45750	www.shiplakemountainhostel.com
15	MARLBOROUGH HOSTEL	Dublin	+ 353 1 8747 629	www.marlboroughhostel.com
16	KINLAY HOUSE CORK	Cork	+353 21 4508 966	www.kinlayhousecork.ie

SPAIN

17	BARCELONA MAR HOSTEL	Barcelona	+34 93 324 85 30	www.barcelonamar.com
18	PURPLE NEST HOSTEL	Valencia	+34 963 532 561	www.nesthostelsvalencia.com

FRANCE				
19	BED & BREAKFAST	Paris	+ 33 14 02 68 308	meyermichael@wanadoo.fr
NETHERLANDS				
20	SHELTER CHRISTIAN HOSTELS	Amsterdam	+31 (0)20 624 4717	www.shelter.nl
GERMANY				
21	FIVE ELEMENTS HOSTEL	Frankfurt	+ 49 (0)69 4005885	www.5elementshostel.de
22	GENERATOR BERLIN	Berlin	+ 49 30 417 2400	www.generatorhostels.com
23	JUGENDGASTE-HAUS	Stuttgart	+49 711 241132	www.hostel-Stuttgart.de
24	EASTERN COMFORT	Berlin	+49 30 66763806	www.eastern-comfort.com
25	ODYSSEE GLOBETROTTER	Berlin	+49 (0)30 29000081	www.globetrotterhostel.de
26	HEART OF GOLD HOSTEL	Berlin	+49 (0)30 2900 300	www.heartofgold-hostel.de
27	LOLLIS HOME-STAY HOSTEL	Dresden	+49 351 810 84 58	www.lollishome.de
28	U INN BERLIN HOSTEL	Berlin	+49 30 3302 4410	uinnberlinhostel.com
29	HEINTZES TOCHTER HOSTEL	Schwerin	+ 49 385 4792968	www.hostel-schwerin.de
30	EASY PALACE CITY HOSTEL	München	+49 89 55 87 97 -0	www.easypalace.de
31	HELTER SKELTER HOSTEL	Berlin	+49 (0)3028044 997	www.helterskelterhostel.com
32	BLACK SHEEP HOSTEL	Cologne	+49 (0)22130290 96	www.blacksheephostel.de
SWITZERLAND				
33	BACKPACKERS VILLA	Interlaken	+41 (0)33 826 71 71	www.villa.ch
34	CITY BACKPACKER HOTEL BIBER	Zurich	+41 44 251 9015	www.city-backpacker.ch

35	RIVIERA LODGE	Vevey	+41 21 9238040	www.rivieralodge.ch
36	DOWNTOWN LODGE	Grindelwald	(0041) 33 853 08 25	www.downtown-lodge.ch
37	GIMMELWALD MOUNTAIN HOST.	Gimmelwald	+41 033 855 17 04	www.mountainhostel.com
38	LAGO LODGE BISTRO	Nidau b.Biel	+41 32 331 37 32	www.lagolodge.ch
39	BACKPACKERS LUCERNE	Lucerne	+41 41 360 04 20	www.backpackerslucerne.ch
40	GRINDELWALD MOUNTAIN HOST.	Grindelwald	+41 33 854 38 38	www.mountainhostel.ch
41	LAZY FALKEN BACKPACKERS	Unterseen	+41 33 822 3043	www.falken-hotel.ch
42	BERN BACKPACKERS	Bern	+41 31 311 37 71	www.bernbackpackers.ch
43	HAPPY INN LODGE	Interlaken	+41 33 822 32 25	www.happy-inn.com
44	BALMER'S BACKPACKERS	Interlaken	+41 (0)33 822 1961	www.balmers.com
45	THE LODGE CHURWALDEN	Churwalden	+ 41 81 356 4054	www.snowmotions.com

ITALY

46	HOSTEL OF THE SUN	Naples	+39 08142 06393	www.hostelnapoli.com
47	RING HOSTEL	Island Ischia	+ 39(0)81987546	www.ringhostel.com
48	PERUGIA FARMHOUSE	Perugia	+39 339 5620005	www.perugia-farmhouse.it

CZECH REPUBLIC

49	OLD PRAGUE HOSTEL	Prague	+420 224 829 058	www.oldpraguehostel.com
50	PRAGUE SQUARE HOSTEL	Prague 1	+420 224 240 859	www.praguesquarehostel.com
51	ARPACAY HOSTEL	Prague	+42 0/251 552 297	www.arpacayhostel.com

POLAND

52	TAMKA HOSTEL	Warsaw	+48 22 213 29 53	www.tamkahostel.pl
53	ATLANTIS HOSTEL	Krakow	+48 12 398 78 13	www.atlantishostel.pl
54	DIZZY DAISY DOWNTOWN	Krakow	+48 12 398 78 14	www.krakowhostel.pl

ROMANIA

| 55 | HOSTEL EOL 777 | Constanta | +40 727 555556 | www.hosteleol777.ro |

LITHUANIA

| 56 | YOUNG TOURIST CENTRE | Vilnius | + 3705 2611547 | www.vjtc.lt |

GREECE

| 57 | PAGRATION YOUTH HOSTEL | Athens | +30 210 7519530 | www.athens-yhostel.com |

NEW ZEALAND

| 58 | BILLY BROWN'S BACKPACKERS | Port Chalmers | +64 3 472 8323 | www.billybrowns.co.nz |

ISRAEL

| 59 | SAFED INN | Galilee | 972-4-6971007 | www.safedinn.com |

CANADA

60	SAMESUNS LODGE BANFF	Banff Alberta	+1 403 762 5521	www.samesun.com
61	SAMESUNS LODGE VAN.	Vancouver	+1 604 682 8226	www.samesun.com
62	UPLACE HOSTEL	Ontario	+1 866 618 1112	www.windsorexecutivestay.com
63	ST CLAIR HOSTEL	Vancouver (see pg 436)	+1 604 684-3713	www.stclairvancouver.com

SEE MAP ON PAGES 336 AND 337 FOR LOCATIONS OF EUROPEAN HOSTELS

Located right downtown close to Chinatown and Gastown. You may walk to restaurants, nightclubs, buses (local for Vancouver Island), skytrain, north Vancouver Ferry, Stadium and Ice Hockey Arena.

This heritage listed building was built in 1911 by Henry Pybus, captain of the Canadian Pacific steamship 'Empress of Japan' which took the blue ribbon while setting the Trans-Pacific crossing record 1887. The hotel originally accommodated railway and ocean going travellers back to both Pacific and Atlantic. A nautical theme is retained, 34 private rooms, 12 per floor, showers on each floor, no dorms, all linen provided, parking facilities in same block.

City bus from airport one block at 'The Hudson Bay Department Store'.

DETAILS

- **Open** - All year, 24 hours. Check in 8-30am/10-30pm, no curfew
- **Number of beds** - 88: 3x4, 12x3, 20x2
- **Booking** - Book ahead if possible
- **Price per night** - From C$44 double bunk room, $49 double room, C$59 triple room, C$79 quad room. Weekly: double C$295, triple C$395, quad C$535. All private.
- **Public Transport** - ALRT from Airport, Greyhound and Rail Station.
- **Directions** - Train station and Greyhound take skytrain to Granville Station, exit Dunsmuir Street. From Airport exit the building, cross the street, board the ALRT to downtown, exit at City Centre Station, right on Georgia, left on Seymour, right on Dunsmuir, next left Richards.

CONTACT: Manager
577 Richards Street, Vancouver, British Columbia V6B2Z5, CANADA
Tel: +1 604 684-3713. Toll free (USACanada) 1-800-982-0220.
sourceentvan@telus.net www.stclairvancouver.com

swiss backpackers
Hostels · Herbergen · Auberges · Ostelli

www.swissbackpackers.ch

Dear Backpacker,

at Swiss Backpackers hostels we offer you a home away from home. You receive a warm welcome, can enjoy a budget, yet comfortable bed, where you can let all the impressions, made every day while travelling, settle. In the self catering kitchens you will find a good atmosphere, not only to cook and eat, but also to get chatting with other travellers. There is no membership required. See for yourself that we provide the quality hostels of Switzerland.

33 hostels in 26 cities all over Switzerland

6677 Aurigeno, **Baracca Backpacker**, +41 (0)79 207 15 54

4008 Basel, **YMCA Hostel Basel**, +41 (0)61 361 73 09, info@ymcahostelbasel.ch

3011 Bern, **Backpackers - Hotel Glocke**, +41 (0)31 311 37 71,info@bernbackpackers.ch

8784 Braunwald, **adrenalin backpackers hostel**, +41 (0)79 347 29 05, info@adrenalin.gl

6558 Cabbiolo/Lostallo, **Humanita Backpackers**, +41 (0)91 830 14 81, info@humanita.ch

7002 Chur, **JBN Hostel**, +41 (0)81 284 10 10, info@justbenice.ch

7075 Churwalden, **The Lodge**, +41 (0)81 356 22 67, info@snowmotions.com

1202 Genève, **City Hostel Geneva**, +41 (0)22 901 15 00, info@cityhostel.ch

3826 Gimmelwald, **Mountain Hostel**, +41 (0)33 855 17 04, mountainhostel@tcnet.ch

3818 Grindelwald, **Downtown Lodge**, +41 (0)33 828 77 30, downtown-lodge@jungfrau.ch

3818 Grindelwald, **Mountain Hostel**, +41 (0)33 854 38 38, info@mountainhostel.ch

1882 Gryon, **Chalet Martin**, +41 (0)79 724 6374, info@gryon.com

7130 Ilanz, **Gasthof Mundaun**, +41 (0)81 925 45 55, info@mundaunpub.ch

3800 Interlaken, **Backpackers Villa Sonnenhof**, +41 (0)33 826 71 71, mail@villa.ch

3800 Interlaken/Matten, **Balmer's Herberge**, +41 (0)33 822 19 61, mail@balmers.com

3800 Interlaken/Unterseen, **Hotel & Backpacker Falken**, +41 (0)33 822 30 43, info@lazyfalken.ch

3800 Interlaken, **Happy Inn Lodge**, +41 (0)33 822 32 25, info@happy-inn.com

3800 Interlaken, **River Lodge**, +41 (0)33 822 44 24, welcome@riverlodge.ch

7031 Laax-Cons, **Backpacker Deluxe Capricorn**, 41 (0)81 921 21 20, info@caprilounge.ch

1007 Lausanne, **Guesthouse & Backpacker**, +41 (0)21 601 80 00, info@lausanne-guesthouse.ch

3822 Lauterbrunnen, **Valley Hostel**, +41 (0)33 855 20 08, info@valleyhostel.ch

6005 Luzern, **Backpackers Lucerne**, +41 (0)41 360 04 20, www.backpackerslucerne.ch

6000 Luzern 6, **Lion Lodge Luzern**, +41 (0)41 410 01 44, info@lionlodge.ch

8212 Neuhausen am Rheinfall, **Zak Backpackers**, +41 (0)52 672 55 21, info@zakzak.ch

2560 Nidau b. Biel, **Lago Lodge**, +41 (0)32 331 37 32, sleep@lagolodge.ch

6430 Schwyz, **Hirschen Schwyz**, +41 (0)41 811 12 76, info@hirschen-schwyz.ch

7554 Sent, **Backpacker Hotel Swissroof**, +41 (0)81 864 17 22, info@swissroof.ch

7500 St. Moritz, **Randolins Backpackers**, +41 (0)81 830 83 83, welcome@randolins-backpackers.ch

9657 Unterwasser, **Saentislodge**, +41(0)71 998 50 25, saentis@beutler-hotels.ch

1800 Vevey-Montreux, **Riviera Lodge**, +41 (0)21 923 80 40, info@rivieralodge.ch

6484 Wassen, **Gotthardbackpacker**, +41 (0)79 306 54 23, www.gotthardbackpacker.ch

8001 Zürich, **City Backpacker/Hotel Biber**, +41 (0)44 251 90 15, sleep@city-backpacker.ch

hospitality
made in
GERMANY

50 independent
quality hostels in
30 cities all
over Germany

BACKPACKER
GERMANY
NETWORK

Backpackers Hostels Canada
Auberges Backpackers Canada

Visit Canada!
Visit ... www.backpackers.ca

NEW ZEALAND!

NZ sets the standard for Backpacker-style accommodation throughout the world. And BBH sets the standard for New Zealand!

BBH has 320+ independently owned & operated establishments at 150 locations around the country, offering a wide variety of experiences which is part of the joy of travel.

BBH Accommodation appeals to budget-conscious travellers who enjoy the ease of meeting others. In addition to the traditional share rooms, the ensuite double and twin rooms that cost less than half the price of a hotel or B&B, have become popular with many older travellers who seek a more informal style of accommodation but still want their own privacy. Everyone can afford to stay longer – especially if they buy our **Club Card** which gives discounts on accommodation / transport and activities.

Standard facilities include:
- Self-catering kitchens
- Laundry
- Lounge areas
- 24 hr Guest Access
- Online Bookings

Our **FREE** 70 page guide contains all the details you need including room styles, current prices, customer ratings & location maps. To order a copy or simply to find out more about us, visit BBH online at:

www.bbh.co.nz

or contact:
BBH, 208 Kilmore St, Christchurch, New Zealand

Wake up in the (BEST) IRISH HOSTELS

{ Beds for all AGES! }

Book Online at
www.hostels-ireland.com

The network of IRISH TOURIST BOARD approved hostels all over IRELAND

INDEPENDENT HOLIDAY
HOSTELS
OF IRELAND

Lakeland Camping Barns

www.lakelandcampingbarns.co.uk

Dry camping in prime locations around the English Lake District. Camping barns offer the opportunity to stay in restored farm buildings at affordable prices. Experience Cumbria's stunning lakes and lofty peaks literally from yc doorstep. All the barns are unique and offer differing facilities. Check out ou individual entries or take virtual tours on the website.

We look forward to welcoming you and your families and friends in 2010.

Barn	Facilities	Page
St John's-in-the-Vale Camping Barn		178
Tarn Flatt Camping Barn		190
Bents Camping Barn		154
Catbells Camping Barn		184
Swallow Barn Camping Barn		189
Murt Barn Camping Barn		186
Cragg Barn Camping Barn		187
Dinah Hoggus Camping Barn		185
Fell End Camping Barn		161
Hudscales Camping Barn		183
Wythmoor Farm Camping Barn		158
Swirral Camping Barn		171

SYMBOLS

 Breakfast bookable in advance

 Shop (miles)

 Pub (miles)

 Shower

 Pets by arrangement

 Electric lighting

Toilets not in main building

Hot water

Campfire

Powerpoints

 Disabled facilities

 Wood burning stove

 BBQ aea

 Cooking facilites

 Heating

Scottish Independent Hostels

Hostels with character throughout Scotland

Scottish Independent Hostels represents over 100 quality hostels throughout the length and breadth of Scotland. Hostels range from vibrant city centre locations to converted barns on tranquil islands, each with its own very special character.
Our Blue Hostel Guide is published every year giving an up to date listing of all member hostels.
For a copy visit our website.

commercial & agricultural | insurance brokers

The Specialists in Hostel Insurance

**FOR A NON-OBLIGATORY QUOTATION,
CONTACT MIKE PATERSON**

Commercial & Agricultural Insurance Brokers, Erskine House,
6b Commerce Street, Arbroath, Angus, DD11 1WB

TEL: 01241 870303
FAX: 01241 877592
EMAIL: mail@caib.co.uk
www.caib.co.uk

Flexible covers tailored to your requirements

Competitive premiums

Competitive finance rates

Free Hostel Risk Management Guide with all policies

Authorised and Regulated by the Financial Services Authority

" Just30 are both proud and delighted to be supporting IHG with the ongoing development and advances with their web presence. "

/eb Site Design · Bespoke Content Management · SEO
E-Commerce · Complete Web Project Management
Small Business Specialists · Rich Internet Applications

44 (0) 1332 207722
ww.just30.com
les@just30.com

gistered in England & Wales, No. 4206938

just30

INDEX

INDEX